OVERCOMING JOB BURNOUT

HOW TO RENEW ENTHUSIASM FOR WORK

BY DR. BEVERLY POTTER

RONIN PUBLISHING

Overcoming Job Burnout
ISBN: 0-57951-000-0
Copyright ©1980, 1985,1993, and 1998 by Beverly A. Potter, Ph.D.

Published and Distributed by:
RONIN PUBLISHING, INC.
Post Office Box 1035
Berkeley, California 94701

Project Editor:	*Sebastian Orfali*
Manuscript Editors:	*Ginger Ashworth*
Cover Design:	*Brian Groppe*
Cartoons:	*Phil Frank*
Text Design:	*Judy July*
Page Composition:	*Generic Type*

Publishing History:
Previously published as
Beating Job Burnout: How To Transform Work Pressure Into Productivity.
Harbor/Putnam 1980
Ace Business Library 1982
Ronin Publishing 1985
Ronin Publishing, 2nd edition 1993
Ronin Publishing, 2nd edition retitled 1998

9 8 7 6 5 4 3 2 1

Printed in the United States of America

US Library of Congress Cataloging in Publication Data
Beverly A. Potter
    Overcoming Job Burnout
    1. Careers.   2. Psychology
    I. Title.

ACKNOWLEDGEMENTS

Thanks to the many friends and colleagues whose encouragement helped propel the creation of this book. I especially appreciate my clients and those who attended my workshops. Many of their burnout experiences and techniques for renewing enthusiasm (with names changed, of course) are incorporated in the pages that follow.

Thank you also, dear reader, for putting your time and energy into this book. May it help empower you and bring you to a renewed sense of fulfillment in your work and your life.

Other books by Dr. Beverly Potter

Finding A Path With A Heart
How To Go From Burnout To Bliss

Preventing Job Burnout
A 50 Minute Workbook

The Worrywart's Companion
Twenty-One Ways To Soothe Yourself And Worry Smart

From Conflict To Cooperation
How To Mediate A Dispute

The Way Of The Ronin
Riding The Waves Of Change At Work

Turning Around
Keys To Motivation And Productivity

Brain Boosters
Foods & Drugs That Make You Smarter

Drug Testing At Work
A Guide For Employers And Employees

TABLE OF CONTENTS

Here's what they say about *Overcoming Job Burnout*

"Remarkably insightful and exciting...offers wise, powerful, useful advice on many levels—good medicine indeed."
—*Miami Herald*

"Dr. Potter's surefire burnout remedy...explains how to succeed in corporate life while 'keeping your souls alive.' "
—*Berkeley Voice*

"Guidelines to help you keep your emotional health *and* your job."
—*Redbook Magazine*

"Self-discovery, goal-setting, planning and dreaming is time well spent."
—*Glamour*

"Potter's remedy for writer burnout."
—*Writer's Digest*

"Worthwhile reading."
—Executive Female

"Tells the individual what he can do for himself."
—*San Francisco Chronicle*

"If it's possible to cure job burnout with a book, this one could do it."
—*Savvy Magazine*

INTRODUCTION

*When Overcoming Job Burnout** was first published in 1980, a malaise of epidemic proportions plagued the American workplace. Rampant inflation resulted in workers earning more but having less. Cumbersome, rigidly structured organizations made it increasingly difficult to do our jobs effectively. The media bombarded us with reports of our inferior production and the Japanese threat. Unemployment was at an all time high. So it was not surprising that so many members of the American workforce were suffering from burnout.

Overcoming Job Burnout was one of the first two major books on the subject, along with Herbert Freudenberger's *Burnout: The High Cost of Success.* Around that time, the term "burnout" made its way from street slang for drug abuser who reached bottom to a commonly used word for the phenomenon ravaging the workplace—the plague of lethargy, despair, nervousness and helplessness gripping people from all walks of life. The sweeping political and organizational changes of the early 1980s contributed, paradoxically, both to the phenmenon of burnout and to the self-empowerment that can counter it. Corporations faced challenges posed by Tom Peters in *In Search for Excellence,* igniting a new spirit of entrepreneurship. Companies experimented with new structures and different employer-employee relationships. Leading organizational experts optimistically claimed we were on the verge of a corporate renaissance.

Much of the optimism, however, proved to be fleeting and illusory. The excesses of the 1980s are still being felt today. Now in the 1990s we

---

* Previously published as *Beating Job Burnout: How To Transform Work Pressure Into Productivity.*

face another kind of workplace crisis. As we move toward a global marketplace we see the secure positions of such giants as Procter & Gamble, IBM and General Motors shaken. Corporate spokespersons, out of necessity for survival, are embracing "change" as a mantra for the approaching century. Words like "downsize" didn't exist before, but in today's economy, it is not uncommon to hear of thousands of workers being laid off by some of the country's leading companies.

In some ways, we feel betrayed by all of these sweeping changes. The promise once held by technological advances, by computers and automated office machines, is now sometimes viewed as a threat. The technological revolution was supposed to lighten our workload and give us efficient clutter-free offices, reduced stress, higher productivity and more leisure. We got something else. Because our new machines enable us to do more, more is expected of us. Whereas a person may have had a secretary to type documents in the past, now that person is given a work station instead of a secretary and is expected not only to type papers but to desktop-publish them as well—and do twice as many. Fax machines were supposed to give us more time. Instead, almost everything must be faxed. A letter received at 9 a.m must be answered by noon rather than the following week.

Judging from my workshops and lectures over the last several years, there seems to be no end in sight to this trend toward frenzied employee overload. Across the board, no matter what profession, no matter what level, virtually everybody says they have too much to do and not enough time to do it.

It reminds me of when I first came across Betty Friedan's book, *The Feminine Mystique,* in the early 1960s. She argued that housewives, when given labor-saving devices like dishwashers, easy-mix recipes and better cleansers, did not see a diminished workload. Rather, work expectations for these women actually increased tenfold because if they could get something cleaner in less time, then that meant they had more time to clean. When I see computers and fax machines, I think the same phenomenon has entered the office. Everywhere people are crying burnout, and burnout has become a household word. You merely have to mention it and people nod knowingly.

While burnout is stressful, it is not, as is often assumed, caused by stress. It is common to find executives recovering from a heart bypass surgery anxious to get back to their desks. While stress is destroying their health, their enthusiasm for work is still strong. Stress and burnout can be likened to fever and pneunomia. The fever can be dangerous and must be treated, but lowering the fever does not cure the pneunomia. Similarly, the stress accompaning burnout is harmful and must be reduced, but focusing solely on stress does not negate the underlying causes of burnout.

Burnout is a destruction of motivation caused by feelings of powerlessness. Power—the ability to influence and accomplish—is essential for well-being and sustained motivaiton. Yet at work, we are often hindered by "damned-if-you-do, damned-if-you-don't" situations. The malaise that results is a painful process that adversely affects work, health, interpersonal relationships, leisure pursuits and self-confidence—as well as ability to perform effectively. Once it begins burnout tends to become a self-propelling vicious cycle that is very difficult to reverse.

The antidote? Developing personal power, an "I-Can-Do" attitude and the ability to influence one's situation. Helping people accomplish this positive transformation is the purpose of *Overcoming Job Burnout.*

Overcoming Job Burnout describes how to avoid or overcome the painful destructive consequences of burnout that lead to declining performance and low self-esteem. Ultimately, the real solution to burnout is not looking over your shoulder trying to shake a monkey off your back but to be looking forward toward a positive and compelling image of the situation you want for yourself. I call this process finding a path with heart. Finding such a path leads to finding meaning and worth in your work and life. I describe the process in my book, *Finding a Path With Heart: How to Go From Burnout to Bliss.*

People who are concerned about burnout want to have a work situation that is more than just okay, more than just putting in time and drawing a paycheck. Such situations may be tolerable, but most people want something more. Therefore, *Overcoming Job Burnout* and *Finding a Path With Heart* should be considered a pair—one showing how to leave behind the negatives and the other showing how to move toward the positives. In *Overcoming Job Burnout* the focus is on getting motivated and staying motivated. Once you are moving, the question becomes where are you going? Answering this question takes leadership—self-leadership which is the subject of *Finding a Path With a Heart.*

Overcoming Job Burnout has been completely rewritten and updated for the 1990s in this new edition. Some things have been added, some deleted. It is restructured in a style more relevant than ever in this time of crisis.

The first part of this book will explore motivation—what dampens it and how it can be reignited. Chapter 1 reviews symptoms of burnout. The causes of burnout are described in Chapter 2. In a nutshell, the "damned-if-you-do, damned-if-you-don't" syndrome triggers feelings of helplessness that can lead to an inablity to stay motivated, and burnout results. The focus of this book is on how to prevent burnout—specific steps you can take to stoke the flames of motivation and keep them blazing. Most important, as you will see in Chapters 4 and 5, is developing personal power, an "I can do it" attitude along with feelings of potency. There are actions you can take that will make a difference.

We will also look at ways you can make your job more compatible with your personal rhythms in Chapter 9 and how to change jobs altogether in Chapter 10. A look at the "Burnout Potential Inventory" in Chapter 3 reveals how much soul there is in your work. How to keep stress within manageable limits is the subject of Chapter 6. How to acquire skills needed to perform optimally is described in Chapter 7 and how to develop supportive relationships that insulate you from burnout and help you to get things done is explained in Chapter 8. In Chapter 11 we will explore ways to command thought processes rather than remain victimized by the limitations of word programs. Chapter 12 covers how to function in seemingly impossible situations without succumbing to burnout. Chapter 13 covers what you can do when you must supervise other people to promote their enthusiasm for working. Finally in Chapter 14 we'll take a look at pathfinding—how to find a path to your bliss.

CHAPTER 1

The Burnout Syndrome

Without work, all life goes rotten,
But when work is soulless, life stifles and dies.
—Albert Camus

*M*any people experience work as drudgery and their jobs as painfully empty. A "soulless" work day can leave people feeling drained and "used up," with little desire to return to that job the next day. Soulless work consumes enthusiasm until motivation goes dry. Skills and knowledge remains intact, but the will to perform — the spirit within — is diminished. Smothering the will, burnout is a malaise of the spirit. In the process motivation, that mysterious force that gets us moving is damaged — in the worst cases, even destroyed.

Hardest hit are service providers like nurses, counselors, and police officers who often become cynical about their work and openly hostile to the very people they're dedicated to serving. Jobs that involve life or death decisions such as being a platoon captain or a heart surgeon have high burnout potential. Managers, team leaders, and others who work with people are also at high risk. Other burnout-prone professions are those that require working under demanding time schedules such as newspaper journalism; those that require exacting attention such as air-traffic controllers; those that involve detailed work, such as proofreaders; those that are "politically incorrect" such as nuclear plant supervisors and IRS agents, for example. *No one is immune from job burnout.* Any person, in any profession, at any level can become a candidate for job burnout.

The question most people want answered first is "Am I burning out?" Chances are if you're asking yourself that question, you are struggling with burnout to some degree. People who find their work invigorating and refueling are filled with enthusiasm for their jobs. The question of burnout doesn't enter their minds. While these people may be experiencing a great deal of stress, their motivation to work is strong. In contrast, burnout is a motivational problem where enthusiasm dies and working becomes meaningless drudgery.

The items in the following quiz give an overview of the burnout symptoms and provide a quick indicator if you're burning out.

AM I BURNING OUT?

INSTRUCTIONS: Review your life over the last six months, both at work and away from work. Then read each of the following items and rate how often the symptom is true of you. When you're done add up your score.

RATING SCALE: 1 = rarely, 2 = occasionally true, 3 = true half the time,
                4 = frequently true, 5 = almost always true

_____   1.   I feel tired even though I've gotten adequate sleep.
_____   2.   I am dissatisfied with my work.
_____   3.   I feel sad for no apparent reason.
_____   4.   I am forgetful.
_____   5.   I am irritable and snap at people.
_____   6.   I avoid people at work and in my private life.
_____   7.   I have trouble sleeping because of worrying about work.
_____   8.   I get sick a lot more than I used to.
_____   9.   My attitude about work is "why bother?"
_____ 10.   I get into conflicts.
_____ 11.   My job performance is not up to par.
_____ 12.   I use alcohol and/or drugs to feel better.
_____ 13.   Communicating with people is a strain.
_____ 14.   I can't concentrate on my work like I once could.
_____ 15.   I am bored with my work.
_____ 16.   I work hard but accomplish little.
_____ 17.   I feel frustrated with my work.
_____ 18.   I don't like going to work.
_____ 19.   Social activities are draining.
_____ 20.   Sex is not worth the effort.
_____ 21.   I watch TV most of the time when not working.
_____ 22.   I don't have much to look forward to in my work.
_____ 23.   I worry about work during off hours.
_____ 24.   My feelings about work interfere with my personal life.
_____ 25.   My work seems pointless.

SCORING:

25 - 50	You're doing well.
51 - 75	You're okay if you take preventative action.
76 - 100	You're a candidate for job burnout.
101 - 125	You're burning out.

Many of the items in the quiz indicate depression and you may wonder what the difference is between depression and job burnout. Depression is a symptom, an emotional reaction, to certain circumstances including certain working conditions. But depression can also have an organic basis including problems of nutrition and brain chemistry. If you got a high score on the quiz it could probably be said that you are experiencing depression. If this depression is serious and unrelenting, it is advised that you consult your physician who can determine if there is a physical basis. Improved nutrition can have a tremendous impact upon your feelings of well-being. In some cases, your doctor may prescribe a medication such as Prozac or another antidepressive drug.

Job burnout could be called job depression. Some people wonder how to determine if the problem is one of general depression that infects ones work, or if it is job depression that infects one's life. Answering this chicken-and-egg type of question is academic. If you got a high score, you must take action to break out of the burnout cycle. Whether the source of your burnout is in your job or your personal life, in either case burnout is a trap because the process wears you down until it becomes too painful to act. By reading this book you're taking an important step toward beating burnout. As you'll discover, the first step is to isolate and identify the situations undermining your motivation. The techniques described in the following pages will enable you to pinpoint the causes of your distress whether at home or on the job.

Burnout is not an all-or-nothing proposition. Like fire, motivation gets stronger and burns hotter, or diminishes and burns out. There is no constant state. On any particular day enthusiasm for work is increasing or decreasing but it does not remain the same. Even the hottest fires will burn out, so we tend them — fanning, stoking, and occasionally adding another log. Like fires, people are not static. When motivation wanes, we burn out. There is no need for alarm as long as you still have fuel, know how to tend motivation, and haven't waited too long.

BURNOUT SYMPTOMS

The symptoms of burnout are neither unusual nor mysterious. In fact, it's difficult to find someone consistently free of symptoms.

■ **Consider John, an employment counselor, who de-scribes his feelings as follows:**

I don't know what's gotten into me. I believe in what I'm doing. I want to help people. But something has happened. Like today, a woman came in for a job referral. Well, she started going over her plight, telling me all the reasons why she couldn't go to the interview. I've just heard it over and over. All the complaints and reasons why she can't get herself together and get a job. All of a sudden I was angry and I said, "Look, I've got problems, too. And they're worse than yours. I've heard your excuses over and over, and I'm sick of it!" I just don't know what's gotten into me. I guess I'm just burned out!

John's story is a common one. Those who work closely with others often seem to lose concern for the very people they are trying to assist and treat them in dehumanizing ways instead, becoming cynical, negative, and sometimes overtly hostile as this employment counselor was. But burnout is by no means restricted to people who deal with other people's emotional, physical, or social problems. The kind of emotional exhaustion John described is experienced by people working in a wide variety of settings.

> We all need to feel productive as human beings. This is not to say that we must have a job working for someone else in order to be fulfilled in life. But the feeling of being useful, of creatively making a difference, of pursuing some task and carrying it out to completion, is crucial. These are basic needs. The consequence of their neglect is boredom and the most painful and debilitating of all human experiences: *loss of interest.* People who lose interest in life are simply wasting away. They are without purpose and they become a burden to themselves and their society as a whole. They suffer severe depressions, self-pity, and physical symptoms of every description, and they eventually can die from this malady. Yes indeed, it is an all-out instinct to be productive and engaged in meaningful work activity. To those who don't follow this instinct, there is the boring life style and the eventual immobilization that come from inaction.
>
> **Dr. Wayne Dyer**
> *The Sky's the Limit*

Loss of interest in work and emotional callousness eventually translate into major organizational problems like absenteeism, substandard work, and high turnover. But more importantly, the victim of burnout can be permanently debilitated by the experience and, in extreme forms, can literally become unable to work. The work skills may remain intact, but burnout leaves its victim unable to become involved in the work: It extinguishes motivation.

Burnout doesn't occur overnight. It is a cumulative process, beginning with small warning signals that, when unheeded, can progress into a profound and lasting dread of going to work.

NEGATIVE EMOTIONS

Occasional feelings of frustration, anger, depression, dissatisfaction, and anxiety are normal parts of living and working. But people caught in the burnout cycle usually experience these negative emotions more often until they become chronic. In the worst cases, people complain of a kind of emotional fatigue or depletion. While no two people respond in exactly the same way, people tend to experience frustration first that may evolve into anger. In later stages we see anxiety and fear, then depression and, in extreme cases, despair.

Frustration

Life is fraught with frustration. There are always some barriers preventing us from getting what we want. In small doses frustration can

be a helpful emotion, spurring us on to try new methods or to find alternatives to a problem. Then we expand and grow. But when frustrations are continual and unsolvable, the stage is set for feelings of futility: "Why bother? There's no point. It's hopeless. I can't do anything anyway." If you feel frustrated most of the time in carrying out the responsibilities of your job, you are experiencing an early symptom of burnout.

■ Consider Don, a software salesman:
I go out and get orders, which is not easy. The sales manager tells me to push quality service. So I do; but as likely as not the home office screws up in delivering the order. The company just doesn't come through with the type of service they promise. I'm caught with having to cool out another angry customer. Usually I'm successful in doing that, and he's happy in spite of the inconvenience. But I lose a lot of credibility. Sometimes customers are so annoyed they cancel the order and all my efforts have been for nothing. This happens all the time and it's getting pretty difficult for me to go out there and do my thing. It's getting so that I don't like this company, and I don't like this job. It's just too frustrating.

When frustrations stem largely from the job situation, intense feelings of dissatisfaction with the job itself can result. Yet many burnout victims blame themselves as they attribute their frustrations to their own failings.

■ Consider Sara, a defense attorney:
I'm here to help these people. And they have heavy problems. I'm supposed to defend them and to get them a lighter sentence. Oh, they all want a suspended sentence, of course! Sometimes I just don't devote myself to working out a good defense like I should. I have a lot of tough cases and they demand time. When one of my clients gets a bad deal

*in the courtroom it nags at me, and I feel like I haven't
given it my best shot.*

Such nagging feelings of guilt exacerbate the original frustrations.
Not only is Sara feeling thwarted in her work but she also feels she is the
cause of the problem. In extreme cases, feelings of guilt can escalate into
bitter self-revolution.

Depression

This tendency to blame oneself for problems arising out of the job
erodes the person's self-esteem, setting the stage for depression.

■ **Sara continues:**
*When Willy got ten years I felt I really had to question
my ability to make a decent case. Since then I've just felt so
down all the time. I don't feel good about myself. I don't feel
good about my work. I don't like my clients and I hate
myself for feeling that way. I can't seem to look forward to
anything. I drag through the day. Things that used to
interest me, like tennis, don't any more. I don't feel like
doing anything. It's a major effort to get up and make it
through the day. I spend most weekends watching the tube
and dreading Monday morning.*

Coping with constant feelings of negativity and futility can run
down the emotional batteries of even the most enthusiastic person. The
result is feelings of profound depression and a kind of emotional and
spiritual exhaustion where you feel like you're running on one watt,
without the resiliency to recharge. While depression may begin as a
response to a job situation, it can become a problem in itself, leading to
poor health and impaired work performance.

INTERPERSONAL PROBLEMS

The negative emotions characteristic of burnout usually affect
interpersonal relationships. Feeling emotionally drained makes inter-

acting with people more difficult, both on the job and at home. When inevitable conflicts arise, burnout victims tend to overreact with emotional outbursts or intense hostility, making communication with co-workers, friends, and family increasingly difficult.

◼ **Sara continues:**
I just don't know what's the matter with me. All in all I like my staff. They're a good group, and they work hard. I don't want to but I get cranky. It's my intention to say something nice, yet I'm critical. Or a couple of them will come in laughing and joking after lunch, and I snap or shoot a dirty look. I don't know why I do it. I don't want to be like this because it doesn't show the way I really feel about them. Irritation just pops out. Then I hate myself and wonder what I'm doing in this job.

Moodiness and irritability over trivial provocations signal impending burnout. You experience a feeling of emotional tautness, as if the slightest inconvenience is enough to make you snap. The process is similar to overloading an electrical circuit: One additional demand for energy, no matter how small, blows a fuse. Emotional overloading makes interacting with others precarious. Getting along with people requires tolerance and patience, but tolerance level drops as the burnout grows.

Interpersonal disturbances are not restricted to working relationships, however. In fact, difficulties may appear in your private life first. Frustrating, conflicting relationships put additional strain on emotional circuits, creating even more frequent blowouts. People need emotional support, and an unsatisfactory personal encounter combined with job frustration can set you up for an emotional meltdown.

Emotional Withdrawal

People suffering from job burnout tend to withdraw from social interactions. This tendency is most pronounced among helping professionals who often become aloof and inaccessible to the very people they are expected to help.

■ **John, the employment counselor, says:**
I just feel emotionally empty. I listen to people's problems all day — problems I can't solve. I do the best I can to offer support and empathy but lately it's getting harder to do. I listen to awful things and feel nothing — like today when Alicia told me what her uncle did to her when she was six. I felt nothing, not even outrage.

I don't know what's happening to me. When I'm not with clients I close my door so none of the other staff will come in to talk. I know I should be interested in people around here but listening to them complain about their case loads and problems with their kids takes too much energy. I used to look forward to the Friday TGIF get-togethers. Now I just go home because I don't have the energy any more.

People often defend themselves against adverse job situations by emotionally withdrawing. But this short-term solution only accelerates burnout because, as you'll see in Chapter 6, a strong social support system acts like a buffer against burnout. Nonetheless, people caught in the burnout cycle withdraw. By cutting themselves off from friends and colleagues they deprive themselves of the support they desperately need.

Emotional withdrawal is common among people in the service professions, like John, the employment counselor. Others such as managers and team leaders who work closely with people often suffer similar symptoms. A natural response is indifference to the people's feelings and problems. Dehumanization is another form of emotional withdrawal: Many helpers begin to think of their clients not as people but as objects. Others will respond to the drain on their emotions with hostility as John did. Still others become aloof and intellectual, talking about their clients as abstract cases in a textbook. All of these attempts to cope actually accelerate the burnout process. When going to work becomes increasingly unpleasant, it becomes an endurance test. A nearly complete emotional shutdown will eventually occur.

HEALTH PROBLEMS

As burnout victims' emotional reserves are depleted and the quality of relationships deteriorates, their physical resilience declines. They seem to be in state of chronic tension or stress. Minor ailments, such as colds, headaches, insomnia and backaches become more frequent. There is a general feeling of being tired and rundown.

■ Don, the software salesman, continues:

I've always thought of myself as a healthy person, but when I look at my track record over this year, I really can't claim that any more. These days it seems like if there's a bug going around I'm sure to get it. This winter I've already had three colds. Hell, I've had the same cold all winter long! And I've been getting indigestion. But that's probably from the tension on the job. What bothers me most is my trouble sleeping. Maybe one night a week I get fairly decent sleep but the rest of the time I toss and turn all night. I just can't get the job out of my head.

Frustration, feelings of guilt, interpersonal conflicts, and even depression are all stressors. In addition to these, burnout victims must also contend with continual physical tension. Burnout takes a physical toll. Burnout victims have more than their share of health problems, from colds, flus, and allergy attacks, to insomnia, cardiovascular and gastrointestinal breakdowns, and other serious health problems.

SUBSTANCE ABUSE

As the occupational "blahs" become chronic, many burnouts seek chemical solutions to overwhelming emotional demands and stresses. People often drink more alcohol, eat more or eat less and use drugs such as sleeping pills, tranquilizers, and mood elevators. Chain smoking and drinking large amounts of coffee and sugar are also common. This increased substance abuse further compounds problems.

■ Sara continues:

My using drugs started out because I was so demoralized about work. Just despondent, really. What happened was I couldn't sleep. I'd be miserable and I'd think about things that happened at work. I'd lie awake for hours, and then I'd be exhausted in the morning. I talked to my doctor about it and he gave me some kind of pill to perk me up. And that worked, I guess. Only, well, then I still couldn't sleep because of the pill. So he gave me a pill to put me to sleep. Now, I'm totally caught in this thing. I take something to go to sleep, and I take something to wake up.

People suffering burnout often use substances in an attempt to self-medicate their anxiety and depression. Not only doesn't this help to alleviate the underlying causes of these distressing feelings, but addiction becomes a risk. If the person does develop a chemical dependency, then the symptoms addiction add another layer to the person's problems, making it even more difficult to overcome.

DECLINING PERFORMANCE

High energy level, good health, and enthusiasm — the necessary conditions for peak performance — are all depleted in burnout. A person may become bored and unable to get excited about projects, or in other cases, the burnout victims may discover that concentrating on projects is increasingly difficult. In both cases efficiency suffers and quality of output declines.

As work becomes more painful and less rewarding, absenteeism is also likely to increase. Even when physically present, the burnout victim is often emotionally and mentally absent from the job. Health problems, substance abuse and interpersonal strain makes it difficult to extend oneself to co-workers and others at work whose cooperation and goodwill is needed to get the job done. As others pull back from the burnout victim, it becomes harder for the person to perform optimally because a solid social support system is generally required for high performance. So it is only a matter of time until there is a substantial drop in the quality of performance. The result is a decline in productivity.

■ **Don continues:**

I used to be one of those red-hot go-getters. I could sell anything to anyone. I was passionate about my work. I took it home with me. I slept with it. I thought about it all the time. I loved it. Now, I've run down. The job has so many frustrations and demands. I don't feel like the same person any more. I go into the office and I don't even care if I do a good job. I just put in my time. I know that the quality of my work has dropped. If I think about it, I feel like hell, so I just don't think about it! I ought to get out of here. But I don't have enough energy to look for another job. I figure I'm really not doing anything here anyway. They're paying me to do nothing, so I tell myself, "I think I'll just stay home today."

The Peter Principle

The infamous "Peter Principle" postulates that people rise through promotion after promotion in organizations until they reach their level of incompetence, where they stay. The person functions, but in a diminished capacity. The problem is usually one of not having the skills to do the work assigned to them. To compensate they tend to adhere rigidly to "the rules" in making decisions, for example.

■ **Consider Adele, a program director:**
I have a rather large staff of individually contracted instructors. When I first started the program, I tried to consider each of their individual situations. I'd bend the rules and make exceptions when I could. At the same time I had the District on my back imposing all kinds of restrictions. Then there were political changes that ultimately resulted in a dramatic decrease in funds. And the cutbacks had to be passed on to the instructors. All of a sudden I could satisfy no one. Everyone was angry and let me know it. I found there was only one way of handling the situation: Stick to the rules! That was a while ago, but I found it to be the best policy. Just go by the rules! When I get complaints and hysterical emotional outbursts, I just tell them, "Look, those are the rules, and there's nothing I can do about it!"

Making unpopular and painful decisions is an emotional strain that can be reduced by rigidly adhering to the rules. Difficult decisions are made easy because rules provide a protective shield from painful ethical questions. Attacks can be deflected onto the organization by pointing to the rules and saying, "I can't help it. I have no choice!" In the process, however, the burnout victim often loses the ability to function in a creative capacity, which stifles innovation and impedes progress within the organization. These subtle consequences of burnout are not felt immediately but can create serious problems in the future.

FEELINGS OF MEANINGLESSNESS

Most people want more from their jobs than a pay check. Virtually everyone wants to do something meaningful — to come home from work feeling that what they did that day on the job served an important purpose. Unfortunately for the burnout victim, working can become meaningless, as they question if working accomplishes anything important.

A strong signal that the burnout victim is sliding into an existential crisis of meaninglessness is evident when the person's statements about work are cloaked with a "so what?" or "why bother?" attitude. This is particularly striking among burnout victims who were once very enthusiastic and dedicated. Enthusiasm is replaced by cynicism. Working seems pointless.

VICIOUS CYCLE

The burnout syndrome takes on a life of its own. Feelings of futility, disappointment, and guilt provoke interpersonal hassles and depression. Emotionally drained, health problems can set in and performance ultimately drops. As performance deteriorates, there is an even greater sense of futility and guilt. A vicious cycle becomes entrenched. Eventually painful emotions give way to lethargy. The person cannot muster enough energy to participate in life; talents remain dormant, knowledge untapped, and potential squandered. The vital driving force has become a whimper. As a malaise of the spirit, burnout attacks and depletes motivation. The cycle rarely stops by itself.

In desperation, the burnout victim may quit one job to seek another. But beginning a new job without first understanding the problem with the first job is a set-up for another disaster. It is easy to unwittingly get into another job with the same problems. Essentially, the new job picks up where the first one left off. Then the second job may promote burnout even more rapidly in the face of fewer frustrations. The burnout victim may once again seek another job, only to find a repeat performance and eventually become unable to work at all.

CHAPTER 2

CAUSES OF BURNOUT

*B*urnout has both physical and psychological effects but it is neither a physical ailment nor a neurosis. Burnout is a loss of will. Motivation is damaged, resulting in an increasing inability to mobilize interest and capabilities.

To understand the causes of burnout we must first understand what sustains motivation. Just as the body needs vitamins and protein for optimal health, certain "nutrients" are also essential to sustain high motivation: Positive consequences or "wins" for good work, and feeling you can control things that influence you. These factors nourish motivation and help overcome burnout.

POSITIVE CONSEQUENCES FOR GOOD WORK

Motivation is determined largely by the consequences of your performance or what happens *after* you act. If your motivation is to remain high, there must be positive consequences or "wins" for performing. Suppose, for example, you take work home from the office and upon discovering this your boss unexpectedly gives you Friday afternoon off. You'll probably experience this as a win for having worked at home, and motivation to work at home will probably increase.

If, on the other hand, your boss criticizes you, saying you're an incompetent who can't get the job done during work hours, chances are you'll stop working at home. In other words, you are likely to repeat actions that result in desirable consequences (wins) and stop doing things that result in negative consequences (punishment).

POSITIVE WINS

Wins can be positive or negative. A "positive win" occurs when you do something and as a result something positive occurs. For example, you make a sale and as a result you get a bonus. If you need the money the bonus is a win for making the sale. If you complete an assignment on time and as a result you experience a feeling of satisfaction, this good feeling is a win. If you look good in a new outfit and as a result receive a compliment from someone you respect, the compliment is a win.

In each case, your motivation to repeat the action that led to the win will probably remain high. That is, if a bonus is a win for you, then you will probably be motivated to make a sale. If satisfaction feels good to you, then your motivation to get work done on time will probably increase. If a compliment from a person you respect is important to you, you're likely to buy more new outfits.

NEGATIVE WINS

A negative win is not punishment. This is a common misunder-standing. Punishment is something that lessens motivation, whereas wins encourage motivation. A negative win encourages motivation by taking a negative away.

For example, suppose you have a headache, which is a negative situation, so you take an aspirin and as a result the headache stops. You just experienced a negative win. A negative win occurs when a negative situation exists and you do something that results in the negative situation going away. Another example of a negative win is when an employee is socializing instead of working (negative situation) so you chew him out (do something) and as a result the employee stops talking and works quietly (negative disappears). In each case, you experienced a win when a negative was removed.

A negative win is like the old joke where a man, who is banging his head against a wall, says, "Oh, this really hurts!" When a second man asks, "Why are you doing that?" the first man replies, "Because it feels so good when I stop!" Like positive wins, negative wins promote high motivation.

PUNISHMENT

When you perform but receive no wins, motivation will usually suffer, especially when you expected a win. Suppose you spend several hours cleaning up the office and putting away papers and books stacked on the floor. You expect your business partner to be pleased but instead she says nothing about the tidy office and doesn't even seem to notice at all. Chances are you will be less likely to straighten up the office in the future.

When you perform and are punished, motivation will almost always decline. For example, suppose after working all weekend on a proposal, your boss flips through it while frowning, points to a word on the last page and says, "You misspelled this word." You'll probably take this response to be nit-picking and lacking of appreciation. Chances are your motivation to work on weekends will be diminished.

WINS AND MOTIVATION

While positive and negative wins keep motivation high, they are not equal. Positive wins generate "working for" motivation, whereas negative wins generate "working to avoid" motivation.

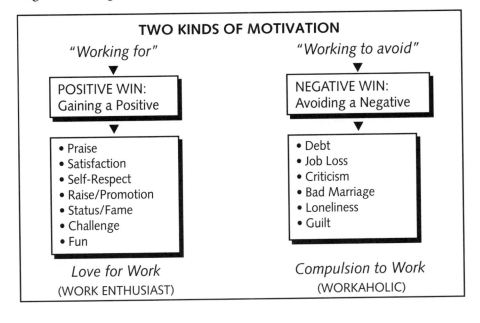

Positive wins create a motivation to gain a positive that generates work enthusiasm or a love for work. Positive wins include praise, feelings of satisfaction, high self-esteem, raises, bonuses, promotions, fame, credibility, challenge, adventure, fun, and anything else that is positive to you. Negative wins create a motivation to avoid a negative and lead to workaholism or a compulsion to work. Negative wins include avoiding criticism, alleviating loneliness, reducing debts, turning off fear, avoiding guilt, getting away from bad relationships, and avoiding anything else that you find punitive and unpleasant.

People often call anyone who works a lot a workaholic. But the time spent working is a less important distinction than the underlying motivation for working so much. Workaholism is propelled by fear-based decisions—*decisions aimed at avoiding* unpleasant situations. By contrast, a work enthusiast works long hours out of enjoyment. A positive motivation pushes forward the work enthusiast who strives to achieve various desirable wins.

Timing of Wins

Timing of a win has an impact upon its power to motivate. The sooner the win, the more powerful its impact. A positive outcome such as recognition that comes weeks or months after performance of a laudable deed has little impact.

■ **Consider Steve, a scientist:**
I worked for months on an electronic switching system. It was interesting at first. But it became paper—just so much paper. Now three years later they tell me they're going to use the system. I suppose I should feel good. But I can't get much satisfaction from it. That project was so far in the past what good is recognition now? It doesn't really mean anything to me.

Delayed recognition and compensation is a problem for many people like grant writers and novelists, for example. When there is a long delay between work and outcome, you can feel unrewarded even when wins finally do come. This happens to vast numbers of workers in modern organizations. Such "devices" as the Christmas bonus are meant to be an acknowledgment for good work, for example. Unfortunately, if the good work occurred in the middle of the summer and the recognition doesn't come until Christmas, the bonus does little to maintain motivation.

FEELINGS OF CONTROL

When we feel in control, we relax because we have an understanding of how to gain the wins we want and avoid negative consequences we don't want. When you are unsuccessful in discovering causal links between your behavior (if I do this) and the world's response (then I can expect that) you can feel like you have little control over what happens to you.

■ Consider Ann, a broadcast executive:

It was because of my broad experience and good reputation that The News Service sought me out. Everything about the job is more than satisfactory except for my immediate supervisor, Burt. Burt is my training supervisor.

When I go on a tour of stations in my region, Burt goes with me. From the minute we leave until the minute we get back, my life is hell. I can do nothing right. We do a lot of driving. He doesn't like the way I park the car, the way I put the luggage in the trunk, the way I hand the money to the toll collector on the bridge. It's just one constant criticism. I know these are trivial matters, but it wears me down and I get so tense. He brushes aside what I do well with no comment.

Recently I spent a whole weekend putting together a presentation for a radio station. I wanted to show him I can do a good job. Broadcasting has been my whole life. I know this business and I do good work. Burt wanted to see the outline of what I was going to present. After he looked at it

he said nothing about my ideas and instead pointed to the bottom and said, "'You've misspelled this word." The presentation was well received. The whole staff was excited. They learned something. All Burt could bring himself to say was, "It was passable," and then he told me to use gestures when speaking. He said nothing about my selling the station manager another contract.

What's worse is that when he wrote up the evaluation of my presentation to the station manager he didn't saying anything at all about the sale. Instead he said I needed to improve my "speaking skills." He made me sound like a failure. Working with Burt is becoming intolerable. I feel like giving up. What's the point in trying? No matter what I do, it's wrong. So why knock myself out?

Ann has been unsuccessful in figuring out what she must do to get a positive response from her boss. Obviously she desires to be acknowledged by receiving compliments or some other type of positive feedback for her efforts—but has been unsuccessful getting it. Ann also desires to avoid criticism and yet feels battered by Burt's criticism.

A sense of uncontrollability or helplessness is the final stage of burnout and is accompanied by depression and feelings of futility. We must believe we are potent, that we have the power to influence what happens to us. I say "believe" because how we see the world exerts a significant impact upon one's susceptibility to burnout. Believing that you can't control what happens to you and feeling helpless is one of the most threatening human experiences. Any time you believe the world uncontrollable, you are in trouble.

Research suggests, for example, that Voodoo deaths may be caused because the victims believed they were helpless. Many concentration-camp prisoners seemed to have died of helplessness. They were told and believed that the environment—the guards—had total power over them. Based on his own experience, Bruno Bettleheim, a renowned psychologist who survived one of the worst Nazi death camps, says that it was when people gave up trying to influence what happened to them that they became "walking corpses."

LEARNED HELPLESSNESS

Psychologist Martin Seligman spent years studying the impact of "controllability" on people and animals. For example, in a typical study matched pairs of dogs were divided into two groups. In the first situation, a naive dog was place in a room with an electric grid floor. This first situation was called "controllable" because the room also contained a puzzle. If the dog "solved" the puzzle, the shock stopped. In this example the puzzle was a lever, which when pushed, turned off the shock.

Since the dog had never been in the room before and it had no knowledge of the shock it was about to receive, the dog was relaxed and friendly as it wagged its tail and wiggled its nose. However, when the electric floor was activated, the dog's demeanor changed dramatically. It jumped and yelped as it ran around the room. We could say that the dog engaged in trial and error as it frantically searched for a way out. In the process the dog accidentally pushed the lever, causing the shock to stop. This is a powerful negative win. Over the next several trials when the dog was put back in the room and the shock turned on, the dog learned very quickly to run to the lever and push it. The dog was highly motivated—albeit by working to avoid motivation. The dog learned that it could do something to control its world.

Most of the species in which sudden death has been seen are wild. Controllability may be a particularly significant dimension of life to a wild animal. When he is taken to a zoo and put in a cage, he is deprived not only of the plains, banyan trees, and ants, but of control. If the argument set forth here is well-founded, the astonishing rate of death in wild animals newly acquired by zoos makes sense. I have heard that 50 percent of the tigers brought from India die en route to the zoo ... Dr. Hal Markowitz of the Portland (Oregon) Zoo had instituted such procedures with his apes and monkeys. Before this, the animals would look almost lifeless at feeding time as they sat near wilted food on the floor. Markowitz placed feeding under the animals' control: at a light signal they now rush to press lever one, race across the cage to press lever two, and then get a bite of food. Experts say they have never seen healthier zoo apes, and the animals have been free from the extensive illness that often plagues less active zoo animals.

Martin Seligman
Helplessness:
On Depression, Development, and Death

The dog in the second group was placed in the same room with the electric floor, only this time there was no puzzle, which when solved turned off the shock. In the "uncontrollable" situation there was nothing that the dog could do to turn off the shock. Just like the first dog, it ran around trying to find a way out. Eventually, it learned that there was nothing that it could do. The dog gave up, and laying down on the floor, it took the shock. The dog was not motivated. The second dog learned that it was helpless.

Later the second dog that had learned that it was helpless was put into the room with the lever (the controllable situation) but made no effort to find a way out. Instead it just lay on the floor and took the shock. Even when the door was left wide open, the dog did not attempt to escape the shock. The dog could not seem to learn that the conditions had changed and that it was no longer helpless.

To summarize, the second dog "learned" that it was helpless and stopped trying to get away. Its motivation to escape was extinguished or eliminated. In the process, dog exhibited a lot of negative emotions: first yelping and growling, later whimpering, and eventually just remaining motionless. Something happened that interfered with the dog's ability to learn when things changed and when it could do something. In effect, the dog burned out.

Powerlessness at work can affect people in the same way. As they learn that there is nothing they can do they experience negative emotions, probably beginning with frustration and anger, later anxiety and guilt, and eventually depression and despair. In the process, motivation

declines. When the conditions change they can't seem to learn and continue acting helpless.

Of course, scientists can't subject people to such experiments so we have no direct scientific data on the effects of powerlessness on human subjects. However, we can speculate that the battered-wife syndrome may be caused by learned helplessness, for example. If the woman believes that she is powerless before an abusive husband, she will probably act like the dog on the grid floor, taking the abuse and not running away when she has the opportunity. People in the ghetto who don't avail themselves of opportunities, such as educational programs, may fail to do so not because of laziness, but because they have learned that they are helpless and, as a result cannot act. Homeless people who are skilled and were once securely employed but now are unable to hold a job, may also be victims of learned helplessness. People who are chronically depressed may have become so as a result of uncontrollable situations. For example, there is a statistic claiming that more Vietnam Vets committed suicide than were killed in the war. Perhaps they were suffering from burnout. Remember the yellow ribbons and the people held hostage over 400 hundred days in Iran? A large percentage of the hostages developed chronic depression. Perhaps it was learned helplessness.

In his research, Seligman discovered that animals who learn to be helpless have little resistance to adverse situations. They often die in as few as ten minutes when placed in a survival situation, whereas animals who have learned mastery continue fighting to survive hours later. This research suggests learned helplessness is literally life-threatening. Research suggests it even triggers a biological suicide mechanism. In some cases biological functions simply slow down or cease; other studies indicate that the body may develop a terminal disease. This notion has been supported by research with cancer patients that suggested that people who are depressed and feel like victims were more likely to get cancer.

An uncontrollable situation can be harmful without being physically painful, however. Feeling helpless can do serious damage to motivation in any situation, even those filled with luxury and privilege.

■ **Consider Bob:**

I'm a V.P. That's my title. I have a plush office and I make a lot of money! It's my father's company, and the way Dad treats me has been the same since I was a child. He streamrolls in and handles everything for me. Once when I was eight I remember deliberately breaking a window. Dad paid for it right away. I didn't so much as get a whack on the ass. I've had everything I wanted—whether I wanted it or not! Dad got me into the top business school in spite of my "weak" academic record. You know, the Good Old Boys' Club? Well, he's president.

I resisted working here, but Dad let me know that if I wanted to continue enjoying the pleasures I'm accustomed to I'd better reconsider. Hell, why bother fighting the old goat? So here I am. When I first started, I tried to put into action some of my ideas and make some changes and start some programs. But Dad, as always, came right in and "fixed" things. Why bother? If he wants to pay me for nothing, it's his money. I go on a lot of business trips, and I meet a lot of foxy women. It's not a bad life at all. I don't get ulcers. Let Dad worry about the market, production, and the board. I enjoy myself!

Surprisingly, Bob's situation is similar to Ann's. While Ann is overloaded with criticism and Bob has an overabundance of occupational goodies, both lack a sense of control. Neither feel they can influence what happens to them. Seligman emphasizes in his research on learned helplessness that it is not the quality of the situation that causes feelings of helplessness and depression. Even though we tend to think that the cause is punitive circumstances, situations filled with rewards can also lead to the same debilitating learned helplessness and depression when the person does not have to perform to get those rewards. Seligman describes research with rats and pigeons in which they could choose between getting food free and having to make certain responses to get the same food. The rats and pigeons choose to work!

As feelings of powerlessness continue, Ann and Bob will both become candidates for depression. Both will probably experience a dramatic drop in motivation to continue trying to command their respective worlds.

Having learned that their efforts cannot influence the world, Ann and Bob may opt for simply plodding along. As the quality of their performance drops, it will feed depression and the vicious cycle will have begun.

VICIOUS CYCLE

Burnout erodes in insidious ways. Most detrimental is the way that experiencing uncontrollability tends to undermine motivation to learn in new situations. Ann and Bob have learned that they can't control their respective worlds so they stop trying to do so, which handicaps their ability to adapt or learn in the future. In this way burnout victims become psychologically "crippled" and burnout becomes chronic.

When Bob and Ann stop looking for ways to control their respective oppressors, they will stop finding them. Their own self-imposed "blindness" will keep them helpless. They will remain helpless because they feel helpless. If, for example, Ann's boss underwent an intensive management-training program and developed good supervisiory skills, Ann may, nonetheless, continue to expect her efforts to be futile. Because of her negative expectations of him, she would probably not be inclined to try her hardest and would therefore provide Burt with little to acknowledge. Even if she were to be presented with evidence that he had changed, she might not see the changes. That is, if Burt acknowledged her performance, she might still discount it as an exception: "Oh, he was just in a good mood. He'll think of something to get me on later."

The same might be true for Bob. If his father retired, Bob's years of training in helplessness might still remain with him, causing Bob to continue to tell himself it is futile to attempt to grab the reins. Having learned not to expect a relationship between his actions and their outcomes, he would probably continue to interpret the world as uncontrollable.

Once a defeatist attitude is learned, it tends to cling tenaciously. Defeated people see only defeat, never success, and thereby remain defeated. Yet, there are ways to escape from the negative trap of job burnout. The root cause of burnout is the *feeling* of helplessness, that there is nothing you can do. Burnout is prevented by an "I-Can-Do" attitude or what I call "personal power." Personal power is a feeling of potency, the sense that there is something "I can do." But before we go into the paths to personal power, let's look at specific kinds of situations that can engender feelings of helplessness.

BURNOUT SITUATIONS

*E*very job has some demotivating aspects. But real "killer jobs" have a preponderance of burnout-promoting situations. In fact, the Japanese even coined the term "karoshi," which means "death by overwork." In working with people in all stages of burnout and recovery, similar situations come up again and again. The Burnout Potential Inventory surveys these burnout-promoting situations.

WHAT IS THE BURNOUT POTENTIAL OF YOUR JOB?

INSTRUCTIONS: Rate how often each situation bothers you at work. Use a scale from 1 to 9 to rate the situations, one at a time, with 1 being "rarely," and 9 being "constantly." Add up the ratings to get your score.

POWERLESSNESS

_____ 1. I can't solve the problems assigned to me.
_____ 2. I am trapped in my job with no options.
_____ 3. I am unable to influence decisions that affect me.
_____ 4. I may be laid off and there is nothing I can do about it.

INADEQUATE INFORMATION

_____ 5. I am unclear on the scope and responsibilities of my job.
_____ 6. I don't have information I need to perform well.
_____ 7. People I work with don't understand my role.
_____ 8. I don't understand the purpose of my work.

CONFLICT

_____ 9. I am caught in the middle.
_____ 10. I must satisfy conflicting demands.

_____ 11.   I disagree with people at work.

_____ 12.   I must violate procedures in order to get my job done.

POOR TEAM WORK

_____ 13.   Co-workers undermine me.

_____ 14.   Management displays favoritism.

_____ 15.   Office politics interfere with my doing my job.

_____ 16.   People compete instead of cooperate.

OVERLOAD

_____ 17.   My job interferes with my personal life.

_____ 18.   I have too much to do and too little time in which to do it.

_____ 19.   I must work on my own time.

_____ 20.   The amount of work I have interferes with how well I do it.

BOREDOM

_____ 21.   I have too little to do.

_____ 22.   I am overqualified for the work I actually do.

_____ 23.   My work is not challenging.

_____ 24.   The majority of my time is spent on routine tasks.

POOR FEEDBACK

_____ 25.   I don't know what I am doing right or what I am doing wrong.

_____ 26.   I don't know what my supervisor thinks of my performance.

_____ 27.   I get information too late to act on it.

_____ 28.   I don't see the results of my work.

PUNISHMENT

_____ 29.   My supervisor is critical.

_____ 30.   Someone else gets credit for my work.

_____ 31.   My work is unappreciated.

_____ 32.   I get blamed for others' mistakes.

ALIENATION

_____ 33.   I am isolated from others.

_____ 34.   I'm just a cog in the organizational wheel.

_____ 35.   I don't have much in common with the people I work with.

_____ 36.   I avoid telling people where I work or what I do.

AMBIGUITY

_____ 37.   The rules are constantly changing.

_____ 38.   I don't know what is expected of me.

_____ 39.   There is no relationship between my performance and my success.

_____ 40.   Priorities I must meet are unclear.

UNREWARDING

_____ 41.   My work is not satisfying.
_____ 42.   I have few real successes.
_____ 43.   My career progress is not what I'd hoped.
_____ 44.   I don't get respect.

VALUE CONFLICT

_____ 45.   I must compromise my values.
_____ 46.   People disapprove of what I do.
_____ 47.   I don't believe in the company.
_____ 48.   My heart is not in my work.

SCORING:	YOUR RISK OF BURNOUT
48 - 168	Low: Take preventative action.
169 - 312	Moderate: Develop a plan to correct problem areas.
313 - 432	High: Corrective action is vital.

Let's look at a number of typical situations that can cause even the most motivated employee to experience burnout. In each case, the ingredients required to sustain high motivation are lacking. We have already encountered the first situation: the critical boss.

CRITICAL BOSSES

The broadcast executive whose boss ignored her proposal and pooh-poohed her presentation is a good example of the critical boss. Encountering negative consequences at one time or another is inevitable. Some criticism is helpful because it lets us know what to improve. But in Ann's situation her boss, Burt, was predominantly negative and miserly in giving her acknowledgement and other wins despite her efforts and good performance. She felt helpless because no matter what she did or how she did it her boss continued to find faults. Compounding the negativity were her feelings of powerlessness. When she asked him directly what she might do to improve her performance, Burt criticized her for asking.

■ Consider Ann's saga:

The News Service automatically renews its contracts unless the contractor puts in a notice of cancellation. You can see the problem. It's easy to forget about it and then discover that the service has been automatically renewed. Some station managers protect themselves by putting in a notice of cancellation immediately after signing the contract. This is logical and, having been a general manager myself, I understand it. This is exactly what one of my clients did. "Ann," he said, "I'm satisfied with the service, but I've placed a cancellation notice to protect myself. It's routine. I always do this, so don't take it personally. I'll probably renew." Naturally, I gave him the standard arguments against his decision, but he was insistent. Afterward, Burt berated me for having accepted the notice. I told him I gave my client all the arguments in the training manual as well as some I'd picked up from the seasoned people. He wouldn't listen, and continued with his harangue. Finally, in desperation I asked him what I should have done. You know what he said? "Ann, if you don't know now, you never will!" Now I ask you, what kind of answer is that? What am I supposed to do? It's like banging my head against a brick wall. I'm bruised and battered, and I'm not getting anywhere. I'm ready to give up. There's nothing I can do right.

Burt's criticism seems to be rooted in something other than Ann's actual performance. Perhaps Burt thinks Ann is a threat to his job; or perhaps he finds having a woman as a broadcast executive unsettling; or there may be something about Ann's personality that he finds particularly grating; or perhaps Burt thinks negativity is a good motivator.

Nonetheless, in most organizations employees must answer to their supervisors. Ann is at the mercy of Burt's criticism. Whatever the reason for Burt's one-sidedness, the basic lesson for Ann is that there can be no way she could succeed. While the failing may actually be Burt's, it is Ann and the news service that suffered. As Ann lost her motivation,

her performance and well-being took an abrupt nosedive. The organization lost a good performer.

Sometimes the constant criticism is not from a boss but from a customer or partner. The result is the same. You can begin to feel that there is no way you can satisfy the person. No matter what you do, he or she finds fault. You feel you can't win. Eventually, you wonder, why bother trying? It is very common to find that positive feedback from associates is absent in most burnout situations.

BEING A PERFECTIONIST

Sometimes it is your own perfectionism that sets you up for burnout. To perfectionists only perfection is acceptable. Anything less than perfect performance is criticized as inadequate. Working with a perfectionist—who could be your boss, a co-worker, or partner—is difficult for most people because no one can meet the perfectionist's standards. A subordinate or partner has the choice, at least in principle, of leaving the perfectionist. But when you are the perfectionist you are stuck with a critical boss—inside your head!

The perfectionist's focus is on rooting out imperfection, no matter how small. As a result he or she tends to ignore progress and what has been done well and instead attacks what he sees as imperfection. Since no one can be perfect—especially on a continual basis—the perfectionist suffers constant self-criticism, which tends to be very demotivating.

LACK OF RECOGNITION

Extremes of negativity and powerlessness are not necessary to burn out motivation. A simple lack of recognition can erode enthusiasm for working. Suppose, for example, you spend a lot of time and energy preparing a report which, when completed, sits for days on your supervisor's desk untouched. How will this affect your motivation?

■ **Consider Gregory:**
I don't know what my problem is. I guess I need those pats on the back. I wish I could be a mover. You have to move fast to get ahead in this world. I used to work hard. And, you know, I enjoyed it. That's when I was in school. I guess it was grades I worked for. Now, I've lost my spirit. I come to work and I do my work and I go home. Nothing comes back. There's no reflection in the mirror. I sometimes wonder if I exist. It's silly to expect anything. It's the government and I'm not special. God knows that! But I can't keep it up—working in a vacuum like this. So I just don't try as hard as I used to. And I still get paid. That's the funny thing. I suppose I should just accept it. Sometimes I think of getting another job. But civil service gives security. And to tell it straight, I just don't have what it takes to get out there and be aggressive. Maybe I never did. I don't like my job very much, though, and it's getting pretty hard for me to keep it up. I wish I could grab a hold of it like before. I miss that old enthusiasm but I just don't have what it takes any more.

Desperation and powerlessness are evident in Gregory's words. He feels it is pointless to seek what he needs. It is futile. He even blames and berates himself for needing recognition. He has stopped trying. Gregory has become another burned-out bureaucrat, perfunctorily carrying out his job. Everyone loses. His usefulness to the organization is greatly diminished. What's worse, he is damaged by the experience. He feels stuck in it, unable to perform and unable to leave and find a more satisfying work environment.

Here again, the root of the problem is in the organization. Many employers operate under the assumption that the paycheck is all people need to sustain peak performance. Too many supervisors are stingy with their acknowledgement and recognition as if these were rare and finite commodities; others righteously boast that they recognize only outstanding performance. Unfortunately, good performance or improved performance goes unacknowledged, reducing motivation to strive for outstanding performance.

INADEQUATE PAY

When you work hard but feel underpaid, you can feel your efforts and outputs are not being adequately recognized. People spend years in college believing that it will lead to personal recognition and well-paid work. If they are paid less than what they had expected, it can be viewed as lack of respect because pay is often used as an indicator of "respect." This can feel punitive and lead to alienation, especially when there is a poor match between the work and the person's values.

Traditionally women have been paid less than men doing the same work. Many women hope to get equal pay through professional training and advanced degrees only to find that they are still paid only about 70 percent of their male counterparts. An ambitious woman can develop a feeling of helplessness when her experience teaches her that no matter how hard she works or how well she performs she'll receive significantly less pay and recognition than a man in the next office who may not work as hard or perform as well.

UNDER-EMPLOYMENT

If you have high aspirations and spent years in college preparing for work but are employed below your appropriate level, you can equate this with a lack of recognition. Baby boomers who must compete with millions of others for disappearing opportunities are particularly prone to this dilemma. Women are often under-employed. It is not uncommon, for example, to find a woman lawyer doing the work of a law clerk or paralegal. Stories abound of Ph.D.s who work in the Post Office because they can't find a job in college teaching. Another example of underemployed people are liberal arts majors who discover they have few marketable skills and must work as waiters and waitresses after graduation. People, who have been laid off when their companies were downsizing and often find that they must subsequently take jobs below their capabilities, can similarly suffer from lack of recognition and be prone to burnout.

AMBIGUITY

Ambiguity is another thread woven into Ann's problem. It results from lack of information about her job and how she is expected to carry it out. Ambiguity can diminish self-confidence. If you don't know what's expected, it is difficult to feel confident that you are doing the right thing in the right way.

■ **Consider Rick's situation:**

Getting this job was a terrific opportunity, and I was thrilled to have it. But I've had a problem getting a handle on the job. It's been a frustrating experience. Samuels—he's the president—built the place up from a one-man operation. Well, he never fills me in on the big picture. I get a piece of it but never enough. A couple of times I thought I had it nailed down. Like the grant proposal last month. I worked on that for weeks, and I thought everything was coming together. I was feeling real good—finally. Betty was doing a terrific job on the research, and Allen conducted a couple dozen interviews. Then Samuels tells me I'm off the track and that the grant isn't a priority project at all. He wants us to put it on the back burner and to move on the Andar project. I just felt really deflated. I worked and I cared and it was all for nothing. I didn't even get to com-

plete what I was doing. This is not an isolated incident. I'm constantly in the dark. I don't know which way I'm going, and I can't pin him down. Lately I've had trouble concentrating. I can't focus. I'm really tense, and I spend a lot of time worrying about my competence.

Rick faces unclear goals and objectives. He doesn't know what the parameters and scope of his job are, what direction he is expected to go in, how his function fits in with the overall organizational goals, or even what the organizational goals are. Rick needs information. Without sufficient information to make decisions and set priorities, he cannot perform the job adequately. His energy and motivation are dissipated in futile, endless trial and error. Every time he thinks he has it figured out and tries again, he finds it's just another error. Ambiguity dampens motivation because insufficient information makes successful performance unlikely. Like Ann, Rick is going through a period of frustration that will probably become futility because he feels powerless.

Information is power. Samuels has a corner on the power and regardless of his intentions, is keeping Rick powerless by withholding the information he needs to perform. Whatever Samuels's—motivation—powerlust or inability to delegate—the result is the same for Rick. He is rendered unable to work effectively. Ambiguity is often caused by a supervisor not knowing how to develop clear goals and objectives or how to communicate them to his workers.

Confusion about job responsibilities and how one's work fits into the accomplishment of organizational goals is especially prevalent in rapidly expanding organizations such as those found in the computer industry. Silicon Valley abounds with stories of multimillion-dollar operations that began in a garage less than a decade before. As profits soar the company mushrooms in several different directions at once. There is ambiguity at all levels; no one has a view of the big picture. People can be confused about their purpose and how their function fits into the overall mission. But whatever the reason is for the information being unavailable, the impact on the workers and on the organization is detrimental.

TASKS WITHOUT END

An in-basket that is always full can feel like a task without end. No matter how long or hard you work to empty the in side of the basket, it quickly fills up again. Other examples include an unending line of customers who eventually become faceless and assembly-line work. A task without end is any job that has no clear beginning or end points.

In Greek mythology, Susyphus was an evil king who was condemned to Hades to forever roll a big rock up a mountain. Each day he strained and struggled all day, pushing the heavy rock up the steep mountain until he finally made it to the top. Each night, as he slept, the rock rolled back down to the bottom of the mountain. Susyphus's task never ended. In today's workplace many people's jobs fits this picture of Hell. Secretaries struggle all day to empty their in-baskets, only to find them full again the next day. People who work under unrelenting pressure or with clients who don't get better can have a similar experience. Eventually, they can develop feelings of futility: "No matter how

hard I work or how late I stay at the office, I just can't make any headway in my job." Every day they push the rock up the mountain only to find it back on their desks again the next day.

Entrepreneurs, sole practitioners, and others who are self-employed easily fall prey to tasks without end. Any project or business of substance can't be accomplished in a day, a week, or even a month. Employees, however, can set aside work at the end of their shift—whether or not it had been completed. People who are their own boss tend to push themselves to complete work, regardless of how long it takes. The self-employed typically work many more hours a week than do their employees, for less pay than their employed counterparts. While employees expect paid holidays and vacations, the self-employed often go for years, even decades without a vacation. Their business becomes a task without end.

When business is growing in the ways that the entrepreneur wants with money flowing in, motivation is high, then going to work is fulfilling. But should the economy take a nose dive, the competition move ahead, or profits otherwise take a downturn, the entrepreneur can develop a sense of futility plugging away at the task without end. If the entrepreneur feels powerless to change it, which is often the case, then burnout is a real threat.

IMPOSSIBLE TASKS

The impossible task is similar to the problem of ambiguity in that a person is not able to perform an assigned task. Unlike ambiguity, however, where lack of information or conflicting messages makes performing difficult, with an impossible task it is clear what is supposed to be accomplished—it is just not possible to do so.

■ **Consider Sara, a defense attorney:**

I have to go to court today to defend a guy on three counts of selling heroin. It's a hopeless case because the guy sold the stuff to two separate police agents. His only defense is: "I didn't do it. I never saw those guys before." His attitude is totally unreasonable. He's not willing to make a deal. So obviously he's going to be convicted and get the maximum sentence. And I'm caught in the middle. I'm trapped between a client who won't cooperate and the people who want to pinch him. I'm his defense attorney, and there's no significant defense. Well, it's very frustrating.

Sara's job is to defend people who are being accused of having committed crimes, yet she is also working with clients who have no real defense. In many of her cases, the client is clearly guilty and often uncooperative—doesn't show up for appointments and court appearances, withholds information, and at times, lies to her. To make matters worse, the size of Sara's caseload precludes her from preparing an adequate defense even when one is possible. There are simply too many defenses to be made. Moreover, the courts and other agencies present other hurdles that compound matters further. In short, it is impossible for Sara to do her job well. Variations of Sara's situation are confronted by helping professionals every day.

INCURABLE CLIENTS

Many service providers, such as social workers, have large caseloads of clients with nearly impossible problems. No matter how hard they try, how much they give or how much they care, the drug addicts continue to use drugs, the welfare recipients can't get work, and the delinquents end up back in juvenile hall.

■ **Consider Frank:**

I work on a hospital ward with drug abusers. I used to find the work fulfilling. I threw myself into it. I cared about those guys. I worked with them, and there were results, or so I thought. A couple would start to shape up, develop some skills, and become more responsible. They'd look good. And after several months of intensive work, it would sometimes be difficult to tell them from the staff. Finally, they'd graduate from the program. I had high expectations. I felt good. I'd helped them! They'd go out into the world and last about three months at the most. Then one day I'd be in detox and there they'd be again.

I'll never forget the first time it happened. Billy Wagner. I put my soul into that guy. And there he was looking exactly the same as he did eight months before when I saw him in detox the first time. I was shattered. He'd done so well. If anyone could make it, he could. Only he didn't. And he's typical. I don't believe people can change anymore. I think these guys are doomed to a lifetime of this and there's not one thing I or anyone else can do. I don't get involved anymore. I can't take it. I'm burning out. It rips my guts out. I know they won't make it, yet I've got to go into the ward every day and convince them they can.

When people helpers are able to provide genuine relief-giving assistance, it can be profoundly satisfying. But when they can't do a thing, it becomes a kind of emotional assault and battery. The burnout symptoms result from attempts to cope with this problem. Emotional withdrawal is common. They may turn on the client, blaming them for their plight; they may become cold and callous; they may turn into rule-worshiping bureaucrats.

■ Consider Jackson:

I work with the homeless and the near homeless. It's my job to rehabilitate them. I'm expected to wave some sort of magic wand and get them to pull their lives together, get off the bottle, get a job or into a training program and set up housekeeping somewhere. My caseload is over 250 people, so I don't have enough time in a day to see each of my clients even once a month.

These people are damaged goods. They'll never live normal lives. And it'd cost tens of thousands of dollars to "rehabilitate" them. My budget is ridiculous. I have about $100 per person. Maybe I'm cynical, but it's a reality. So I'm suppose to single-handedly make them right? Well, it's a joke—a sick joke! I've got to sit here every day and some-how face these people who come to me to help them. I can't help. So maybe I get them into a flop-house for a week. Maybe I get them a two-week meal ticket. Then what?

Closely related to the impossible task is the "no-win" situation. With the impossible task you are expected to do the impossible; in the no-win situation you are presented with demands that are possible to achieve but mutually exclusive. This motivation extinguisher can take a number of forms.

INCOMPATIBLE DEMANDS

Incompatible demands means that satisfying one results in failing to satisfy another. Further, you are expected to satisfy both demands. Actually, it is a lose-lose situation because there is no way you can win. Every time you win, you simultaneously lose. These kinds of situations are often called damned-if-you-do damned-if-you-don't because no matter what you do you are "damned."

If you report to two bosses you can be confronted with incompatible demands. One boss may want speed while the other wants quality, for example. Producing both may not be possible. Jobs that require working across departmental boundaries are also plagued by incompatible demands. Marketing wants one thing while manufacturing wants another. Anyone interfacing between unions and management struggles with this problem.

■ **Consider Ralph:**

I'm the best machinist in the shop and everybody knows it. Sometimes I wish I was just an average Joe because people expect the impossible from me. It's the foreman. He wants precision work. And I can do precision work. He wants me to cut to an accuracy of 1/100th of an inch, and I can do this. But quality takes time. This is what I tell John, and this is what he wants. When I take the time and I put out a top-notch product, he turns around and gets on my back because he wants to move items. He wants quantity. He wants speed. He wants to get the bucks. Well, I try to explain to him that he can have one or the other but not

YOU'VE GOT TO CHOOSE

both. I say, "Okay, okay, John. I'll do it. I'll work as fast as I can." I work fast and I don't get accuracy. With speed I can maybe do cuts to 1/50th of an inch and that's damn good! But there are complaints. The fit's not perfect. And John's down on my case because of quality. Well, what am I suppose to do? I tell him I'm not superman, and he doesn't understand. I just can't win so I've stopped trying.

Ralph is in a double bind. When he satisfies John's demands for quality he fails to meet the demand for quantity; when he meets the quantity he fails to meet the demand for quality. In other words, Ralph works and works. He tries to perform as he's directed, yet he never actually receives the payoff he desires or has been promised. Basically, Ralph faces the same problem as Ann. He is continually receiving negative consequences for his performance and appears powerless to change this. A person in a losing situation will try only so long and then give up.

Conflicting demands from different sources can be equally devastating.

■ **Consider Janis, a production foreman:**

I'm caught in the middle and it's hell. I get management down on me and they want production. That's how they make money. They want these guys working at maximum output and if they don't it's my head on the block. So when I go down to the production line and try to get these guys to work harder, I run into the union steward. He's saying, "Come on, Janis, cut a little slack and give us a break, will you. Lighten up!" And I get these pressures and subtle threats from him. So I'm pretty unpopular with the guys and I spend a lot of time wondering if I've got a job.

Janis's position is like Ralph's. No matter what she does, she loses on one front or the other. She must walk a precarious tightrope strung between two superpowers: management and the union. It is a losing situation. She is powerless when it comes to maximizing wins and minimizing negatives.

■ **Marvin, a middle manager, says:**

When I hitched on here the company was growing fast. We had the product people wanted and my future was unlimited. I moved up fast. I felt good about what I accomplished. But lately I get a suspicion that some of the others around here are throwing sand in my tanks. I think they're jealous because of how fast I've come up. A couple of the guys on my team drag their heels. They just don't pull their people together and meet their objectives. They don't see how they interface with the others. And I've got to pull it all together. Of course, the boys upstairs, they're looking more at the big picture, and I've got to look through their eyes, too, if I'm to make things work around here. I've been told I've got to be more "seasoned" before I can make the next step up. Well, it's tough to juggle it all. And sometimes I wonder if some of them want to hold me back. Anyway, I've come to a roaring halt here. I've leveled out. You can't stand still, you know. You either go up or you go down. I sure don't want to go down. I want to keep winning.

Marvin faces a multitude of conflicting demands. His position at the middle of the organizational ladder puts him at the crossroads between focused task objectives and broad-range future planning. When he centers on one, the other is neglected. When he attempts to think like the "big boys," those below feel he is not giving proper supervision. When he attempts to work with his team, guiding them on a day-by-day basis, those above feel his vision is myopic and that he needs seasoning. His ambition compounds his dilemma. Marvin wants to get ahead. To do so he must satisfy the conflicting demands placed on him. Furthermore, because many see him as ambitious, they may feel like steppingstones and retaliate by limiting their cooperation. So while Marvin seems to have a great deal of power because of his position, he feels like a monkey in the middle, unable to grab the ball and run.

CONFLICTING ROLES

A similar dilemma is one of conflicting role demands. This can be a woman executive who is expected to be supermom, superwife, and star employee or a manager whose company expects her to travel and whose family wants her at home.

■ **Consider Rosie's situation:**
This morning William, the director, said he has an urgent project and wants me to stay late. I told him that I couldn't work late because my husband and I have tickets for dinner and the theater which we bought over a month ago. My husband's really been looking forward to it. William only said, "Yea, a typical woman, always putting the family first!" What he said really irritated me but I worry about my job with all of these lay-offs. So I called my husband and explained that I had to work late and wouldn't be able to make the dinner but I hoped to make the play. As you might imagine, he was pretty annoyed and said, "That's typical. Your job always comes first!" I just can't win.

Rosie faces conflicting roles. Her boss expects her, as a highly paid professional, to make personal sacrifices to meet company deadlines. Her husband expects her to put their plans before the job. Often, as on the day she had to choose between meeting her boss's request to stay late to work on the project and her husband's desire to enjoy the dinner and outing they had planned, Rosie faces mutually exclusive demands. Like the others, Rosie feels powerless. She has little to say about her boss or her husband's expectations; they are imposed upon her. Of course, many men suffer similar conflicts between responsibilities to their families and the demands of their jobs. As men increasingly take on responsibility for raising children, these kinds of conflicts will probably become more common among fathers.

VALUE CONFLICTS

If you work in a sensitive field such as police work, IRS investigation, military, weapons research or nuclear power, you may face value conflicts. You may believe in what you do and you strive to do a good job, yet everywhere you go people criticize you for the work you do.

■ **Consider Jeff's situation:**

I love my work and I'm really excited about some of the developmental projects I'm working on. I feel I'm doing a good thing for the world because I'm contributing to some real scientific breakthroughs. The snag is that the projects I work on cause pollution and this causes me a great deal of conflict. I'm really concerned about ecology and sometimes I get upset about it and think perhaps I should quit and get a job elsewhere. The problem is that this is absolutely the best job I can possibly get. There isn't another lab anywhere where I would have as much freedom and as many challenging projects as I have here. And a lot of the things that I do can be used in other capacities. Yet, I know that toxins are a by-product of my experiments. And it really gets to me sometimes.

Jeff's moral values conflict with his career objectives. He cannot satisfy one without forfeiting the other. While his win-lose situation may be self-imposed, it is no less frustrating than those experienced by Jane, Ralph, and Janis. Jeff feels powerless because of the way he sees the world and the choices he has made. Personal strivings often exacerbate the win-lose situations the world flings at us.

In short, many burnout victims are confronted with situations in which they are pressured to meet several incompatible demands because of double-binds or damned-if-you-do damned-if-you-don't situations. The devastating impact of these crazy-making situations on the human psyche has been well documented in psychological journals. In fact, there is an entire theory of schizophrenia based on the double bind. Win-lose dilemmas make us feel crazy and place a tremendous drain on motivation. Those caught in such a situation will eventually stop trying to meet the conflicting demands, and will become burnout victims.

FEELINGS OF MEANINGLESSNESS

Not all burnout victims suffer losses and feel themselves a failure, however. Some come to it through success. They seem to achieve all the desirable goals. Yet, these bountiful rewards fail to provide the lasting satisfaction promised to this existential burnout victim who feels empty, undernourished, and helpless to fill the void. This is the most insidious form of burnout. None of the symptoms are manifested as warning signals in the early stages. There is only a tiny nagging inner voice saying, "I am living a meaningless life."

■ **Consider Richard Alpert, the Harvard professor who partnered with**
and jumped headlong into LSD experimentation:
I was at perhaps the highest point of my academic career. I had just returned from being a visiting professor at the University of California at Berkeley. . . . I had been assured of a permanent post that was being held for me at Harvard. . . . I had research contracts with Yale and Stanford. In a worldly sense, I was making a great income and I was the collector of possessions. I had an apartment in Cambridge that was filled with antiques, and I gave very charming dinner parties. I had a Mercedes-Benz sedan and a Triumph 500 CC motorcycle and Cessna 172 airplane and an MG sports car and a sailboat and a bicycle. I vacationed in the Caribbean where I did scuba diving. I was living the way a successful bachelor professor was supposed to live in

the world of "he who makes it"... . Something was
wrong.... Here I was, sitting with the boys of the first
team.... and in the midst of this I felt here were men and
women who, themselves, were not highly evolved beings.
Their own lives were not fulfilled. There was not enough
human beauty, human fulfillment, human contentment. I
worked hard and the keys to the kingdom were handed to
me. I was being promised all of it. I had felt I had got into
whatever the inner circle meant.... But there was still that
horrible awareness that I didn't know something or other
which made it all fall together. And there was a slight panic
in me that I was going to spend the next forty years not
knowing, and that apparently was par for the course. And
in off hours, we played "Go," or poker, and cracked old
jokes. The whole thing was too empty.... I experienced
being caught in some kind of a meaningless game.... And
in the face of this feeling of malaise, I ate more, collected
more possessions, collected more appointments and posi-
tions and status, more sexual and alcoholic orgies, and
*more wildness in my life.... *

Baba Ram Dass
Remember: Be Here Now
Copyright 1971, Baba Ram Das, The Lama Foundation,
Reprinted by permission

Albert continues to describe attempting to fight his malaise through psychedelics. Finding LSD a false path, he became a seeker. During this journey Richard Alpert became Baba Ram Dass.

WORK OVERLOAD

Work overload means having more work than we can perform in a given amount of time. Overloaded people are harried. They have too many tasks to do and decisions to make and are constantly behind schedule, worrying about time and deadlines. Work overload is physically stressful. But work overload, in and of itself, does not cause burnout as long as people feel they can control what happens and they receive adequate wins. For example, you may be very tired, you may be "stressed out," but your motivation can still remain high. Whereas, an overload of work that is ambiguous, punitive, or characterized by the other situations just described is a set-up for burnout.

Whether or not an overloaded person burns out depends upon how he or she sees the work. If the person views it as a challenge and feels able to meet that challenge, burnout is less likely. He or she might develop health problems as a result of the continuous physical drain, but interest and motivation to work would not necessarily be extinguished. Instead the person may continue working with furor and enjoy doing so. Similarly, the person who sees a difficult situation as an opportunity to learn new skills is also less likely to burn out. On the other hand, people who feel helpless in the face of overload are at high risk of burnout. People overloaded with the types of work described earlier are prime candidates for burnout. An overload of win-lose situations or impossible tasks, for example, compounds the overload problem and speeds up burnout.

BUREAUCRACY

Burnout is not the result of personal weakness or some neurotic vulnerability. We are all susceptible. Given the wrong conditions, anyone can burn out. Any time you work in a situation in which you feel you have little or no influence, you risk burning out. The frightening fact is that most jobs constitute such situations. In organizations, controllability is not distributed equally: It is allotted to a few. Yet a feeling of having influence or control over our treatment is necessary for high motivation and peak performance.

Abraham Zaleznik and his colleagues at the Harvard Graduate Business School investigated this paradox in an analysis of 2,000 high-status workers in three occupational groups: management, staff, and operations. They found that, like power, burnout symptoms were not shared equally. Those in operations had significantly more health problems, emotional distress, and job dissatisfaction. Managers, in contrast, had a consistently low symptom rate. Digging deeper, they found that operations people reported feeling frustrated by the vague goals and objectives set by supervisors who they viewed as technically ignorant. Ralph, the machinist who's story we heard earlier, is an example. Being technically ignorant, his supervisor, John, presented Ralph with incompatible demands for speed and accuracy. The environment that the operations people described was highly competitive, demanding peak performance and fraught with potential failure.

More than those in the staff or management groups, operations people experienced a great deal of conflict between their jobs and their personal lives. While management also encountered conflict and ambiguity, they reported less frustration than the operations and staff groups. Zaleznik's group theorized that the ability to influence consequences helped minimize the impact of ambiguity and damned-if-you-do damned-if-you-don't situations. Managers are typically less susceptible to burnout because their decision-making power gives them more influence over their situations, which in turn acts as insulation from the negative aspects of the organization. Having an ability to influence personal power helps prevent burnout.

Not all managers are equally protected, however. Organizational specialist Robert Kahns and his associates have shown that the middle manager is more susceptible to burnout than managers at other levels. The middle manager is typically caught in a psychic squeeze between the incompatible demands of those above and below and his or her own intense achievement strivings. Marvin, the middle manager who was caught in the middle between thinking like the big boys and dealing with the daily details is an example. Middle managers must learn to tip-toe through a psychologically precarious minefield. One false step can mean a motivational blowout. In a downsizing economy middle management positions are the most likely to be eliminated. Many middle managers feel unemployable, which instills a profound sense of helplessness.

In fact, the organizational structure minimizes personal power. Zaleznik concludes...

> Bureaucratic practices set limits to the assertion of power by individuals in the organization, but the possession of power in organizations reduces the harmful consequences of bureaucracy to the individual. Therefore, survival in bureaucracies falls to those individuals who know how to negotiate a double-bind situation, while advancement in bureaucracies falls to those individuals who can make an opportunity out of a paradox.
>
> **Abraham Zaleznik**
> *Behavioral Science*

Organizations maximize their survival by minimizing the power of individuals. Powerful individuals can change the organization or leave it, which threatens the organization's existence. Organizations resist change: they strive for stability and predictability. It is the pyramid or bureaucratic structure itself that renders individuals powerless. But as we have seen, powerlessness is toxic to individuals. For individuals, powerlessness demotivates and eventually kills the spirit. Individuals must have power, the capacity to influence what happens to oneself and to make what one wants to happen more likely.

SKILL DEFICIT

The modern organization can be toxic to anyone who enters. The extent of the impact on any one individual depends in large part on that person's position and how he or she responds. Some burn out completely; others are scalded but continue to function in a reduced capacity; while others buffer themselves. Successful defense depends upon a person's coping skills. The victims described earlier might have been able to prevent burnout if they had more refined defenses. Ann, for example, might have been able to increase her personal power with better communication skills. She didn't know how to draw out Burt's expectations nor how to best communicate with him. Similarly, Gregory needed acknowledgement from his supervisor but he did not make this known. The same holds true for Rick, who was unclear about his job parameters. Had Gregory or Rick developed assertiveness skills, they might have been able to prevent burnout. How you perceive and think about work is very important. Rosie would not have been as susceptible to her boss and husband's barbs had she altered her concept of herself as a woman. Likewise, it was Sara, the defense attorney, and Frank's, the drug counselor, expectations of themselves and their clients that made their tasks impossible. Improved career decision-making skills might have helped Jeff with his moral conflict over creating pollution and prevented his burnout. On the other hand, Marvin's (the middle manager) survival and advancement could have been maximized by using all of these skills. And all of these victims needed to increase their resistance through learning how to manage their own stress.

While the larger solution requires a broad-based alteration in the organizational structure and environment, this is an unrealistic hope at this time. Clinging to such an expectation is folly: You may burn out first. Survival in the organization depends on how you see and respond to it. When faced with a threat—physical or psychological—defense is an automatic response. Unfortunately, burnout victims who resort to self-destructive coping tactics such as drug-usage or emotional withdrawal tend to eventually surrender to helpless thinking. While these tactics buffer the fledgling spirit temporarily, ultimately such defensive maneuvers accelerate burnout. Learning productive coping skills is required. By increasing personal power through skill building, you can prevent burnout. How to do this is the subject of the remainder of this book.

CHAPTER 4

MOTIVATION AND LEARNING

*T*he future grows out of the present moment. What you do or don't do now creates the conditions and environments of your tomorrows. By applying systematic problem-solving steps to your daily encounters with the world, you can gain control over your future.

When we feel we have no control over events in our lives, motivation to continue performing decreases and burnout results. The antidote is personal power, skills that render us in command of ourselves and what happens to us. Personal power insulates us from the negative effects of many work situations. We are able to refuel ourselves by gaining the needed acknowledgement and other wins independent of the boss or the organization.

Understanding the principles of motivation and how we learn increases personal power. We can use the principles to engineer ourselves to change in ways we choose and to actualize our potential. This chapter describes these principles of learning. There are many technical points and it is easy to get bogged down. You might skim through this chapter, then go on to the how-to chapters which draw upon the learning principles. When you want to go into a particular self-change technique in more depth, you can return to the relevant section in this chapter.

SELF-CONTROL AMBIVALANCE

Self-control ambivalence is the first issue burnout victims must confront and resolve. The only way to prevent burnout and to turn the process around once it has begun is to become captain of your ship.

The first step, then, in beating job burnout is making the decision to take command and direct your moments. But it is here that we run into self-control ambivalence. The urge to rebel against control is so engrained that when we attempt to take command of ourselves, we often blindly rebel. Then, attempting to gain control again, we resort to patterns of self-punishment, thereby reaffirming our fears of being controlled.

> I suggest that what produces self-esteem and a sense of competence, and protects against [burnout], is not only the absolute quality of the experience, but the perception that one's own actions controlled the experience. To the degree that uncontrollable events occur, either traumatic or positive, [burnout] will be predisposed and ego strength undermined. To the degree that controllable events occur, a sense of mastery and resistance to depression will result.
>
> Martin Seligman
> *Helplessness*
> *On Depression, Development, and Death*

Another kind of ambivalence deals with the tender issue of responsibility and choice. We have no manual for managing our motivation. Too often we allow others to control our choices. Much self-control ambivalence is rooted in ignorance. Few of us took classes in decision making, self-observation, or personal problem solving in high school, a time when we needed it most. So we fumble along, slowly rediscovering the basic principles of how we function.

HOW ENVIRONMENTS SHAPE US

We respond to specific events in the world. If you perceive an event as dangerous, your body will activate in preparation to deal with that danger: to fight it, run from it, or otherwise overcome it. We respond mentally and physically to pleasurable experiences as well. Through these experiences, we learn about the world, and our place in it: what to expect from it, and how to adapt to it. A certain degree of learning occurs with each subsequent encounter modifying us somewhat. It is this fluidity that enables us to adapt to a changing world. And it is also through this process that we develop habits. This is how we are shaped by the environment. Sometimes what we become works well and our habits, lifestyles, and workstyles operate in such a way that we succeed and gain satisfaction from doing so. Other times, in the case of job burnout, we may have habits that interfere with optimal functioning and result in dissatisfaction and demotivation.

But we don't have to be passive responders to our environment. We can arrange our world in specific ways to learn specific things we decide to learn. Of course, to a certain degree we already intuitively use certain learning principles to manage ourselves. While we rely on them to survive, and get what we want, we seldom think about them or use them systematically.

In a sense human beings are like highly sophisticated computers. Like computers we can be programmed. We call these programs habits. But there is at least one notable difference between people and computers. Both can be programmed, but a person can "self-program." While we have the capability to self-program, we haven't been given an operating manual and aren't trained to actualize all the "computer's" potential. If we know the basic operations, however, and how to implement them, we can work with the computer in sophisticated ways. The same applies to us. It is easy to program and deprogram ourselves, provided we know how to use the basic operations.

You can look at how you operate within your world in terms of "programs" you follow. We're all born with functioning and survival programs that are written into our "basic operating system." We learn other programs through our interactions with the world. As you will see, burnout is partially a problem of acting in programmed ways—responding to events in the world in learned ways—that can end up harming you.

HOW WE LEARN

Behavior occurs between two environmental encounters—that which happens right before and that which happens right after the behavior. These are the two points where we make contact with the world—the learning points.

The event that comes right before a behavior is called the "prompt." Prompts signal that a certain behavior is appropriate and trigger you to take specific actions. Neutral events become prompts through a learning process. A familiar example illustrates how this works. As you prepare your pet's dinner, he probably paces around the kitchen, licking his chops in anticipation. The sight and smell of the food prompts this impatient behavior.

Now suppose each time you prepared your pet's meal you use a particular can opener. In couple of weeks you might notice him salivating when you use the can opener to pry off the top of a can of olives. The can opener has become a prompt through direct association with the pet food. Next, you notice your pet getting excited when you open the drawer where the can opener is stored. The drawer has become a prompt through association with the can opener.

Many an exasperated mother has employed this learning trick to speed up toilet training by turning on the water when putting the child on the pot. Soon the sound of the running water alone prompts the child to use the toilet. Unfortunately, learned responses have a way of lingering on. Twenty years later, when standing beside a babbling brook with his sweetheart, Junior may not be so happy with his response to the sound of running water!

Words make particularly effective prompts. If a child is slapped, for example, she'll probably respond with anxiety due to the pain of the slap. Imagine Jane yells "Bad!" as she slaps Susie. If this happens enough times, the word "bad" can become a prompt for anxiety. "Bad" signals a threat of pain. Jane no longer has to slap Susie to make her cower in fear; a word is sufficient. If Jane should call Susie a "stupid bad girl," "stupid," because of its association with "bad," could become an anxiety prompt. The association does not need to be limited to close proximity

in time; it can be based on similarity of any kind. Words similar to "stupid" or "bad" could become anxiety prompts.

Whenever a powerful emotion such as anxiety (or anger, fear, joy, enthusiasm, sexual arousal, and so forth) is involved, learning occurs quite rapidly. And it can be literally contagious. Anything physically present—anything you think about or anything reminiscent of the emotional event—can potentially become a prompt for the emotion. You don't have to be aware of this happening; in fact, most people are not. Yet it provides the basis for the emotional response. You sense the prompt and your body responds instantly so that you are ready to act. Through this simple programming procedure, routine activities can have the power to mobilize you to deal with a threat. Making a decision, for example, always implies the threat of criticism. Because of this association, having to make a decision can become an anxiety prompt. This can spread contagiously to deadlines, for example, giving them the power to also trigger anxiety through their association with decisions.

This example hints at how easy it is for your world to gain control over you!

On the other hand, this type of learning, which is called classical conditioning, is a sophisticated survival mechanism. We scan the world continuously, responding to anything that signals potential danger. We don't stop to think. We have the capability for immediate action. Anxiety is the internal signal telling us of a possible threat, so most of us are extremely sensitive to anything that prompts anxiety. If we can avoid the anxiety, we can avoid the possible harm. This is a simple and effective formula in the short run. Unfortunately, whatever we do to avoid anxiety can become a deeply engrained habit—so deep, in fact, that a once harmless habit, like having a beer after work or kicking back in front of the TV—can become an addiction. This brings us to the second programming point: what happens after the behavior.

PROMPTS MUST PREDICT

The prompt is "learned" only if it is a useful predictor. For example, if you see rain clouds on the horizon and put up the top on your convertible to avoid getting drenched in a downpour, you'll probably run to put up the top the next time you see similar clouds. Rain clouds have become a reliable predictor of rain. Clear sunny skies prompt something entirely different. It's through such prediction that all of us weave our way through the world. We rapidly appraise the threat or pleasure potential from the data coming in through the senses and act to our best advantage. If our predictions are good, we are successful in maximizing pleasures and minimizing pain. Then our friends tell us we're living the good life!

Prompts don't automatically stimulate us. Rather, at a level outside awareness, we are rapidly appraising the prompt's associations, which we then act upon. But because we're unaware of these instantaneous judgments, they are nearly the same as an automatic knee jerk. For a prompt to take on power, it must be a good predictor. To establish its predictive potential, a specific type of outcome must follow the prompted behavior.

If the outcome during prompt learning is pleasurable, you'll probably feel like repeating the associated behavior next time you encounter that prompt. If, on the other hand, there was a negative or painful outcome, you will feel like avoiding such an outcome in the future. Anything that was associated with the painful experience can become a prompt, in that it signals potential danger and warns you to escape. Suppose, for example, that the child who was slapped is usually called "Susie" except when her mother is angry with her. Then she calls her "Susan." If Susie is playing in the garage and hears her mother call out, "Susan, come in the house immediately!" she is likely to feel frightened and might try to hide from her mother. Having heard "Susan," she knows that she may be slapped.

OUTCOMES CONTROL BEHAVIOR

Outcomes influence how we act in the future. Behavioral psychologists say behavior is "controlled by its outcome" because we are more likely to repeat behaviors followed by positive outcomes than those followed by something negative. Most of us use this principle intuitively. We reward behaviors we want to continue and punish those we want to stop. This type of learning is called "instrumental conditioning." A behavior can meet with one of five possible outcomes: two positive, two negative, and one that is usually neutral.

POSITIVE OUTCOMES

What we most commonly think of as a positive outcome involves *turning on or the addition of something good* in our lives. Examples are when someone compliments you ("Hey, George, what a great idea!"), when you get a bonus, or when you feel satisfied. Any behavior that meets with a positive outcome is likely to be repeated again in the future. And if when you do repeat the behavior, it usually meets with positive outcomes, the associated prompts will be considered good predictors of forthcoming rewards and will be maintained. Eventually the behavior will become a habit.

Another kind of positive outcome is less obvious but equally powerful and potentially sinister. Such an outcome occurs in situations in which your actions result in *something negative being turned off or removed*. This is best illustrated by the jogger's response to the question: "Why do you jog?" "Because it feels so good when I stop!" Anything you do that turns off some kind of a pain is likely to be repeated. For example, suppose you have a headache which is painful and take an aspirin. If the pain goes away you will probably take another aspirin the next time you have a headache. We all want to have as little pain as possible. Any time we can avoid it, we usually try to do so. Herein lies the danger: Whatever we do to turn off "bummers," we're likely to do so again and again until it becomes an engrained habit, whether or not danger of the bummer continues to exist. We have become controlled by our own escapism! Each time we avoid or escape the discomfort, we feel better momentarily. We may have averted a bummer or have been lashing out at windmills! Either way, the result is the same: We feel better because the threat, real or imagined, has been averted.

It is extremely difficult to break a cycle of avoidance once it is established. Thus, it is important to pay close attention to anything you do that turns off pain, and anxiety in particular. If your avoidance involves a potentially self-destructive behavior, you can be in trouble. For example, if you have a couple of drinks to relieve anxiety you can run the risk of becoming an alcoholic. Actions that begin as temporary protective measures can become self-perpetuating destructive habits.

NEGATIVE OUTCOMES

There are two types of negative outcomes. The most obvious is what we typically think of as punishment: *something unpleasant is turned on or added.* Slapping, criticism, pain, or anxious feelings are examples. Another type of negative outcome occurs when *something pleasant or desirable is taken away or turned off.* Having our pay docked or a friend give us the cold shoulder are examples. And we usually respond to negative outcomes anxiety and fear. We are inclined not to repeat actions that meet with negative outcomes.

NO OUTCOME

The final possibility is no outcome at all: *Nothing happens.* Behaviors that have no outcome are typically not repeated very often. Psychologists call this extinction. But if you think about it, it is rare that "nothing" happens, because everything is relative. If you expect a positive outcome (you complete a report early and expect your boss to be impressed but get only silence instead), you may get no outcome but it feels like a negative outcome because something you want and expect is withheld.

HOW HABITS ARE FORMED

Reviewing, the prompt is a signal telling you the best course of action. It is a sign of what's ahead so you can adjust your actions. Thus, if your response to the prompt—the behavior—has met with a positive outcome, the positive feelings that accompany the successful behavior will become associated with the prompt. If your efforts have met with a

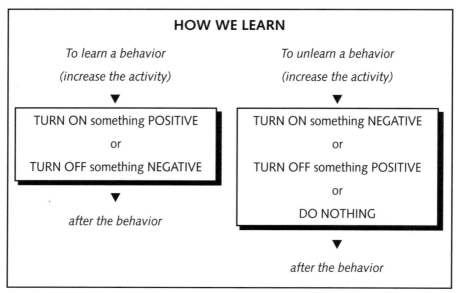

negative or no outcome, negative feelings that accompany failure and disappointment become associated with the prompt. In both cases, positive or negative, a habit can be formed where you respond the same way each time you encounter the prompt.

This is a highly effective survival mechanism. You don't have to stop to think or analyze. You appraise and act, often without conscious awareness. But this mechanism can also cause problems: Certain habits, no longer of value, can linger on in full force to direct your current behavior.

ANALYZE YOUR PERSONAL PROGRAMMING

Equipped with these fundamentals, you can identify your personal "programming" through systematic observation and data recording and draw parallels between what happens in your world and how you respond. When studying these parallels, look for patterns. The patterns reveal habitual responses.

IDENTIFY PROMPTS

When you notice an occurrence of the behavior or emotion under consideration, stop for a moment. Look at what happened *just before* it.

What prompted the behavior? What's associated with it? Jot this on a card or in a notebook. Don't rely on your memory. You may think you'll remember these things, but you usually won't. Write them down as soon as you can. After you've collected several examples, look for patterns. This will tell you a great deal about what can spark you to perform at your peak and what can throw you off center.

IDENTIFY CONTROLLING OUTCOMES

The controllers are the outcomes of your actions. Look at what happens *after* you respond to the prompt. When studying stress and emotional responses, the most important outcomes to monitor are avoidance and escape outcomes. Prolonged stress is physically harmful to your body and feels uncomfortable. We have a natural, built-in mechanism that makes us strive to return to the norm as soon as possible. Anything that turns off stress and brings us back within the normal range falls into the escape type of outcome discussed earlier in this chapter.

> For the most part, what we fear is not real—it is merely our mind *imagining* something awful that has not yet happened. . . .
>
> Seldom do we do the thing we fear, so we never discover if our projection of disasater was accurate. In fact, when we *don't* do the thing we are afraid of, we breathe a sign of relief *as though it actually would have taken place.* "That was a close one!" we say, even though we never actually got close to anything but a string of our own negative thoughts.
>
> Eventually, we begin to avoid all things and thoughts that even *might* produce the fear of fear. It becomes a many-layered fortress—fear defending fear defending fear defending fear—and inside: nothing.
>
> John-Roger & Peter McWilliams
> *DO IT! Let's Get Off Our Butts*
> *A Guide to Living Your Dreams*

Remember, turning off a negative outcome can be dangerous. If there are a number of burnout prompts in your work environment, such as work filled with ambiguity, losing situations, and little recognition and if you react to these prompts with stress, whatever you do to turn off that tension will probably be repeated. Eventually you may use the avoidance response to head off displeasure at the pass. By avoiding the unpleasant situation you can avoid the unpleasant feeling. The avoidance prompt signals that displeasure is likely. So you avoid by taking some action to turn off negative emotions before they start.

Avoidance

This process can take on a life of its own and you'll continue to avoid even when there is no longer a real threat of pain. Turning off the threat of pain is a positive outcome or win that maintains or controls the avoidance habit. Think of the different things you do to turn off negative feelings as a vulnerability. If you use a potentially self-destructive response to lower stress or reduce anxiety, for example, you are vulnerable because you are likely to use it again. Thus, such behaviors as

smoking, overeating, excessive television watching, and even emotional withdrawal can gain control of you through this process. Avoidance patterns are difficult to turn around. It is important to use beneficial behaviors such as relaxation or assertiveness to turn off unpleasant feelings. These will yield a sense of personal power.

Forewarned is forearmed. Any time you're off center, remember to notice what you do to bring yourself back. Any time you feel very anxious, uptight, or afraid, notice what you do to calm down or turn the negative off. Anytime you feel lethargic or bored, notice what you do to perk yourself up.

Analyze your work performance with the same technique. Notice what happens *after* you perform. For example, suppose you interview a client. What happens after that interview? When you complete a report and give it to your supervisor, what happens? What happens when you make efforts to perform? You can expect behaviors followed by negative outcomes to disappear. It has nothing to do with character, or willpower. A built-in survival mechanism automatically stops you from continuing to act in ways that bring pain. Pain, both physical and mental, is your message that danger exists as a threat to your survival.

> However one defines success, it's a fact that those who experience more of what they desire in life seem to be people who do not back away from problems, growth, or difficult tasks. . . .
>
> The easiest way to observe our avoidance patterns is to look at our response to anything demanding: a new task, something tedious and repetitive, a co-worker's request, deadlines or routines, rules or restrictions, or the demands of the job at hand. . . .
>
> It isn't easy to spot our own avoidance patterns. "Put a snake in a box," an old adage goes, "if you want it to learn its shape." This means that as the snake hits itself against the sides of the box, it begins to discover its own form. I do not know about snakes, but people can teach themselves about their peculiar brand of work avoidance and resistance by observing themselves objectively as they go about their daily routines. Routines are our own "boxes," and often these will bring to the surface valuable information about the Big R (resistance).
>
> Marsha Sinetar
> *Do What You Love, The Money Will Follow*

Chuck, a design engineer, recorded his activities at work for several days. The table lists information he gathered from one day. In the middle column, Chuck listed what he did; then in the first column he noted what prompted him, and in the third column recorded the outcomes of his actions. Later he filled in his analysis of the controlling potential of the outcomes.

CHUCK'S ACTIVITY CHART			
Prompt	**Behavior**	**Controlling Outcome**	**Analysis**
Deadline	Give completed design proposal to Ralph a day early	1) Ralph comments on poor spelling 2) Not hassled for being late again 3) Felt satisfied with proposal	Negative turned-on (–) Negative turned-off (+) Positive turned-on (+)
Directive from Ralph	Call ACADA about proposal	1) Put on hold 2) JR on vacation 3) Feel irritated	Negative turned-on (–) Positive turned-off (–) Negative turned-on (–)
Feel restless	Go to Cafeteria	1) Visit with Joe 2) Calm down	Positive turned-on (+) Negative turned-off (+)
Ralph hovering around	Sketch out TRS design	1) Ralph backs off 2) Dissatisfied with design	Negative turned-off (+) Negative turned-on (–)
Call from production	Talk to Prod Mgr about needs & report to Ralph	1) Ralph says I'm wasting time again! 2) Feel angry	Negative turned-on (–) Negative turned-on (–)
Feel Angry	Read Sci-Fi Mag	1) Calm down 2) Entertained	Negative turned-off (+) Positive turned-on (+)

A quick review of this one day in Chuck's work life reveals he has few positive outcomes, and only one of these is helpful in sustaining motivation. This was when he felt satisfied with his proposal. Otherwise, the other Turn-On-Positive outcomes are either his socializing with Joe or his being entertained by the science-fiction magazine. Both of these rewarded "goofing off." All the other positive outcomes were Turn-Off-

Negatives, which promote avoiding. For example, sometimes goofing off resulted in calming down, so we could predict that Chuck will goof off in the future when he feels tense or anxious. The goofing off is fun and prompts him to relax. One activity—sketching out the THS design—deserves note. The prompt for doing this was Ralph, Chuck's supervisor, hovering around which is probably an implicit threat. Following this, Chuck worked, not to achieve something, but to avoid a potential hassle. While the avoidance of a hassle is a win, it is dangerous because it encourages avoidance by removing something negative. This erodes Chuck's ability to work for something and encourages him to work to avoid instead.

Looking at his data, it's not too surprising that Chuck is not motivated to work when there isn't a threat of something negative. Ultimately, he can end up essentially being "programmed" to work to avoid, which, of course, is not conducive to creativity or enthusiasm and is part of the burnout process.

If, when you do an analysis of your own work experience, you find that much of your work is done to avoid negatives, take it seriously. It is a burnout warning signal.

■ BURNOUT WARNING SIGNAL ■

Frequent Negative Wins: Outcomes that turn off or take away pain and anxiety.

The striking thing about Chuck's day is the large number of negative outcomes. A couple of these came when Ralph was critical. In other cases, the negative outcome was Chuck's own reaction—his anger and irritability, or his expecting some kind of positive acknowledgement and not getting it. It's likely that Chuck's efforts to work will diminish, and he will be less motivated to try. In addition, as his work becomes associated with pain, aggravation, criticism, and anger, the work—like the can opener with the pet—becomes associated with negative feelings. Chuck's work itself could become an anxiety prompt. If this happens, he will be caught in the burnout process. Increasingly Chuck will respond to work projects with anxiety, which he will probably turn off by goofing around. When the quality of his work suffers as a result, his supervisor will criticize him even more. The escalating negativity would then strengthen association between work and pain, leading to even higher stress and more necessity to escape by goofing off.

That Chuck's work meets with so many negative outcomes is another burnout warning signal. As noted before, we tend to stop doing whatever leads to punishment, which is what behavioral psychologists call negative outcomes. Punishment inhibits the punished behavior and is accompanied by anxiety and other negative emotions such as anger and depression. Thus, if Chuck's work continues to be punished, his motivation will decline along with his productivity. Chuck is in danger of burning out.

■ Burnout Warning Signal ■

Frequent punishment: Outcomes that turn on or increase pain and anxiety.

Why do we continue to repeat certain actions even though we know better or have decided to do otherwise? Why can't we muster the energy to do our work? By observing the patterns of outcomes—what outcomes follow our actions—you can gain insight into what controls you and how your habits are maintained. This type of analysis will yield information on what maintains our habits.

After a period of careful systematic study, you will know a great deal about yourself and what makes you tick. You will be able to know whether or not you are burning out. You will have laid the ground work to turn the process around. Additionally, understanding the principles of learning and behavior change increases your ability to manage other people effectively. In short, you will have build your personal power because you will have a greater ability to influence your future.

CHAPTER 5

PACE YOURSELF
THE FIRST PATH TO PERSONAL POWER

Self-reverence, self-knowledge, self-control,
These three alone lead to sovereign power.
—Alfred Lord Tennyson

*B*urnout victims experience a sense of powerlessness at work and feel helpless to change it. Personal power which is the ability to influence what happens to you is empowering and combats burnout. Managing yourself effectively is the first path to personal power. By using basic principles of learning you can building and sustain high motivation and peak performance. Similarly, you can reprogram bad habits that sabotage achieving your goals.

PACE YOURSELF

PACE stands for four steps for "deprogramming" bad habits and learning more effective self-managing skills: Pinpoint, Analyze, Change, Evaluate. By following these steps you can pace yourself through your moment by moment encounters with the world. It is a guide for shedding old habits and learning new ones.

■ PACE ■

P = Pinpoint
A = Analyze
C = Change
E = Evaluate

P = PINPOINT

Pinpointing means narrowing the focus of your observation to a very specific behavior. Precision is necessary to change a habit. The behavior that you desire to change must be clearly defined. You need to know exactly what it is that you will change. A statement like this social worker's: "I'm ineffective, I'm not sensitive to my clients," is too vague. We can't get a handle on such a description. There is no starting point for analysis or change. You need a precise description for the behavior you want to change: Effective when? On what projects? What does effective "look" like? Does effective refer to the number of clients processed? The degree of client improvement?

ASK THE YES/NO QUESTION

To satisfy the yes/no principle you must be able to stop at any moment and answer with an unambiguous "yes" or "no": "Is this an instance of the behavior I'm observing?" If you hesitate or qualify your answer, then the definition needs to be sharpened. A more precise definition of "sensitive" might be "asking feeling questions of clients." Such a definition makes systematic observation easier and more reliable. It also helps Sue, the social worker, to focus in on her concern with her work and performance.

DESCRIBE A BEHAVIOR-IN-A-SITUATION

People do not act in isolation; what you do occurs within a context. What goes on around you plays a key role in what you do and how you do it. Thus, a pinpointed definition includes the conditions under which the behavior occurs. Where does it occur? Who and what are around? Sue selected the intake interview as the situation: "Asking feeling questions (the behavior) during intake interviews (the situation)." This may seem like a lot of effort. But definitions alone are illuminating and are the cornerstone of a self-change program. The time spent at this stage saves you from muddling along and getting lost in frustration later.

A = ANALYZE

There is a tremendous temptation to rush into a change plan, skipping over the critical step of collecting information and looking for patterns. The goal at this step is to determine how the behavior you want to change functions. Success in a self-change program depends on the thoroughness of the analysis because a strategy for making a change is rooted in it. A sloppy analysis yields an inaccurate picture of what's going on and will cause budding feelings of personal power to wither.

It is essential to determine how the behavior functions within the situation. This is accomplished by observing specific interactions with the environment. Remember that it's through encounters with the environment that habits are formed. We typically think of environments as something "out there," but the environment can be something inside—your
—which includes what you think, feel, fantasize, and your physical sensations. Like events in the outer world, internal events can prompt us to do certain things or serve as a reward for certain actions.

BE SYSTEMATIC

Being systematic is important. Record encounters with your environments, external and internal, to enable you to step back and objectively review emerging patterns. Data will reveal how the habit you want to change works. An easy way to do this is to keep an "encounter diary" in which you record each occurrence of the behavior in question, and note what happened just before (the prompts) and just after it (the controllers). This is similar to the method Chuck used when he made a general analysis of his work interactions. The difference is that Chuck observed several behaviors, and here you should record only the pinpointed behavior.

ASK THE CAN DO/WILL DO QUESTION

This question asks, "Can I actually perform as I desire? Do I have the skill? Do I know how to carry out the action?" If the answer is "No,

I do not have the skill to act as I wish," it is a No-Can-Do behavior. You need to learn skills for carrying out the actions. If, on the other hand, you answer: "Yes, I have the skill to act as I wish but I do not do so," you are looking at a No-Will-Do behavior. Here you are doing too little of what you want to or too much of what you don't want to do. With No-Will-Do behaviors—things you can do but don't—look closely at prompts and controllers to determine what inhibits you from doing what you know how to do and desire to do, but do not do.

ANALYZE PROMPTS

What stops you from acting or feeling as you want? What does your data reveal? Prompts can inhibit performance in four ways. First, the prompt can be fear or anxiety. Here, rather than triggering the behavior you wish, it probably sets off avoidance and negative emotional responses. Second, tension and stress can be a prompt that interferes with performance and can also trigger avoidance and negative emotions. Third, there may be prompts for the wrong behaviors, those you'd prefer to be rid of or to engage in less often. Chuck found, for example, that his irritation and restlessness were prompts for "goofing off." Finally, there may be no prompt at all for the actions you desire. You may procrastinate writing a report because there is no deadline to prompt you to write.

■ DYSFUNCTIONAL PROMPTS ■

1. The prompt triggers fear or anxiety.

2. The prompt is stress.

3. The prompt triggers undesired behavior.

4. There is no prompt for desired behavior.

ANALYZE OUTCOMES

What happens after the behavior controls the likelihood of a repeat performance? There are four basic ways in which controlling outcomes can interfere with sustained enthusiasm and peak performance. First, there may be no outcome at all for the desired activity. We know that when there is no positive outcome for an action we are not inclined to repeat it. When Ralph gave no acknowledgement for Chuck's completing the design proposal early, Chuck became less likely to be as conscientious about deadlines in the future or about completing proposals carefully.

The second situation is one in which there is a positive outcome but it comes before the behavior is performed. Rather than "If-Then," the relationship between behavior and outcome is "Then-If." Here the positive outcome carries little motivational clout. Third, the behavior desired, which in the long run will lead to a desired work style, might be punished or followed by a negative outcome. An example was when Ralph criticized Chuck for "wasting time" after he reported talking to the production manager. Lastly, an undesired behavior—one that eventually detracts from performance, health, and enthusiasm—might be leading to wins or positive outcomes and thereby encouraged by the environment. As much as you might "will" not repeating an undesired act, you are likely to continue doing so when it's being rewarded. Overeating is a good example. Everyone who has ever been on a diet knows the pleasure of sneaking a forbidden treat and its devastating impact on willpower and the waistline. Chuck's goofing off is another example. His irritation and restlessness trigger the goofing off. The positive outcome for goofing off, like overeating, turns a seemingly harmless indulgence into a self-destructive habit.

■ DYSFUNCTIONAL CONTROLLERS ■

1. The desired behavior extinguished. There is no outcome.
2. The positive outcome comes before the behavior.
3. The desired behavior is punished. It meets with a negative outcome.
4. An undesired behavior is rewarded. It meets with a positive outcome.

C = CHANGE

When you have a good understanding of how the behavior pattern you want to change functions—what triggers it and what perpetuates it—you are ready to develop a self-change program. As you read on you may think the techniques or steps seem simple. But PACE is a systematic approach, guiding you in selecting what to do when and how to get yourself to carry through. You can determine the best way to go about changing the target-behavior pattern from analysis of the data collected. For example, if a No-Can-Do behavior surfaces, where you don't know how to perform the behavior you desire, learning a new skill is indicated. With a No-Will-Do behavior, you can intervene at the prompt point, the control point, or both.

CHANGING PROMPTS

You can use these principles to change yourself. You can arrange your environment so that it will prompt you to act in ways that will bring wins essential for sustaining your enthusiasm for working. There are three strategies for changing yourself by changing prompts. You can avoid the prompt. Here the undesired behavior wouldn't be triggered. A second strategy is to create a new prompt, one that triggers desired behaviors. Finally, you can change how you respond to the prompt. This strategy involves desensitizing yourself to the prompt, so that you "unlearn" your habitual response.

Problem: The Prompt Triggers Anxiety or Fear

When analysis indicates that fear or anxiety are inhibiting performance or prompting undesired behaviors such as timidity, snapping at people, or procrastination, you must take way the prompt's power to trigger these problem emotions. Desensitization is the first strategy to consider. How to desensitize fear and anxiety is described in Chapter 6. In a nut shell, the technique involves reducing your sensitivity to the prompt. This is accomplished by learning to relax in the presence of the prompt, beginning with mildly disturbing situations and moving to more disturbing ones.

Problem: The Prompt Triggers Stress

If general tension or high stress levels are revealed as the performance saboteurs, then relaxation training is likely to be the most appropriate first step. Several techniques for relaxing are described in Chapter 6.

Problem: The Prompt Triggers Undesired Behavior

Suppose, for example, you were observing your smoking habits and you discovered that the cigarette machine in the lobby of your apartment building triggers the desire to buy and smoke cigarettes. You could adopt a different route to the work area by-passing the lobby and cigarette machine. If you don't see cigarettes for sale, you're less likely to feel like buying them.

Strategy: Avoid the Prompt

When your analysis reveals that the prompt triggers undesired responses, the first change strategy to consider is to avoid the prompt. Suppose the behavior pattern that is burning you out is an interpersonal conflict. One common tactic is avoiding the person, which is a viable solution if it doesn't interfere with the rest of your work. If the troublesome person is not central to your work duties, by all means avoid him or her. On the other hand, if the person's job interfaces with your own, avoiding becomes a self-defeating defense rather than a solution. You can't avoid a central part of your work and expect to perform at your peak or to achieve positive outcomes.

Strategy: Change the Prompt

An alternative to avoiding the prompt is changing it. The dieter who purchases only "approved" foods when in the supermarket is employing this strategy. Later, when peering into the frig, there will be only celery sticks and carrots to munch on. The eating prompt has been changed from chips to carrots.

The person who wears earphones to block out tension-producing noise is another example. Listening to soothing music that relaxes is substituted for aggravating sounds. How to alter the environment to change prompts is described in Chapter 6. Restructuring the tasks and responsibilities of one's job which will be discussed in Chapter 9 falls into this category. New job demands are prompts that trigger a different set of behaviors.

Another strategy for dealing with prompts that trigger undesired behavior is to alter the prompt itself. The effectiveness of this approach is limited to what you can realistically change. You cannot directly change other people. (If they would just act as you desired, you'd have no problem!) Give up the notion. Your control is limited to your own behavior. Thus, when analysis shows that interactions with another person bring negative outcomes, trying to change the prompt (the person's behavior) probably won't work. In fact, rather than solving the problem, you may actually aggravate it.

Strategy: Change Your Response

When an encounter with a prompt that triggers undesired behavior is inevitable, that is, when avoidance won't work and you can't change it, try the third way: Change your response to the prompt. In this strategy reworking the association between a prompt and your actions becomes the focus of change. This may mean learning a new skill, eliminating fear responses, or altering your thinking and the way you perceive prompts. How to do this is discussed in Chapters 6, 7 and 11.

The power of the prompt is equal to its ability to influence you. Changing your response to the dysfunctional prompt yields the most personal power. When you learn to respond differently to a person or a situation, it no longer controls you. It can't trigger an action or a feeling. You are free of it. The habit is deleted and you need never concern yourself with it again because you reclaimed the prompt's power over you.

Strategy: Prompt an Incompatible Behavior

Another approach is to change the situation so that it prompts a neutral or positive behavior that will be incompatible with the one you want to eliminate. "Incompatible behaviors" are behaviors that are opposite, mutually exclusive of the undesired behaviors. That is, you can do one and only one at a time; you can't do them both at once. For example, deep relaxation is the opposite of tension; laughing is the opposite of crying; working on reports is the opposite of "goofing off." The idea is to substitute prompts that trigger a behavior that is opposite to or incompatible with the undesired behavior. To block out goofing off, for example, Chuck should concentrate on prompting behavior aimed at developing and completing designs.

Manage your prompts: Use the environment to help rather than trying to "will" yourself to not act. Arrange prompts to "grease the skids" of your change. The trick is to trigger a behavior opposite of the undesired one.

Problem: There Is No Prompt for the Desired Behavior

A general prescription for beating job burnout is to nourish enthusiasm by adding positive, healthy wins for productivity. Such outcomes may often be available, but we do not always act in ways to obtain them.

If your analysis reveals a No-Will-Do behavior where you know how to perform but are not doing so, the breakdown may be the failure of the environment to prompt you. For example, having become accustomed to structured training, the new professional just out of graduate school often flounders and withdraws upon encountering a "laissez-faire" world. The rewards are available but the prompts are absent. The teachers aren't there to set assignments and deadlines. So the intelligent and talented graduate sits frustrated in the new job, waiting for someone to come along and turn the switch. Sue, the social worker, was one such person. She excelled in her internships under close academic supervision. Her professors pointed out each step in the learning process. But upon joining the ranks of the work world, she discovered her new boss had little supervisory skill and even less interest in her work. She was on her own. It was self-supervise or stagnate.

Sue realized if she wanted to maintain her interest in her casework, she had to be effective. She pinpointed effectiveness to include being more sensitive to clients, developing new projects, trying out new techniques, and evaluating herself. Her analysis revealed no prompts for these activities. She had to provide them herself.

Strategy: Create a New Prompt

Once Sue's problem was clear, she advised herself as she did her clients, using her goal-setting skills. To increase her sensitivity to clients, she set an objective, for example, to increase the number of feeling questions asked during the intake interview. She knew how to ask feeling questions but there was no prompt to remind her. It was a No-Will-Do behavior. To correct this she wrote "Ask a Feeling Question" in bold print on a 3 x 5 card, which she placed against the clock on her desk where she alone could see it. This was a physical prompt, reminding her each time she looked at the clock (which she did frequently, especially with reticent clients) to ask a feeling question. This strategy is like tying a string on your finger as a reminder to buy paper towels when shopping. Many people use list-making as a prompt to get their busywork out of the way. They need merely glance at the list to be reminded of what needs doing.

Begin by artificially arranging a situation so that you remember to act. This gets the ball rolling. But if you want the behavior to continue, to take on a life of its own, it must be followed by a positive outcome: a win. Remember, one prescription for beating burnout is to refuel by increasing positive outcomes. So prime the pump. Get yourself to act; then the world will have something to respond to.

When Sue increased the number of feeling questions she asked during client intake, for example, she was more successful in being sensitive and developing rapport, an ingredient of effective casework. The rapport served as a win that encouraged her to ask more feeling questions. With bad habits, wearing strings on fingers or writing messages to yourself are not necessary. They seem to come naturally. By coordinating prompts and controllers, you can manage yourself so that the behavior you consciously select eventually feels natural, too.

The basic formula is to select a suitable prompt, then act out the desired behavior, and none other, in the prompt's presence. Make sure the association between the prompt and the behavior is clear-cut. Finally, arrange for a desired positive outcome each time you act. The outcome cements the association between the prompt and the behavior. With each repetition, the association strengthens.

■ HOW TO CREATE A NEW PROMPT ■

1. Identify suitable prompt.
2. Perform desired behavior and none other.
3. Provide a positive outcome.

Consider another example. Chuck wanted to do more writing such as developing proposals, writing up projects, and keeping notes, but he had difficulty concentrating, actually getting to it. He knew that if he did the writing it would enhance his productivity. He wanted to do it, he knew how to do it, but he didn't do it. After a lot of fiddling and fussing he would begin to write but become distracted almost immediately by a phone call, his in-basket, or restlessness. Part of Chuck's problem was that there was nothing to prompt him to write.

Chuck needed to develop writing prompts that would trigger his attention and help him concentrate on writing. Here's what he did. He found a quiet conference room that was rarely used and designated it as his place to write. The change strategy involved making the conference room his writing prompt. To do this he had to build an association between being in the conference room and writing, so that eventually when he entered the area just being there prompted Chuck to write. The objective was to "feel" like writing when in the conference room. To do this, he arranged to write in the conference room for short periods of time, such as fifteen minutes. He did nothing else. He did not contaminate his writing prompt with undesired behaviors such as reading a sci-fi magazine, chatting with a colleague, or goofing off. When he felt the urge to do these activities, he left the writing area. After each brief period of writing, Chuck arranged to receive an immediate win in order to cement the prompt-behavior association.

If you try this strategy it may feel artificial, even forced at first. As Chuck was successful in implementing his change plan, he slowly increased the amount of time spent in the writing area and it became easier to concentrate on writing. The conference room became a prompt for writing.

If you can't set aside a specific area, you can try using a ritual such as cleaning off your desk as a prompt, or using a specific time of day, or using a ritual plus time such as telling your secretary to hold calls every day from 9 to 11 a.m. This is a strategy Sue used successfully to increase the quality of her case recording. She found she frequently put off writing notes summarizing sessions with clients until they dwindled to a couple of abbreviated sentences. Sue recognized this as a first indicator of performance deterioration. She wanted to write thorough case notes but there was nothing to prompt her to write them. Instead her day passed with opening and answering the mail, making referral phone calls, and so forth. There was nothing to prompt her to write the notes.

These are not discrete strategies. You may have a couple of causes checked under prompts. For example, tension may undermine your performance quality and simultaneously trigger the undesired behavior of snapping at co-workers. Strategies may dovetail or overlap.

MANAGE OUTCOMES

Events following the behavior are called "controlling outcomes" because they influence the likelihood of that behavior occurring again. These controllers cement associations between the prompt and the behavior. The cementing quality is the prompt's prediction-ability. The prompt is a signal of what outcome is likely to come. When the controller is a positive outcome, something pleasurable, associations can take on prompting power. Encountering the prompt, you rapidly appraise the situation, determine what type of outcome is likely to follow, and act. Prompts are particularly important when the outcome is negative. The sooner you know a negative outcome is imminent, the more likely you are to be able to escape it. Managing outcomes—events that follow behaviors—is a key step in changing habits. The general rule of thumb is to arrange positive outcomes for desired, enthusiasm-generating activities; no outcome, or possibly a negative one, for off-target activities such as procrastinating and goofing off.

With this general principle in mind, analyze the controlling outcome in operation with the burnout behavior you want to change. Look for a pattern, and compare it to this guiding principle. How does it deviate from this standard? Does it turn off motivation? If so, you'll want to change it. There are several ways controllers can squelch motivation and set you up for burnout.

Problem: There Is No Outcome for Desired Behavior

When there is no pay-off for the desired behavior, we can expect that behavior to occur infrequently, if at all. If the person expects a win for performing and receives nothing instead, the absense of an outcome can be experienced as a punishment. Behaviors that are punished tend to decline rapidly in their frequency. One principle of learning called extinction states that a behavior that meets with no response will "extinquish" or stop occurring. An example is the person who works hard to complete a report by the deadline and receives no acknowledgement for doing so. Chances are that he or she will not try as hard in the future to get reports done on time.

Strategy: Prompt Desired Behavior Then Give Win

When there is no positive outcome for the desired behavior, the solution is clear-cut. Acknowledgement and other wins from the world are needed to encourage you to perform. Arrange for a positive outcome to follow the behavior you desire to increase. For example, when Chuck gave his proposal early to Ralph, his boss—clearly a desirable behavior—there was no positive consequence. Ralph is not likely to change. By concentrating on Ralph's failing and bemoaning how the world "should " be, Chuck accomplishes nothing except keeping himself in an agitated state, which will eventually give way to a sense of helplessness and

lethargy. If Chuck wants to protect himself from the dampening influences of "extinction," he needs to provide his own win. Once Chuck took a closer look at what was happening and what he needed, he was able to thrive in spite of Ralph's indifference. He paced himself with self-acknowledgement. The increased confidence and sense of competence that resulted was a psychological booster fortifying him against burnout.

Problem: The Positive Outcome Is Before the Behavior

This situation is logically impossible, of course. An outcome is something that comes after a behavior. If it comes before the behavior, it is not an "outcome"—which is precisely the point. Only outcomes can control behavior, not random positive events. Positives are surely desirable, but in order to influence motivation and turn around burnout, the wins must be outcomes, results of your action. You gain a sense of mastery, the feeling of control over your world. The feeling of being able to influence, to maximize pleasures and escape pain, is the essence of personal power. Mastery, or control, is the antithesis of the helplessness experienced during burnout. From mastery grows confidence and enthusiasm.

Strategy: Set Up an If-Then Contingency

If you notice that many positive occurrences in your data are noncontingent (they come before the behavior or when you don't perform), look at them again. Do you grant yourself little indulgences throughout the day, such as coffee breaks, an extra fifteen minutes at lunch, or a personal phone call? These indulgences can become positive outcomes simply by placing them *after* a desired behavior. Don't take away these privileges; instead make enjoying them contingent (if I file ten folders, then I get a cup of coffee) on doing what you have decided to do.

For example, Myra, an independent insurance agent, didn't like making out client reports and analysis forms. She often made herself miserable because she let them pile up and then had to sacrifice her precious weekend catching up. This one small part of her job was casting all of her work in a drab shade of gray. Myra's one pleasure was spending about an hour and a half in the afternoon at a coffeeshop reading the paper and sipping expresso. Her coffeehouse visits were a pleasure that had potential for being a motivator. She made an agreement with herself: *if* she completed all the R & A forms for the day, *then* she could go to the coffeehouse. Not only did Myra manage to put a halt to her procrastinating but she also enjoyed her coffee and paper even more. She had tapped the motivating potential of her afternoon pleasure by making it contingent upon finishing the forms.

Problem: The Desired Behavior Is Being Turned Off

Anything that meets with a negative outcome is eventually going to turn off. We simply do not continue doing the unpleasant, if we can help it. Unfortunately, organizations often discourage the very activities employees were hired to do; a double bind that is both confusing and frustrating. Seeing your motivation slip through your fingers and feeling helpless to stop it is worse.

Consider the following example. Beth, a bright and creative management trainee, made an excellent suggestion for an innovative approach to the development of training material. Henry, the supervisor, responded to the suggestion by saying, "It has its interesting aspects," and directing her to "Go work it out and draw up a detailed proposal for my review." Writing up a detailed proposal is at least a little burdensome. Not everybody is going to sit down at the keyboard and whip out ten or fifteen pages of text and charts and graphs. While Henry may have intended the assignment as an acknowledgement of Beth's suggestion, it was a turn-off to her because it meant a lot of extra work. She quickly learned to keep her ideas to herself.

Strategy: Give a "Win" for Desired Behavior

Beth was distressed that her enthusiasm was drying up. She could see it was in part because of the additional work it earned her. Once pinpointed, she dealt with the problem by learning how to assertively communicate her concerns to Henry. Together they reached an agreement where he would brainstorm ideas with her before telling her to "write it up." Simultaneously, Beth worked out a self-reinforcement program in which she silently evaluated her own suggestions and acknowledged herself for having made it.

Again, the strategy is to eliminate the negative outcome and provide a positive one for actions you wish to promote. Negative outcomes tend to have unpleasant side effects: anger, fear, anxiety. When we encounter a negative outcome, our bodies go on alert because there is a potential danger. These feelings tend to become associated with the situation and your behavior at that time. Consequently, any time you want to encourage a behavior, such as speaking up in a group or making suggestions, that has been suppressed by negative outcomes, it is a good idea to erase these old emotional response habits at the same time that you provide positive outcomes. If overlooked, such fears and anxieties can act as inhibitors.

Problem: An Undesired Behavior Is Encouraged

Chuck's goofing off, for example, was encouraged by its built-in enjoyment. Fudging on expense accounts, smoking, or talking to a friend on the phone are the same phenomena. The general formula here is to ignore the undesired activity and to provide a positive win for its opposite. Ignoring is a better approach than self-punishment.

Behaviors that don't meet with a win eventually fade out. And by ignoring them, you don't run the risk of learning negative emotions that might interfere with your work. Rather than chastising himself for goofing off, Chuck focused on developing the opposite activity and providing a win for working on his design proposals, for example.

Strategy: Ignore Undesired Behavior and Give "Win" for Its Opposite

The win for the undesired activity should be blocked because it encourages the undesired behavior. However, when the undesired behavior is inherently pleasurable, it is impossible to make this separation. For example, the taste of chocolate is itself a win for chocolate lovers. You can't separate the win (the pleasurable taste) from the act of eating the chocolate. Many people attempt to do so by reprimanding themselves, but such punishment should be avoided because it generates negative emotions.

An alternative is to intervene simultaneously at the prompting point. For example, Chuck examined his data and realized that his goofing off was inherently pleasurable: he enjoyed talking to Joe and reading science-fiction magazines. It helped him relax. He reduced goofing off by removing some of its prompts. His data revealed that he usually goofed off when feeling restless or angry. These emotions were his goof-off prompts. By using the techniques we'll review in Chapter 6 Chuck learned to subdue his restlessness with deep breathing and relaxation rather than going to the cafeteria, for example. He also took a course in time management and learned how to use self-imposed deadlines to prompt the opposite of goofing off, working on his designs.

GUIDELINES FOR ARRANGING OUTCOMES

When and how often to arrange for positive outcomes is another consideration. Wins have the strongest impact when they come immediately after the behavior you want to influence. The longer a delay, the weaker the influence. An acknowledgment coming six months after the deed has little motivating power.

How often to give a positive outcome depends on the behavior. In the beginning, give yourself a positive outcome or win every time you perform. As the new behavior strengthens, slowly begin weaning yourself. Continuous acknowledgement renders us vulnerable because, if the positive outcome is abruptly cut off, performing will rapidly stop. In contrast, when the rewarding outcome is unpredictable the behavior it controls is resistant to burning out. A good example is playing with slot machines or other forms of gambling. Sometimes a lever pull brings coins; more often it doesn't. Intermittent wins keep us dropping in coins and pulling the lever.

Create a Want List

The Want List, as the name suggests, is a list of things and activities you want. When you have such a list, you can give yourself something you want after you've performed in a particular way. Getting something from the Want List serves as a reward or a "win." We're more likely to repeat actions that bring wins. Using a Want List enables you to tailor rewards to your mood and the moment.

WANT LIST		
What I Do A Lot	**Activities I Like**	**Things I Want**
Drink coffee	Reading the paper	Classical & jazz CDs
Drop into Dottie's office	Eating out	New shirt
Comb hair	Dancing	Mountain bike
Talk on phone	Go to movies	Running shoes
	Sleeping late	
	See friends	
	Walks on beach	

A side benefit of using the Want List is that creating it helps to clarify what you want. Oddly enough, simply listing what you want increases the chances you will get them. Some people who have publicly posted their "Want Lists" have found that people they work with or live with began to reward them by fulfilling their wants.

How to Make a Want List

The Want List has three categories: (1) What you do a lot, (2) activities you like, and (3) things you want. Wants need have no limits. Items listed can be small or large; material, social, personal, or work activities.

Remember burnout can be prevented by developing a sense of personal power. This is accomplished by giving yourself wins when you perform as you want. Not only do you get more wins in your life but you build your feelings of control. This simple formula contains the means for psychological well-being.

Revitalization begins by deliberately arranging to get positive outcomes. You immediately begin getting what you want. This motivation booster fuels forward motion. Personal power is feeling able to influence the world or able to get what you want as a result of your actions. This is the opposite of helplessness. The key is to make getting what you want *contingent* upon your taking a small step. Don't worry about how small the step is, as long as it is movement toward the goal. Satisfy your wants. Burning out is characterized by a pronounced absence of satisfaction. And turning around burnout is no easy task. It has a negative momentum that requires a great deal of energy to stop.

DEVELOP A CHANGE PLAN

Finally it is time to set forth a plan for change. The plan includes a goal with small step objectives for reaching it. It also specifies what win or reward you'll receive for reaching your goal.

SET A GOAL

Goals are important. They give you something to strive for, to aim at. Without a goal you are a ship at sea without a destination going around and around, never making headway. Set a reasonable, attainable goal. Many people set themselves up to fail by setting their sights on the unachievable. You can always increase, modify, or revamp your goals.

SELF-CHANGE GUIDELINES		
Prompts (Before Behavior)	**Behavior**	**Controllers (After Behavior)**
IF...	IF...	IF...
■ **Fear/Anxiety** a) Slowly approach feared situation while remaining relaxed. b) Approach feared situation while engaging in behavior incompatible with fear, i.e., eating, sex, following instructions, relaxing, laughing, etc. ■ **Tension** a) Train self to relax. Use workshops or self-help books. b) Eliminate tension-producing thoughts. ■ **Prompt triggers undesired behavior** a) Avoid prompt. b) Change prompt. c) Change reaction to prompt. ■ **No prompt for desired behavior** a) Use a prompt to cue. b) Use situation control: Engage in desired behavior only in specific situation, then folow with a win.	■ **No Skill (No-Can-Do)** a) Set goal to learn desired behavior, break into small steps; set objective for each step; give wins as objectives are reached. ■ **Too little of desired behavior (No-Will-Do)** a) Set objective for slightly more than currently doing; give win each time meet objective. When reach new level, increase requirements to get win slightly. When reach goal level, slowly change from getting win each time to only sometimes. ■ **Too much of undesired behavior** a) Perform a behavior incompatible with or opposite of undesired behavior, follow with win and give no outcome (ignore) for undesired behavior. b) Use prompt to trigger behavior incompatible with (opposite of) undesired behavior and avoid prompts for undesired behavior.	■ **No win for desired behavior** a) Prompt desired behavior, follow with win. ■ **Win comes before desired behavior** a) Set up contingency: If perform desired behavior, then give win. If don't perform desired behavior, then no win. ■ **Desired behavior is punished** a) Give win for desired behavior and desensitize fear/anxiety prompts created by punishment. ■ **Undesired behavior is rewarded** a) Ignore undesired behavior; give win for opposite behavior b) Avoid or ignore prompt that triggers undesired behavior, plus use prompt to trigger incompatible (opposite) behavior.

The best way to assure a viable goal is to look at how often you are now performing the behavior in question. Count it. If you have already done a good job pinpointing, counting should be straightforward. You can keep a tally on a file card you carry around. (Try golf counters, available in sporting goods stores. They are a mechanical tally worn on the wrist and look like watches.) After several days of counting, look at the frequencies. Are you engaging in this activity more than you thought, or less? How often you are currently performing the behavior is your "baseline." A baseline describes the level at which you are performing before implementing any change plan. The baseline is used as a basis of evaluation. It is the measure with which you compare your performance during and after your change plan. The baseline also gives you a level for establishing your first objective.

> **The name of the game is action. Doing. Overcoming your inertia and *acting* will give you a whole new lease on being creatively alive. Action is the single most effective antidote to depression, anxiety, stress, fear, worry, guilt, and, of course, immobility.**
>
> **Dr. Wayne Dyer**
> ***Pulling Your Own Strings***

SET AN OBJECTIVE

Objectives are steps on the path, a series of markers toward the goal. The goal is where you want to go; objectives get you there. They guide you in determining what to do or not do in the moment.

■ BEHAVIOR OBJECTIVE ■

I will _____
(WHAT)

when _____ for _____
(SITUATION) (HOW MUCH)

Goals are reached by taking many steps and meeting many objectives. An objective is a statement of what you will do to achieve the next
step.

Pinpoint What You Will Do

Remember from the earlier discussion of the PACE self-change
program that the first step is to pinpoint the behavior to be changed. A
pinpointed behavior is one that is described so clearly that you can
answer the yes/no Question: "Am I doing it now?" Or "Is this an example
of it?" When you can answer "yes" or "no" without hesitation, the "what"
of the objective has been clearly stated. For example, Sue, the social
worker, wanted to increase her effectiveness by building rapport with
the client during intake. Drawing people out with "feeling questions"
was one way to accomplish this. She pinpointed a feeling question to be
a question that asks for another person to communicate feelings.
Examples include "How do you feel about . . . ?" and "Do you feel . . .
(angry, sad, good, etc.) about . . . . . ?" In listening to taped intake
interviews, Sue could easily decide if any particular question was a
feeling question.

Describe the Situation

Objectives describe the situation where you will carry out the
objective and/or the prompts for what you will do. In this way you know
exactly what you will do and when you will do it. Sue, for example, would
ask the feeling questions during intake interviews. She might also ask
questions that elicit feelings when talking with friends, but these would
not be part of her objective.

Take a Small Step

Finally, an objective specifies at what standard you will perform. It
states how long, at what level of quality, to what degree, or how many
times you will act. The rule of thumb for success is to set the objective
for a small improvement over a short time period. Don't set yourself up

to fail by demanding enormous changes. Instead, begin at your current level of performance with the first objective. For example, from data she collected during intake interviews, Sue found she was asking two feeling questions on the average. In her first objective she started with asking two feeling questions during the next two intake interviews. This was an objective that got the ball rolling and Sue knew she could meet.

The feeling of accomplishment in meeting small achievable steps sets a success cycle into motion and will go a long way to bolster you against burnout. Once you've begun your change plan by setting an objective at your current level of performance, then proceed in small steps. Ask yourself for small improvements only. For example, Sue's second objective required that she ask at least three feeling questions in the next intake interview. It's similar to practicing yoga. In yoga, you assume a posture that you can do without undo strain, then you stretch a little bit. You don't demand too much or try to force yourself into a position.

REWARD YOURSELF

Sue looked over her Want List and decided that she would buy a particular magazine she wanted as a reward for meeting her first

I PACE MYSELF

objective. She also decided she would silently acknowledge herself after each feeling question she asked. This immediate positive outcome bridged the gap in time between acting and getting the magazine. Self-acknowledgement has other benefits. Sue paid more attention to feeling questions she and others made during daily conversations as well as in the interviews. This kind of heightened awareness facilitates rapid learning. Also using self-acknowledgement while seeing yourself succeed strengthens its power to motivate you.

DISCIPLINE AND COMMITMENT

Good intentions alone are not enough to change behavior. You must act. There's an old saying: "The road to hell is paved with good intentions." Good intentions don't ensure that things will go right.

This brings up the issue of commitment and discipline. To succeed you must have commitment—good intentions and discipline—a way to motivate yourself to carry out your good intentions. One obstacle is the tendency to rebel, which gets in the way of doing what we want. A bigger obstacle is simply not knowing how to manage oneself.

WRITE A SELF-CONTRACT

A simple technique for building commitment and discipline, called a "self-contract," is a written agreement with yourself stating what you will do. A self-contract is something like a New Year's resolution in that you are making a resolve to do something or change in some way. It differs, however, from a New Year's resolution in a few notable ways. First, New Year's resolutions tend to be global statements like, "I will be more receptive to change," or "I will lose weight and take care of my health." By comparison, the contract contains a pinpointed statement of what you are going to do, when and where you will do it. "I will ride the exercise bike for ten minutes when I get home from work."

Describe a Win

The contract describes the outcome. It states what reward you will receive when you meet the objective. New Year's resolutions are rarely stated as contingencies: if I do X, then I'll get Y. The contract has a term or termination date, whereas the resolution is open-ended: "I will stop smoking" as compared to "Today I will not smoke during breakfast." The contract teaches you that you can do what you decide to do. You can be without smoking for one day during breakfast. You can successfully do what you determine. Your self-esteem and confidence in yourself grow. By comparison, the open-endedness of the resolution sets you up to fail. Most smokers don't stop "cold turkey" which is what the resolution demands. If you go all day and then have a smoke your resolution has failed. You learn that you can't do what you decide to do. Your self-esteem and confidence in yourself can decline.

```
┌─────────────────────────────────────────────────────────┐
│                     SELF-CONTRACT                         │
│                                                           │
│   I agree to _____  │
│   _____ │
│                          OBJECTIVE                        │
│   When I complete this I will _____   │
│                                       WIN                 │
│                                                           │
│   _____                                      │
│   CONTRACT TERM                                           │
│                                                           │
│   _____      _____   │
│        DATE                        SIGNATURE             │
└─────────────────────────────────────────────────────────┘
```

Make the contract for only as long as you are sure you can stick to it. This might be an hour, a day, or a week. For example, the person riding the exercise bike for ten minutes might write a contract to do so for three days. When the contract term ends, you are free to decide if you want to renew it.

> A human being is the kind of machine that wears out from *lack of use*... for the most part we gain energy by using energy... mental and spiritual lassitude is often cured by decisive action or the clear intention to act. We learn in high school physics that kinetic energy is measured in terms of motion. The same thing is true of human energy: it comes into existence through use. As... Fritz Perls, founder of Gestalt therapy, use to say, "I don't want to be saved, I want to be *spent*."
>
> George Leonard
> *Mastery: The Keys to Success and Long-term Fulfillment*

Write It Down

Write down the agreement with yourself, your self-contract. This promotes commitment. It's helpful to have a friend, co-worker, or mate witness and sign the contract to provide self-imposed peer pressure. Try using the self-contract. It is surprising how effective such a simple technique can be.

E = EVALUATE

Seeing progress toward your goal provides nourishing feedback and promotes continued movement. It feels good to succeed. Sometimes early change is hard to see. Suppose, for example, you wanted to think more positive thoughts and fewer negative ones. And suppose you counted positive and negative thoughts before starting any change program and you were thinking 500 negative thoughts and 25 positive thoughts a day. Suppose in the early stages you reduced your negative thoughts by 20 percent to 400 a day and increased your positive thoughts by 20 percent to 30 a day. A 20 percent change is considered good progress, but without some sort of objective evaluation, it might be hard to see it.

Proof of progress in black and white can help, especially in the beginning. Progress in a self-pacing program is something you can feel good about regardless of the negative factors that exist in your work situation.

Suppose evaluation reveals you haven't made the progress you had hoped. You can take immediate trouble-shooting action. There is no need to drag an ineffective change plan on for weeks and weeks, becoming discouraged and frustrated. You can act immediately to do something else. Absence of change isn't a fault or something to feel guilty about; rather, it indicates a need to go back and systematically reexamine each PACE step. Maybe you didn't state the objective clearly so that you didn't know when to do what. Perhaps you demanded too much of yourself. Perhaps some other aspect of the action plan needs revamping. Evaluation is an intricate part of pacing yourself. By focusing on your goal and looking at your progress toward it, you can keep yourself on-target.

If you have pinpointed the behavior carefully and collected a baseline rate (counted the frequency of the behavior before implementing your action plan), then evaluation is simple. Continue counting how often you engage in the behavior after implementing your change plan and compare this to your baseline. The evaluation is a comparison of how often you are performing the behavior now with how often you were performing it before implementing your change plan.

If the behavior is not clearly pinpointed, it is difficult to evaluate. For example, when Sue, the social worker, said, "I'm not effective," it was difficult for her to establish a baseline. She could not count instances of effectiveness. On the other hand, when she pinpointed effectiveness as asking feeling questions in intake interviews, it was a straightforward matter to count the number of feeling questions and log their frequency on a graph.

Graphs are a convenient way to look at your evaluation. The pictorial quality makes comparison easy. Evaluation is a-count-ability: becoming accountable to yourself.

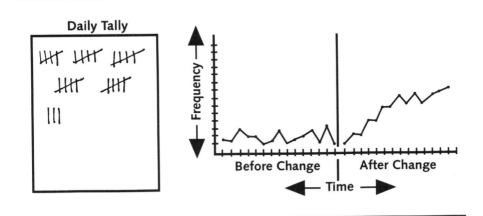

PACE is a general guide for implementing a self-change program. The following chapters will discuss specific types of techniques to use at the C step of PACE.

CHAPTER 6

MANAGE STRESS

THE SECOND PATH TO PERSONAL POWER

*P*ersonal power, the capability to influence the world around you in the ways you desire, is the opposite of helplessness, which causes burnout. While we have little control over other people, we do have control over ourselves — something we tend to forget when we're feeling helpless. We can move, walk, decide, choose, look at things from different perspectives, set goals, and learn skills. Numerous capabilities lie dormant in each person, waiting to be developed. As we develop our capabilities, we gain a sense of mastery and control.

The experience of mastery changes everything. Because striving for mastery focuses your attention on areas in which you are skilled, a sense of confidence and being in command of yourself develops. Building personal power comes from developing your capabilities, your powers. It means learning how to get what you need. To the extent you are able to do this, you are powerful.

We know that exercise, or the lack of it, shapes the body by developing some muscles and ignoring others. Weight, skin tone, and hair shine depend on the food we eat. There is a tradition of commanding and altering the physical self. Most of us have acquired some good skills along with many poor habits. Control over one's basic operating system, the autonomic systems that run our bodies, is also possible. We have all had experience doing this. You know you can make yourself nervous or calm, for example, but may not know exactly how. Most people understand that chemical means like coffee, alcohol, or drugs can alter tension levels, but may be less knowledgeable when it comes to using one's internal responses.

Managing stress involves learning to influence your basic operating system in such a way that you perform at your peak more of the time, withstand greater stresses, and have more resistance to negative forces. Unfortunately, most people do not develop "command-ability" and respond willy-nilly to the world instead.

WHAT IS STRESS?

Stress is a physical response to certain encounters with the environment. Change, pleasant or unpleasant, is such a stressor. Change requires adjustments that open the possibility for failure. Change brings uncertainty. We can make predictions about what will occur but we can never be certain. Change raises doubts. We wonder if we took the right course. Change is threatening because we might not like what happens.

Our bodies do certain things automatically. We don't have to think to breathe or blink, for example. These automatic responses make up your "basic operating system." When we encounter a stressor, the bodies' basic operating system responds with what is called "the general adaptation syndrome." There are three stages: alarm, resistance or adaptation, and exhaustion.

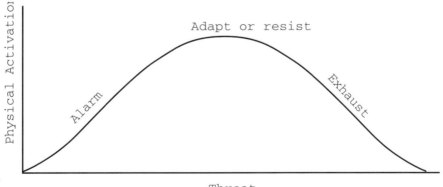

ACTIVATION LEVEL AND OPTIMAL RANGE

The fight-flight response is appropriate if you are confronted by a robber in your home, or by some other threat to your life. But often this response, or some of the characteristics of it, is triggered inappropriately by a situation which is stressful, but not life-threatening. You my be suffering a chronic stress response worrying over unpaid bills. The ultimate result of not paying your bills may be death: if you go bankrupt your creditors might come and shoot you; if you fail to pay your utility bill the heat may be turned off and you might freeze to death. These possibilities are neither immediate nor likely, but your body cannot distinguish between the hypothetical threat you imagine, and an immediate geniune one. Consciousness has developed to the extent that stress responses can be triggered by emotions, ideas, memories, and expectations. Abstract thought produced in the sophisticated, higher centers of the brain (cerebral cortex) can trigger the automatic survival reflexes located in the lower centers.

John Mason
Guide to Stress Reduction

During the alarm stage, the body activates, preparing to fight or flee. Meeting this demand requires physiological changes in the adrenal cortex, hormone secretions, heart rate, breathing, and muscle tension. The energy demand on the body is tremendous. These responses exact a toll called "stress." Out of self-preservation, we move into the second stage: resistance or adaptation. At this stage we resist the stressor while seeking a way to nullify it. The level of physical activation drops somewhat from the peak reached during alarm and continues at a moderately high level. During the resistance phase we search for ways to influence the world in ways we want. When we are successful in dealing with the stressor, functioning becomes easier and activation drops back to its former maintenance level. But when—as in the case of burnout—the stressor continues unchanged, activation level remains high. Continued physical demands combined with the repeated failure to control the situation is experienced first as frustration. If there is no way to turn off the stressor, the frustration turns into futility. Soon comes exhaustion, the third stage of the stress response.

A medical example makes it easier to understand the relationship between stress and burnout. Stress does not cause burnout any more than a fever causes pneumonia. The fever is a symptom and not the cause of the pneumonia. While getting rid of the fever will not stop the illness, an unchecked fever can be serious and will compound the destructiveness of the pneumonia. So the fever must be treated. You could think of stress as being the "fever" of burnout. Eliminating stress alone is not going to stop burnout. But stress wears down your physical resources and is associated with illness. So like a fever, stress needs to be controlled.

WHAT CAUSES STRESS?

Things that stress us are called stressors. Many stressors are universal. For example, fear and anxiety are stressors. Loud noise, like low-flying airplanes, screaming of sirens, and jack-hammering in the street are stressors. Anything that threatens our safety is a stressor. Some stressors are learned. For example, some people become very agitated when they must give a speech or tell someone what to do.

Business Week magazine once reported an interesting study of stress in race-car drivers. It seems that some researchers at Emory University measured drivers' stress levels when they were traveling at two hundred miles an hour out on the racetrack, then while they were waiting in pit stops as someone else serviced their cars. **Conclusion: the drivers experienced far more stress when they gave up control and sat idle.**

William A Charland, Jr.
Career Shifting
Starting Over in a Changing Economy

The most ubiquitous stressor is change. Any change, even change for the better, is stressful. With change comes fear, uncertainty, and doubt — sometimes called FUD. Change requires learning and adjustment to new conditions. There is always the potential that we won't like the change.

Another potent stressor is loss of control and feeling helpless. When we can't control situations, circumstances could turn against us, for example. Loss of control is very threatening to most people.

Stress and Performance

Activation level is the degree of activity in your basic operating system that includes heart and respiratory rates and muscle tension. Understanding the relationship between activation level and performance is central to managing stress. Notice that when activation is low, when you're bored or drowsy, for example, quality of performance suffers. A similar drop in performance occurs when activation is high, when you feel panicky, for example. On the other hand, a moderate level of activation is optimal for peak performance.

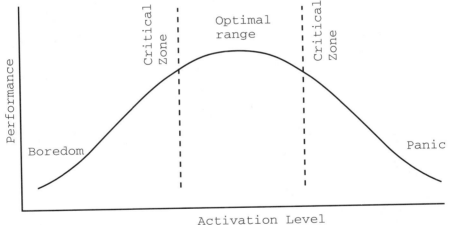

ACTIVATION LEVEL AND OPTIMAL RANGE

CREATE A PERSONAL STRESS LOG

The first step to managing stress is to identify situations that stress you and gather information on what prompted the stress and how you respond to it. Then you can see your response habits and develop a plan for change.

PERSONAL STRESS LOG

Instructions: When you feel frustrated, worried, pressured, angry, excited, anxious or upset, stop and look at yourself and the situation. Create a personal stress log. Describe the situation, including who was involved, when and where it happened. Rate your distress level, using a scale from 1 to 10, with 1 being "very little distress" and 10 being "extremely upset." Describe your response to the distressing event including what you were thinking, how you felt and what you did.

When	Prompt: Situation	Distress: Level	Response: Thoughts, feelings, actions

After you've collected data on your stress for several days, review your personal stress log, looking for patterns. See if there are generalizations that you can make about when you experienced distress. What situations, people, times, or days seem to prompt it? For example, you might notice that deadlines are a reoccuring theme. Or perhaps there is a person or kind of event that appear several times in the log.

Look also for patterns in your responses. Pay particular attention to responses you use over and over. You might see a pattern of avoiding certain situations or overeating when anxious for example. From this analysis you can begin making a plan for managing stress. When you know you are going to encounter a situation you know is stressful to you, you can prepare for it in advance. For example, if you know that speaking with a particular person on the phone always upsets you, before calling him you might spend a few minutes breathing deeply and and reminding yourself that you are not the target of this person's anger.

STRESS PATTERN ANALYSIS

Instructions: Describe patterns you found in your personal stress log. Next to each pattern describe your usual response to it. In the third column write ideas you have for handling the situation differently so that it is less stressful.

Stress pattern:	My usual response:	Possible plan of action:

SENSING ACTIVATION LEVEL

Learning to sense activation level from moment to moment is essential to managing stress. "Oh, I know when I'm stressed out." you may say. But this is not always the case. In fact, most people do not accurately read their activation levels and are not aware of how inaccurate they can be. To illustrate this, try the following experiment:

TENSE-FIST EXPERIMENT

Procedure: Make a very tight fist with your left hand and continue holding it tightly for 60 seconds.

Observe: Notice the sensations in your left hand. Notice what you feel, where you feel it, and how intensely you feel it.

Procedure: Continue to hold your left hand in a tight fist for 60 seconds. Then, while still holding your left hand in the tight fist, make another very tight fist with your right hand.

Observe: Notice the sensations in your right hand. Compare the way that your right hand feels with how your left hand feels.

If you're like most people, you probably noticed that the strength of the sensations dropped as you continued applying tension to your left hand. That is, when you first made a fist in your left hand the sensations of tension were very strong but the sensations dropped off considerably in only 60 seconds of holding your hand in a tight fist. The contrast became evident when you made a fist with your right hand: the sensations were much stronger in the right hand than in the left one. This is generally the case for everyone. When we first tense our muscles it feels uncomfortable, but the discomfort rapidly fades. This phenomenon where sensations diminish is called adaptation.

One way to assess activation level is to notice the degree of tension; in your muscles. Generally, the more activated your systems, the more tense your muscles. However, because sensations of tension can drop off, it is easy to misread tension levels and miss a vital stress warning signal. It's much like driving your car with a broken temperature indicator. You know how serious that can be!

BIOFEEDBACK

Biofeedback is a popular method for sensing activation. A device measures one of the autonomic processes in the body — the brain wave (EEG), muscle activity (EMG), galvanic skin response (GSR), or skin temperature. Through a sound or digital display, you are given feedback on your level of activation and told how it compares to the optimal range.

Biofeedback can be quite effective in increasing awareness of what is going on in one's basic operating system, but the method has a couple of serious drawbacks. Biofeedback devices can be expensive. Typically the feedback training has a narrow focus. Devices that measure muscle tension, for example, are limited to working with one, at most two, muscles at a time. A subtle drawback is that some people can begin to think they need a machine to give them information about themselves. It is not always possible to have the device handy when you want to check on yourself.

A small weather thermometer can be used as a biofeedback device. If you want to try it, use a thermometer that indicates decreases as well as increases in temperature. Medical thermometers record increases only. To record your skin temperature, hold the bulb between your thumb and first finger. The thermometer will give you feedback on the temperature of your fingers. When activation goes above the optimal level, blood is withdrawn from the hands, feet, nose, and ears to supply the increased demands of your heart. When the blood is withdrawn, temperature goes down. If your finger temperature is below 98.6° F, you are activated. The thermometer is inexpensive and convenient because you can carry it with you most of the time.

SELF-OBSERVATION

Self-observation is an alternative method of sensing activation level and requires no mechanical devices. The first step is to learn to discriminate between sensations of tension and those of relaxation. The following experiment illustrates how this works.

SENSING–TENSION EXPERIMENT

Procedure: While lightly tensing, make a fist with your left hand. The degree of tension should be just enough to notice.

Observe: Like a scientist, objectively and dispassionately notice what you feel in your fist. For 7-10 seconds watch exactly where and how the sensation of tension feels for you.

Procedure: Create contrast in the sensations by quickly releasing the tension and consciously relaxing the muscles in your left hand.

Observe: Objectively watch what you experience in your left hand. In a detached manner, compare how your hand feels when relaxed with how it felt when tense.

■ How to Sense Tension ■

Tense ➤ Observe

Relax ➤ Observe

Compare ➤ Tension vs Relaxation

Learning to identify tension in your muscles involves systematically tensing and relaxing various muscle groups throughout your body, one at a time, while studying how the sensations feel. The objective is to learn to identify small amounts of tension so that you can then take action to reduce the tension and thereby bring your activation level back into the optimal range.

STUDYING–TENSION AND RELAXATION

Instructions: Find a place where you can be comfortable and won't be disturbed for about a half hour. Lying on your bed, couch, or a futon on the floor is good. Alternatively, you can sit in an overstuffed chair. Kick off your shoes and loosen your belt and any tight clothing. Tense and relax each muscle, one at a time, as follows. With eyes closed, tighten the muscle just enough to notice the tension. It is important to learn to detect light tension, so *do not tense tightly*. While holding the tension for about seven seconds (except for the feet — hold these for three seconds), study the physical sensation of tension in the muscle.

Next, *quickly release* the tension from the muscle and relax it as much as you can. Study the sensation of relaxation for ten or more seconds. Compare the sensation of relaxation and tension. Then tighten the muscle just enough to notice the tension a second time. Again, study how and where the tension feels for you and compare the feeling of tension to the feeling of relaxation. Then quickly release the tension and relax the muscle as much as you can. Study the way relaxation feels and compare that feeling to the way that the tension felt.

ARMS AND HANDS

Hand and forearm: Make a fist.

Biceps: Bend the arm at the elbow and make a "he-man" muscle.

FACE AND THROAT

Face: Squint eyes, wrinkle nose, and try to pull your whole face into a point at the center.

Forehead: Knit or raise eyebrows.

Cheeks: While clenching the teeth, pull the corners of your mouth to your ears.

Nose and upper lip: With mouth slightly open, slowly bring upper lip down to lower lip.

Mouth: Bring lips together into a tight point, then press mouth into teeth. Blow out gently to relax.

Mouth: Press the right corner of your mouth into your teeth and push the corner slowly toward the center of your mouth. Repeat for the left corner.

Lips and tongue: With teeth slightly apart press lips together and push tongue into top of mouth.

Chin: With arms crossed over chest, stick out your chin and turn it slowly as far as it will go to the left. Repeat for right side.

Neck: Push your chin into your chest at the same time as pushing your head backward into the back of your chair to create a counter-force.

UPPER BODY

Shoulders: Attempt to touch your ears with your shoulders.

Upper back: Push shoulder blades together and stick out chest.

Chest: Take a deep breath.

Stomach: Pull stomach into spine or push it out.

LOWER BODY

Buttocks: Tighten buttocks and push into chair.

Thighs: Straighten leg and tighten thigh muscles.

Calves: Point toes toward your head.

Toes: Curl your toes.

———————————————

It is important that you tense only the muscles in the area that you are studying while keeping other muscles relaxed. For example, to tense your biceps you bend your arms at the elbow and make a "he-man" muscle. While doing this let your hands hang limp. If you make a fist at the same time that you bend your arm and make the "he-man" muscle, you are tensing two muscle groups rather than one. Doing this makes it harder to study the sensation of tension in the biceps.

Remember, the idea is to discriminate between two feelings—tension and relaxation—so that you can recognize each. It is something like holding a heavy rock in one hand and a lighter rock in the other and "weighing" the two. Discriminating a very heavy rock from a much lighter one is easy. But if you work at it you can eventually learn to identify small differences in weight. The way that you do this is by comparing one against the other. To train yourself to identify small amounts of tension, you study the sensations in a tense muscle, then compare that feeling to how the muscle feels when relaxed.

It takes about twenty-five minutes to go through your entire body slowly and systematically tensing and relaxing your muscles. You must practice to learn to discriminate, so do the exercise or segments of it as often as possible. If you do it every day, that's very good. You can develop an internal monitor by observing the sensations in your entire body at least three times a week for two or three weeks. Study the more tension-prone areas, such as muscles in your face or shoulders for five to seven minutes each day. In as short a time as two weeks you will notice you are much more tuned into your activation level. The more you practice, the better your internal monitor will become.

I recommend self-observation over biofeedback. Of course, if you have access to biofeedback equipment, by all means use it. It provides a helpful adjunct to self-monitoring. As you explore the various facets of personal power, you will see that the essential ingredient is self-observation.

HOW TO RELAX

Relaxation is the opposite of high activation or stress. The biological processes occurring during relaxation allow the body to repair, rest, and prepare for optimal functioning. With practice anyone can learn to relax and use it at specific times to control stress. Personal power increases when you can relax at will. For example, when faced with a crisis situation, if you can keep activation within the optimal range for peak functioning you will remain alert and have all your resources to draw on to deal with the situation. Confidence grows because you know you can remain cool regardless of provocation. You feel in command instead of helpless. In this way ability to manage stress contributes to personal power.

BREATHING

Deep breathing is one of the easiest and fastest ways to reduce stress. Slow, steady, smooth, deep breathing will immediately lower activation level. You might assume that people breathe correctly. After all, it's natural. But many people breathe shallowly, which is incorrect because all the air is not forced out of the lungs. During inhalation the diaphragm contracts and descends, increasing lung capacity. During exhalation the diaphragm relaxes and moves upward, forcing the air out. If you are breathing correctly your abdomen should go out when you breathe in. When you breathe out the abdomen should go in. Check to see if you are breathing properly by placing your hand on your abdomen and noticing what happens as you breathe. Does your hand go out when you inhale and in when you exhale?

To develop your ability to breathe deeply, which fosters relaxation so that your body can rest and repair, do the following exercise for five to ten minutes each day.

BREATHING EXERCISE

Step 1: Breathe in slowly for four seconds; hold the breath for four seconds; exhale slowly for four seconds; hold for four seconds.

Step 2: Count the breaths from one to four as follows: 1 - Inhale; 2 - Exhale; 3 - Inhale; 4 - Exhale; Begin again with 1.

Step 3: Focus all your attention on breathing and counting.

Hold your hand on your abdomen the first couple of times you do this exercise to make sure you are breathing correctly. As you gain skill and lung capacity, slowly increase the time at each phase to six, then eight seconds. Some people prefer counting "1 and 2 and 3 and 4" with "and" coinciding with the hold phases. When you find your attention wandering, just let the distracting thought go and bring your attention back to the counting.

Anytime you notice yourself getting overly excited or feel tense, you can relax with a few minutes of deep breathing.

RELAXING MUSCLES DIRECTLY

Training yourself to relax is a simple process that takes about three weeks and has two important components. First, you must learn to identify tension in the muscles. Without this sensing ability or "internal monitor," you will not know when to relax. Second, when you have identified tension, you command the tension to be released.

The Relax Command

Learning a "relax command" can be done while you develop your internal monitor. Begin by selecting a word to use to command yourself to relax. The actual word doesn't really matter. It can be any word, but "relax" is a good word because it already has the association. When we're tense other people use "relax" to urge us to calm down. They say, "Hey, George, come on and relax. Just relax, pal." However, you might want to use a different word such as "calm down," "quiet," "chill out," or any word you prefer.

After selecting a word to use as a relax command, create a strong and clear association between the command word and the physiological sensations of relaxation. The objective here is to associate your word with the feeling of releasing tension.

HOW TO TRAIN THE RELAX COMMAND

Step 1: Select a command word for programming.

Step 2: Tense the practice muscle for 7-10 seconds.

Step 3: Think the command word just as you quickly release the tension from the muscle.

Practice associating the command word with the release of tension. Use the tensing and relaxing procedure described above. This time systematically go through the muscles in your body, tensing the muscles one at a time, then think the command word, "Relax," just at the moment when you quickly release tension. Each time you do this the association between the relax command and the release of tension becomes stronger. Thinking the relax command should come just an instant before actually releasing tension.

Learning the relax command can be easily integrated into the development of your internal monitor as follows: Tense the practice muscle, study the sensation of tension, think the relax command, release the tension, study the sensation of relaxation, and compare it to tension.

HOW TO RELAX AT WORK

After practicing in a quiet spot for about two weeks, slowly transfer the relaxation training into your daily routine. The key word here is *slowly*. If your first attempt to use the relax command is during an emotional encounter you are likely to be disappointed in the result because the situation will probably overwhelm the command and confidence in your ability will drop.

Begin by transferring the relaxation practice into your daily routine. Instead of a coffee break, for example, you might close your office door, turn off the lights, and spend five minutes practicing the relax command with one or two muscle groups. Or you might practice during times when you are waiting for the elevator, hanging on hold on the phone, or sitting in someone's waiting room. Next, use the relax command in mildly tension-producing situations such as riding the bus home from work. This is an ideal way to unwind for the evening. Or try it before making that phone call you have been putting off. Remember, begin using the relax command with mildly disturbing situations. When you sense tension, take a deep breath, focus on the tense muscle, think the relax command, and consciously release the tension. As you notice success, slowly increase the disturbance level of the situations.

USING YOUR IMAGINATION

Your imagination can be a powerful stress-management tool. To show you how this works, try the following experiment.

IMAGINATION EXPERIMENT

Imagine sitting on the grass in a lovely little park that is nicely landscaped and well cared for. You have brought a cloth to sit on, a bottle of mineral water, some cheese, bread, and fruit. It is a warm spring day. There are butterflies flying and a couple of bees busily working in the nearby clover flowers. You can smell newly cut grass. Your lunch is delicious.

Stop. Notice how you feel. Using a scale from 1 to 10 with 1 being very relaxed and 10 being very tense, rate how you feel after imagining yourself picnicking in the park.

Return to your picnic in the park. Again, imagine enjoying your delicious lunch as you luxuriate in the warm spring weather. Suddenly you hear a distant noise. Coming your way is an old pickup truck followed by a large cloud of dust. The truck screams to a halt at the curb near you and eight frolicking teenagers jump out of it from all sides. They cheer on their two large dogs, a Doberman and a pitbull, who run frantically after one another. The kids prop a portable radio blasting rap music against a nearby tree and scatter out for frisbee. Excited by the flying frisbees, the dogs yelp and try to catch one in their snapping jaws. Suddenly a misguided frisbee flies just a few inches over your head. Pursuing the frisbee, the two dogs are running straight toward you.

Stop. Notice how you feel. Using the same scale from 1 to 10, rate your tension level after imagining the noisy scene and the dogs running toward you.

How did you feel when you imagined the first half of the scene? How about during the second half? If you are like most of us, you felt calm and relaxed when imagining enjoying a delicious picnic. Just imagining the warm sun, the butterflies, and enjoying the cheese and water relaxed you. When the teenagers arrived you probably noticed your muscles tense. Perhaps your heart rate increased and breathing quickened.

This exercise illustrates that what we imagine can be as powerful as what is actually present in the moment. In other words, *our bodies respond to the images in the mind as if those images were real.* Your body responded as if you were really in that park and not just imagining it. This is a key to using your imagination to manage stress. You can control activation with the kinds things you picture in your mind. By imagining pleasant calming situations you can reduce your tension level.

THE PLEASANT FANTASY

Stress can be lowered quite rapidly by taking a few deep breaths and imagining a pleasant fantasy. It is best to have a well- developed fantasy to call on rather than to ad-lib. Waiting until a threatening situation is upon you to select a pleasant fantasy is risky. The situation may overwhelm you before you're able to think up an effective pleasant fantasy. Alternatively, when a pleasant fantasy has been well rehearsed, you know exactly what to imagine and can turn to it immediately. A pleasant fantasy can be anything: a real situation, such as hanging in a hammock in your backyard, or an invented one such as riding on a billowy white cloud. There need be no limits. The only requirement is that imagining it relaxes you.

Writing Your Fantasy

Select a situation that you find relaxing for your pleasant fantasy. Review the fantasy in your mind and then write down one or two paragraphs describing the fantasy in detail. Describe the setting. Add as much detail as you can about what it looks like and what is there. Think in terms of the five senses. What do you see? Hear? Feel? Smell? Taste? Add these to the description. For example, if your fantasy is lying on the beach on a warm summer day, you might see the waves, sun, and other sunbathers; hear the waves lapping the shore and seagulls screeching; feel the warmth of the sun and the blanket under you; smell the salty water; and taste a cool soda. The more the fantasy stimulates your senses the more power it will have to relax you.

After writing the first draft of your pleasant fantasy, close your eyes, relax by breathing deeply for a couple of minutes, and imagine your fantasy. Imagine all the details you wrote on the paper. Bring it to life making it as vivid as you can. It may be easier to imagine in one "sense" than another. You may be able to hear things in your imagination, for example, but not able to smell anything. Very often people report that they can imagine situations but can't "see" anything in their imagination. If you can't see anything, then just *imagine* what you would see. Likewise, if you can't smell anything in your imagination, then just imagine what it would smell like if you could smell it. Do the same for the other senses.

Be active in the fantasy. Do not look at yourself as a character on a TV screen; instead put yourself *into the situation*. Imagine yourself inside your body during the fantasy.

After imaging your fantasy for two or three minutes stop and add more detail to the written description of the fantasy scenario. What did you find in your fantasy that you did not write on the paper? Add these to the description. This is your pleasant fantasy. You can use it to reduce your tension.

Your pleasant fantasy must be powerful to be effective in quieting tension in difficult situations. You can increase the power of your fantasy by adding details from all the senses and by associating it with deep relaxation. The good time to work on the power of your fantasy is at the end of the deep-muscle-relaxation-training sessions. When you have systematically relaxed all of your muscles and are deeply relaxed, then bring your fantasy to mind. Project yourself into the situation and make it as vivid as you can. Remember to notice what you experience in each sense. Notice how relaxed you feel.

The more often you imagine yourself in the pleasant fantasy, the more relaxing power the fantasy will have. Slowly transfer use to your daily life by following the same gradual procedure used to generalize the relax command.

ENGINEERING THE ENVIRONMENT

Think back a moment to the pleasant picnic in the park that was interrupted by the teenage frisbee players with their two dogs. Things in the first part of the scene promoted relaxation whereas things in the second part of the scene were stressors. The environment has the power to stimulate us in different ways. The more uncertain the environment, the more it contains the possibility of danger. Uncertainty is a stressor. Environments with a lot of information to be processed are also stressing. Because we don't know what's out there, all the senses must operate. We mobilize into alertness, the optimal level to process information.

According to researcher Albert Mehrabian the amount of uncertainty and information in the environment is the "load" of the environment. (Mehrabian's fascinating research into the impact of environmental factors is described in his book *Public Places, Private Spaces.*) Environments that are certain, known, or regular, where things are familiar and there is little new information, are low load. Environments that are new, unusual, irregular, unknown, or contain a lot of new information are high load. By manipulating environmental load you can increase or decrease your tension level. You can translate this principle directly into increased productivity.

Up to this point the emphasis has been on how to reduce dangerously high activation. But there are times when lethargy or boredom prevails. Underactivation, like overactivation, can inhibit performance. Consider Celia: She must prepare a report containing a lot of figures every Friday afternoon, and Fridays are not conducive to report writing for her. She's tired from the week, anxious to move into the weekend, and bored of the repetitive reports. Her activation is way down and she just can't quite find the energy to work on the report. Consequently, she ends up making a lot of errors and doing an inefficient job. Celia needs to stimulate or increase her activation, bringing it up into the optimal range. To accomplish this she could try engineering the environment.

Look again at the figure on page 102. Notice that prolonged high activation will finally give way to exhaustion. In the figure on page 105, you see that a moderate activation level is optimal for peak performance. By increasing or decreasing the load of your environment you can keep yourself in that optimal range. When your internal monitor tells you that you are in the high critical range, for example, you can lower your activation and bring yourself back into the optimal range by reducing the load of your environment. Similarly, when you are bored you can increase your activation and move into the optimal range by increasing the load of your environment. Most of us understand this principle intuitively. The problem is that we often use potentially harmful methods of increasing or decreasing activation levels such as taking coffee, alcohol, or drugs. By making simple changes in your environment, on the other hand, you can regulate your stress for optimal performance — and health.

MUSIC

Most people don't realize that mood can be altered faster with music than with drugs. Try a simple experiment. Look through your collection of cassettes or CDs and select an instrumental with a simple, repetitive melody and a slow, even beat. Then select a second piece that has a fast, changing beat with a strong percussion emphasis, the more chaotic the better. Relax yourself until you feel calm. Play the low-load music and notice your internal reactions. How does it feel? What is your activation level? After a minute stop the music and relax again. Now play the high-load music and notice how you respond. Most likely you noticed a sizable increase in activation in less than a minute when listening to the music with a fast beat.

Music pulls our heart strings. We respond both physically and emotionally. You might feel nostalgia when listening to *Pomp and Circumstance*, like dancing when listening to a disco tune, or maudlin listening to a love song. Celia might increase her efficiency filling out the report forms if she had a radio in her office and switched it to an upbeat station. The high-load music would bring her activation up to the optimal range and the increased alertness would help her perform at her peak. On the other hand, work requiring intense concentration can raise activation dangerously high. Here Celia would do better to turn the dial to a station that plays calming music because low-load music lowers activation level.

COLOR AND DESIGN

Soft, muted colors and regular designs are low load and have a calming effect. Bright colors such as reds, yellow, oranges, and bold designs in clashing colors are high load and stimulating. Like music, color and design can be used to regulate activation. Jack, for example, was fascinated by abstract paintings. He put one on a wall in his office. On the other side of his office he placed a painting of a Hawaiian sunset. Whenever he needed to calm down he projected himself into the sunset; when he needed a boost he looked instead at the abstract.

The color and style of your clothes affects those around you. For example, when I lead a stress-management workshop I often wear a dress that is dark blue with a simple Oriental flower on the bosom. Watching the flower with its blue background all day has a calming affect on the participants. On the other hand, in another workshop I might wear a brighter, more high-load outfit.

You can't change the decor of your office or home as easily as pulling off a dress—or can you? With the flip of a light switch you can change the load of any environment and your mood. Compare the affects of a soft-white light to that of a harsh-white one. And what about other hues? You might experiment with lights. This principle is used routinely in the theater. If you've been backstage you probably noticed banks of colored lights that can be turned on to help create the mood needed for the play.

I discovered quite by chance that I could transform a dreary, depressingly gray day into a bright one simply by wearing glasses with yellow lenses. Having lost my dark-brown tinted sunglasses I wore ski goggles with yellow lenses to protect my eyes while riding my Vespa motorscooter one cold windy March day. Typically, I avoided riding in adverse weather, but I had no choice. My car had been stolen and "totaled" the night before by joyriders. All indicators suggested a bad day! Yet, I arrived at my destination feeling light-hearted, unaffected by the chill. I wasn't even depressed about having no car. Everything changed, however, when I pulled off the goggles. Not only did the world change back from yellow to gray again, but the temperature seemed to drop 15 degrees. With my cheerful mood evicted, I immediately felt victim of an unfair world. After that experience I understood the cliche "looking at the world through rose-colored glasses." Do not underestimate the power of color and light!

PEOPLE

Of all things in the world, people are probably the highest load. Even our closest friends can be unpredictable. A group of people, especially strangers, are extremely high load. Without realizing it, you probably use this factor to regulate activation. It is stimulating to go to a party and stand in a crowd of people for entertainment. Other times you might want to get away, to "get your head together," so you go on a walk in the woods to avoid people. Celia could have used this principle to help her complete the boring reports. Rather than sitting in her familiar, sterile office, she could have packed up her papers and gone to the cafeteria to write the report. The comings and goings of people, their talking and movements, provide a more stimulating environment. This may have perked her level up enough to put her into the optimal zone.

I've found when I have tedious, repetitive tasks that just have to be done, I can do them best in a coffeehouse, listening to the music, watching people go by, and drinking coffee. On the other hand, writing that requires intense concentration is best done late at night in the isolation of my office.

BATHS

Baths are another age-old method of modulating body tempo. Stretching out in a tepid bath will relax you every time. Alternatively, when you need to be perked up it is best to take a cold shower. For instance, if you have trouble getting started in the morning you might take a cold shower first thing. Or, if you are tense when you arrive home after work, a warm leisurely bath or dip in a hot tub will probably do the trick.

FOOD

Food is a powerful regulating tool. Any kind of spicy or unusual food is stimulating, whereas bland and familiar foods like mashed potatoes have the opposite effect. A quick look through an herb and tea book will suggest many alternatives to drugs. Cayenne pepper and ginseng, for example, are two natural stimulants; milk and valarian tea are relaxants.

Level of hunger is also important. A mild degree of hunger is stimulating. After a large meal, on the other hand, you might get drowsy because your energy has been detoured to digestion. I used this regulation principle when I first began leading workshops. At that time, performing in front of a group of people who may have been hostile and were certainly studying me was highly activating. I prevented overactivation by getting up an hour early and treating myself to a large breakfast of eggs, pancakes, and hash browns at a local cafe, leisurely reviewing my lesson plan, and then slowly driving to the workshop. The bulky meal and the sense of command (from having extra time) brought my activation back into the optimal zone. I could perform at my peak.

As time passed, however, I was no longer nervous when leading workshops. In fact, there were times when the last thing I wanted to do was to get up early in the morning and spend the day teaching. I needed to have my activation increased if I were to perform well. I traded the long breakfast for an extra hour of sleep. Grabbing a slice of toast, a piece of fruit, and a vitamin pack, I left for the session on a nearly empty stomach. The mild hunger was just enough to push me up into the optimal range and the extra rest boosted my stamina.

EXERCISE

Exercise is a popular method of regulating activation level. When you are bored or depressed, vigorous exercise is a very good way of picking yourself up. On the other hand, when you are already highly stressed, a mild light exercise such as a walk around the block will help release tension so you can relax.

FANTASY

Fantasies have unlimited potential for regulating activation. You can imagine real environments as well as the implausible. Use adventuresome or sexual fantasies to perk yourself up, and fantasies about eating a wonderful ten-course meal or your "pleasant fantasy" to relax.

INCREASING STRESS TOLERANCE

Unrelenting activation wears out the body's resources and eventually gives way to the third stage of stress: exhaustion (see the figure on page 102). This always happens if you don't act to reduce chronic high activation. You simply can't tolerate it forever. You can, however, influence tolerance level. For example, a sense of being in command, having choices, having fun, and feeling pleasure all increase tolerance, enabling you to withstand higher load, greater threat, and more activation for longer periods of time. In other words, you can tolerate more job pressure and frustrations in situations where you have personal power and feel in command. Research has shown that while management had greater stresses than those in operations or service, operations and service nonetheless had the higher rates of stress-related diseases. The increased tolerance is attributed to authority or the ability to control what happens to you. The manager's authority buffered them so that they were somewhat insulated from the effects of stress.

■ STRESS BUFFERS ■

Being in command

Having choices

Having fun

Feeling pleasure

Gaining meaning

The same is true with pleasure. When we're doing something that feels good or that we consider to be "fun;" we can tolerate higher activation. Consider a roller-coaster ride and what you actually feel when you shoot straight down at 60 mph. This would be a truly terrifying feeling you would never repeat if you didn't view it as fun. Sexual intercourse is another example. Here, too, you can withstand higher activation. I'm sure you can think of other examples. The opposite is true of passivity, helplessness, and pain. Situations in which you feel passive or powerless or experience pain lowers activation tolerance.

OVERSTIMULATION

Have you ever had this experience: Tired from an unusually demanding day, you drink a cup or two of extra strong coffee, hoping it will revive you. Instead, you fall asleep shortly afterward. The caffeine seems to help bring on sleep. How can this be? Are you an exception, immune to the stimulant? There is a simpler explanation. Think about what happens when you're on the edge of the high critical zone (see the figures on pages 102 and 105) and you consume a stimulant. The additional boost pushes you into the exhaust phase so both performance and activation drop, while extracting a physical toll. You experience an activation shutdown caused by stimulation overdose. This method of regulation is common. Often used stimulants include coffee, amphetamines, sugar, nicotine, and vigorous exercise. Without realizing it, you might be using one or more of these stimulants to overdose yourself. Sally, for example, did well in her demanding job but there was residual stress. One of her great loves — and weaknesses — was German chocolate cake. She fell into the habit of picking up a piece at a neighborhood dessert shop after work. At bedtime she snuggled up with a book and luxuriated in the rich sweet chocolate. She always fell to sleep immediately. The sugar in the cake may have overstimulated her, pushing her into exhaustion.

You may wonder why vigorous exercise is included in the list of stimulants. We tend to think the more exercise the better, but this is not necessarily so. Again, when you have been highly activated all day, vigorous exercise would not be advised. You could exhaust yourself. Some people get into an exercise regime, sticking to it rigidly without checking their internal monitor to see what they actually need at the moment. It is better to take a reading on yourself and then adjust the nature of your daily exercise. On days when you are depressed, a strenuous workout would be advised; on days when you're pressured, light exercise might be what you need.

SELF-OBSERVATION

Again, the key to managing stress is an effective internal monitor. If you want to fine-tune yourself you must become aware of yourself. Observation of your internal responses tell you what you are experiencing now, how tense you are, and what you need.

As you develop the sensitivity of your internal monitor and learn to manage stress responses, your personal power will increase. You will feel more in command of yourself and more able to handle difficult situations. As a result you'll probably take on more challenges and act with greater confidence when handling them. Other people will sense your confidence and respond to you with greater respect.

ERASING FEAR

Fear is a special kind of stress characterized by heightened activation, negative emotions, and a strong urge to run from the feared object. It is always uncomfortable. Because we are programmed for survival, we attempt to turn fear off and to avoid anything that prompts it. Fear works well and keeps us away from many dangers, but it also has a great potential for imprisoning us. Each time you give into the urge to escape or avoid, you are reinforcing the strength of the fear. By escaping, you remove yourself from the feared object; by avoiding, you prevent encountering it at all. In either case you have turned off something negative. As we have already seen, this strengthens the association between the object and your fear of it. Once a habit of avoidance is set you need never encounter the feared object again to maintain the fear. The avoidance habit can become self-perpetuating. Each time you manage to avoid an encounter the association is reaffirmed because you have turned off the threat of feeling fear. For example, suppose while taking a riding class you were kicked by your horse after one of the classes. Being kicked certainly could elicit fear. The fear could be reinforced if you thought of going to class, felt mildly anxious, then decided to skip class. Even though you didn't confront the horse again, the fear was strengthened. This is how fears linger on from childhood.

DESENSITIZING YOURSELF

Fear responses can be desensitized by substituting an opposite emotional response. Arrange to experience an emotion that is opposite or incompatible with fear while being in the presence of the object of your fear—the fear prompt. Because the two emotions are opposites, the experience of fear is blocked. This weakens the association between the fear and the prompt, because the prompt is now being associated with a different emotion. For example, because you cannot feel joy and fear at the same time, you can use the feeling of joy to desensitize some fears. Create an artificial situation that makes you laugh. The laughter stimulates joy, which blocks fear. This is the same strategy we were taught as children when we were told to "whistle a happy tune whenever feeling afraid." There are many activities that can be used in this way: being curious, dancing, eating, solving problems, sexual response, being relaxed, and focused attention. By deliberately engaging in these incompatible behaviors in the presence of a fear prompt, the association between the prompt and the fear is broken. For example, if you were afraid of flying on airplanes, you might eat a favorite meal at the airport while watching planes takeoff and land. The pleasure of the eating would block the fear. The most frequently used activity for desensitizing fears is relaxation. When you have trained yourself to relax you can use your new skill to erase fear responses.

Make a List of Situations to Desensitize

Select a mild to moderate fear that involves one general theme such as fear of flying, making speeches, or spiders. On a piece of paper write down several specific situations that make you fearful. Include the full range from very mild to extreme reactions. Don't race through this step. It requires a lot of thought to make sure you get a representative sample of situations. When you have a sizable list (10-15 situations) rate each situation on a scale from 0 to 100 in terms of how much you fear it. Let 0 represent absolutely no fear at all and 100 represent the most extreme fear reaction you can imagine. On a clean paper, rewrite the list beginning with the least-feared to the most feared situation. These become your desensitization steps.

Use Your Mental Stage

Take some time to relax. It is important to be deeply relaxed during desensitization. You will be using your imagination. You could think of your imagination as a stage where you can reenact experiences and act out new behaviors. Set the props for the first situation on the list you want to desensitize, the one rated as least-feared.

Step on to the stage and project yourself into the feared situation. It is important that you remain *completely relaxed* while you do this. If you feel any tension or fear — even a small amount — stop the scene and switch to your pleasant fantasy, until you are completely relaxed. Then begin again with the least-feared scene. Continue in this manner until you can go through the feared scene while remaining *completely relaxed.* When you can do this, move to the second situation on your list and repeat the process. You will probably do only one or two situations each time you work on desensitization. Don't try to do too much. Remember, this is a time to move like a tortoise, slowly. Begin each new session by going through the last desensitization scene.

CHAPTER 7

BUILD SKILLS

THE THIRD PATH TO PERSONAL POWER

It's a fact of life. For the rest of our careers, you and I
will be working in the midst of an economic revolution.
. . . the best strategy I know for directing the course of our careers
these days is to focus on our skills. Skills are our best bridge
to the new economy, as well as to the talents that lie within us. . . .
Which leads to my . . . point. A career is a continuing education.
The bottom-line benefit in most jobs is what we learn,
not what we earn.
—William A. Charland, Jr.
Career Shifting: Starting Over in a Changing Economy

Remember when you were a young child, eagerly learning life's basic skills like how to climb stairs or tie your shoe, cross a busy street or count to twenty, and later how to drive a car or dance? Chances are with each feat you felt a little bigger and stronger. Each ability enlarged your horizons and your personal power. You could do more and have more of what you want.

Mastery, learning how to do something and doing it well, feels good. You like yourself more and get positive feedback from others. When you feel powerful you approach difficult situations with an I-can-do attitude. Difficulties are a chance to exercise your "muscles." They become a concern only when you think you can't handle them. When you lack the skills to deal with troublesome parts of your work, people may point to you as an example of the Peter Principle because you

appear to have reached your "level of incompetence." Your days are a struggle. Your efforts are aimed at avoiding situations that require the skill you lack so you won't look bad. In other words you avoid negative outcomes rather than pursue positive ones. When you don't have the skills to handle the challenges of your job you feel incompetent, incapable, and helpless to change it. No-can-do becomes an uncrossable ravine between you and your goals.

Without the appropriate skills you can't succeed in tasks required of you. Wins are possible, but you are unable to perform in ways necessary to receive them. No-can-do becomes no-can-get. We can't predict what skills the future will demand, so having certain specific skills is less important than knowing how to acquire them when needed. A frequent villain behind burnout is poor problem-solving skills. The burnout victim doesn't know how to pinpoint what is dragging motivation down or how to develop a plan to change it.

IDENTIFY WHAT YOU NEED TO LEARN

It is important to pinpoint what stands between what you are doing now and what you must do to gain the wins you want. While your ultimate goal is to achieve a certain outcome, you get there by focusing on your moment-by-moment behavior. You cannot learn outcomes, only behaviors. The outcome is the end result you desire; the behavior is what you do, the actions you take to achieve this result. For example, completing a report on time is an outcome; making an outline and dictating the report are behaviors that create a completed report.

SKILL-BUILDING CHECKLIST

Instructions: Review your Personal Stress Log (page 106) and your Stress-Pattern Analysis (page 107). For each situation and pattern consider what actions you might have taken or what abilities you might have exercised to reduce the distress. Think of others who would have handled the situation more effectively. Think of what skills he or she would have used. For each situation or pattern, check the skill identified. Some skills may be checked several times. When finished, tally the number of checks for each skill. Circle the five skills with the most checks. These are the skills you need to learn.

_____ Assertiveness	_____ Mentoring
_____ Decision making	_____ Networking
_____ Listening	_____ Leading meetings
_____ Information gathering	_____ Managing time
_____ Team playing	_____ Goal setting
_____ Delegating	_____ Relaxing
_____ Giving support	_____ Self-starting
_____ Getting support	_____ Self-acknowledging
_____ Public Speaking	_____ Writing
_____ Specific technical skills	_____ Planning
_____ Negotiating	_____ Mediating
_____ Supervising	_____ Giving feedback
_____ Using feedback	_____ Prioritizing
_____ Other	_____ Other
_____ Other	_____ Other

PINPOINTING THE CHAIN OF BEHAVIORS

Failing to pinpoint the behavior you need to learn or racing through this stage can result in a shot-gun approach of trying one thing after another that doesn't work until you finally give up. Your motivation to even try to solve the problem could burn out in the process.

Typically, a series of behaviors is required to reach the desired outcome. Consider Jeff, who sells contracts for surfacing driveways and parking lots. Even though he is hardworking, conscientious, and puts in long hours, the number of contracts he lands has been way below what he wants. He is frustrated, discouraged, and feels like a failure. Burnout is likely. To halt this vicious cycle Jeff needs to identify the chain of behaviors that lead to a sale.

To determine the required behaviors and their sequence, begin with the outcome you desire and work backward, step-by-step, through the required behaviors. The process works like this:

Question: "What specifically must I do to get a signed contract?"

Answer: "I must ask for a signature."

Question: "What prompts me to ask for a signature?"

Answer: "The prospect's positive enthusiasm: smiling, nodding affirmatively, making positive comments about the deal."

Question: "What must I do to obtain the prospect's positive enthusiasm?"

Answer: "I must present a persuasive sales pitch."

Jeff continued with such an inner dialogue until he worked his way back through the entire process of making a sale. Here's what he found: The behaviors interlock like a chain. It's dynamic and moves on its own toward the outcome you're seeking as long as there are no breaks in the flow. Don't become discouraged if you can't figure out the chain. This is often the case. Fortunately, there are a number of information sources, the slowest and least successful being trial and error, which involves trying one thing after another and seeing what works. In theory you will eventually hit upon the right formula. But eventually can be a long time. You could burn out first! A more effective method is observing the chain in action. Find somebody who is successful in achieving your desired outcome. Watch exactly what that person does, step-by-step. You might even take notes.

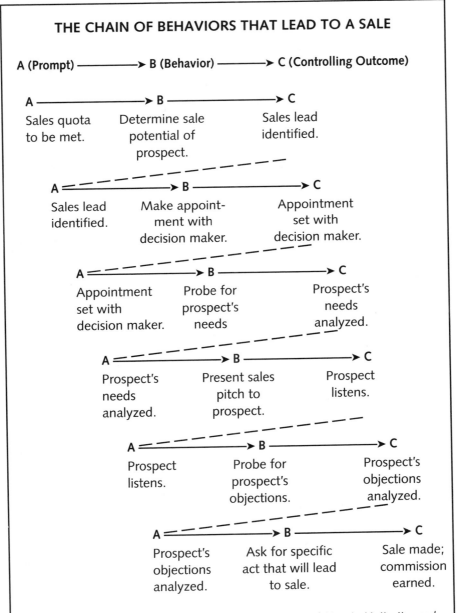

THE CHAIN OF BEHAVIORS THAT LEAD TO A SALE

A (Prompt) ————————→ B (Behavior) ————————→ C (Controlling Outcome)

A ————————————→ B ————————————→ C
Sales quota   Determine sale   Sales lead
to be met.   potential of   identified.
                   prospect.

A ————————————→ B ————————————→ C
Sales lead   Make appoint-   Appointment
identified.   ment with   set with
                   decision maker.   decision maker.

A ————————————→ B ————————————→ C
Appointment   Probe for   Prospect's
set with   prospect's   needs
decision maker.   needs   analyzed.

A ————————————→ B ————————————→ C
Prospect's   Present sales   Prospect
needs   pitch to   listens.
analyzed.   prospect.

A ————————————→ B ————————————→ C
Prospect   Probe for   Prospect's
listens.   prospect's   objections
                   objections.   analyzed.

A ————————————→ B ————————————→ C
Prospect's   Ask for specific   Sale made;
objections   act that will lead   commission
analyzed.   to sale.   earned.

A lot of learning takes place through watching other people which is called "modeling." The person you are watching is called the model. Think about how people learn a sport. The instructor models the skill, like how to swing a tennis racket, then the student attempts to duplicate the motion. Learning through modeling goes on all the time, usually without our realizing it. It is through modeling that we learned most of our social skills as we grew up, for example. When you are new in a job, it's through modeling that you learn "the way we do things around here." You notice what others do that works and soon you're acting in a similar fashion. Unfortunately, models will not always be available or you may not have an opportunity to watch them perform.

If you can't watch, ask. Ask your model to describe each behavior in the sequence. This is what Jeff did. He invited Bill, one of the "star performers," to have a couple of drinks. Over cocktails he encouraged Bill to talk about how he approached his customers. Jeff asked questions such as, "Give me an example of what you would say then," or "What do you do next?" or "How did you do that? What did you say?" Jeff's goal was to get specifics about what Bill actually did and when he did it.

If you find yourself isolated or cut-off from those who have the skills you need, don't despair. There are other ways you can go about identifying the specific behaviors you need to learn. Molly, for example, was a floor supervisor in a candy factory. Being in a position of authority

was new to her. She felt unsure and was having a hard time giving assignments or telling people what to do. Simply stated, Molly didn't have "boss skills." It was a small family-owned company and all the other supervisors were relatives of the owner. Their skill at giving directives wasn't much better than Molly's. She was cut off without good models to study. Fortunately for Molly and others caught in the same dilemma, there is bountiful information available.

Self-help books are valuable information sources for behavior chains. Such books break down a process like making decisions or being assertive into "discrete steps." Typically, each behavior in the chain is described with do's and don't's. For example, in my book *Turning Around: Keys to Motivation and Productivity*, I describe chains of behaviors involved in several core managing skills, such as how to elicit information, give directives, lead groups, and resolve conflicts.

Workshops are another excellent source of information. Molly attended a community-college class I taught on how to give directives, where she learned the chain of behaviors involved in giving an effective directive: Describe the situation, ask for information, direct, then check out. The behavior links were described and demonstrated, then Molly practiced the four steps for giving directives with others in the class.

ANALYZE THE BREAKDOWN

After you have identified the behavior chain, you must locate the broken link. Observe yourself carefully, looking for the step you leave out or don't perform well. Be aware that it's not always easy to watch yourself when actually performing. You may get caught up in the situation and forget to watch. An alternative is to use your imagination. This is what Jeff did. In his mind's eye he watched Bill sell a customer. Then Jeff imagined himself as he usually handled a customer. Jeff looked for behaviors Bill performed but that he did not.

How you watch is also important. Your imagination is powerful. What you imagine feels real. In fact, research has shown that we can learn skills through mental practice. Of course, we all know this. That's why we mentally rehearse encounters beforehand. Negativity during this process is dangerous. By criticizing and judging your performance, you could implant anxieties and fears that could become insurmountable barriers to acquiring the skill. Take care to avoid doing this. While viewing yourself, be objective, nonjudgmental, and dispassionate. Simply watch; just observe yourself. Only after you have completed your entire performance and leave your "mental stage" should you make comparisons with your model. Think like a scientist: Be objective when making this comparison, in the same manner as when you compared the sensations of tension and relaxation in your muscles. Emphasize what you did well. A nice side-benefit of this self-study is that by remaining relaxed while watching your not-so-perfect performance, you can desensitize yourself to "performance anxiety" which frees you to learn the skills you want to acquire.

TEACHING YOURSELF A NEW BEHAVIOR
DETERMINE A SMALL STEP

Jeff's situation was pretty straightforward. In comparing his own approach to Bill's he discovered the vital missing link. He wasn't actually asking for the sale. Once he pinpointed this to be the problem, he set an objective to ask the customer for a sale after presenting his pitch during

his next call. He was surprised to discover what an impact this had on his sales. Signed contracts immediately increased.

Most "no-can-do" problems, unfortunately, are more complex than this. They usually involve a series of intricate behaviors that are not being performed. This is what Molly discovered in the giving directives workshop. She found that the language she was using was deferential rather than authoritative. Thus, she needed to learn a new vocabulary and a new way of using it. Not an easy task. She also learned that she tended to jump into a directive too fast without giving the employee any frame of reference or opportunity to ask questions. For Molly's skill-building to be successful she must break these complex behaviors down into small steps. Proceeding slowly is the most effective approach. Avoid the temptation to try to accomplish too much too soon. You will get further by taking small steps.

Molly's first small step in learning to give effective directives was to write down what she wanted to say. Then she used the four-step procedure she practiced in the workshop to give Betty Lou, the employee she felt most comfortable directing, a routine directive. It would have been foolish as her first step to attempt the procedure with Butch who often challenged her. Remember, when you determine steps make them so easy you know you can perform them. It doesn't matter how small the step is as long as taking it leads to some improvement or movement toward the end result or final behavior. For example, if you were learning to play tennis you wouldn't start your first practice session attempting a volley with a seasoned player; rather, you would begin practicing your forehand at the backboard. Carry this same principle over into all of your skill-building situations.

SET AN OBJECTIVE

Set a behavior objective (see Chapter 5) for each small step. The small step provides the "what" part of the objective. Make sure you decide exactly when you are going to carry out this behavior and how much or how long you will do it. Once again, ask only a little of yourself at a time. This is something new and requires effort. Require only as much of the new behavior that you feel totally confident you can actually

perform. When you have your objective nailed down you are ready to use your imagination or mental stage to rehearse.

PRACTICE

Before going to your mental stage relax yourself. It doesn't matter whether you use deep breathing, muscle relaxation, or any of the other techniques. What is important is that you are in a state of deep relaxation each time you practice on your mental stage. This deep relaxation is conducive to learning new behaviors.

With all props in place step onto your stage and slowly walk through the behavior specified in your objective. Go in slow motion and focus your attention on the behavior and carrying it out accurately.

Be inside your body and notice how it feels to perform in this manner. Notice all the information coming in through your senses. See your behavior work for you. Have others in the scene respond as you desire and have your behavior yield the result you are seeking. Focus attention on what you did right during the rehearsal and acknowledge this. This is most important. You might go through this practice several times. Don't expect only one mental practice session to work.

DIRECT YOURSELF

When you rehearse be both actor and director. While you are performing in slow motion, direct yourself through the behaviors. Direct your expressions, direct your words, direct your feelings. Silently talk yourself through the steps. This helps you keep on track and remember exactly what you intend to do. You are going through a new behavior, which isn't easy.

A word of caution: Self-directing is one of those things that helps a great deal up to a point. Used to excess, it can become an impediment because it encourages you to evaluate your performance while putting a filter between you and the actual experience of doing something. Nonetheless, self-directing can help you in learning new skills. One of the difficulties in learning a complex skill is that we must do so many different things at the same time. Talking yourself through each step helps with coordination. When learning dancing, for example, it's helpful if you count the steps, "two forward, now hop to the right," for example. But that's not dancing. At some point, and very soon, you have to stop talking and dance!

Another benefit of self-directing is that it can block out negative talk. Do not be critical and negative toward your performance while practicing. This will impede learning. In fact, it may implant something you don't want at all. Block out extraneous thoughts so that you focus all of your attention on the practice. Self-directing helps to do this. While you are thinking about and following your directions, it is difficult to be worrying and criticizing yourself. And directions need not be restricted to words. You can also direct yourself by "seeing" yourself doing it right. Images can be even more powerful than words when it comes to learning.

PRACTICE AT WORK

Practicing on your mental stage embeds the new behavior at a level deep in your mind. However, if you are going to have a new skill, at some point practicing at work becomes necessary. The practice on the mental stage makes it easier.

Continue practicing the small-step behavior on your mental stage until you can go through the behavior while feeling completely relaxed and confident in each act. When you reach this point, transfer practice to your work situation. Be conscientious about this; don't rush through it. If you set an objective for doing something three times, do it three times. Don't short-change yourself by carrying out the objective halfway. You'll only undermine your own progress and everything will come tumbling down. Build a firm foundation of solid practice. If you have set a small-step objective—one that is reasonable and that you know you can perform—you should have no problem practicing in your real-life work setting.

GIVE YOURSELF WINS

Learning proceeds fastest when the small-step behavior is followed by a powerful win. Now is the time to indulge yourself. Each time you enact the small step, go to your Want List and select an appropriate activity or commodity. When you complete the objective itself, satisfy a more significant want. Reward yourself. Avoid moralizing, telling yourself, "I should be able to ... and don't really deserve to ..." This will defeat your learning. A positive win is necessary. Remember, learning a new skill—changing yourself—is not easy. It takes a lot of effort. Putting out the effort to change deserves indulgence.

One way you can turn small gains into wins you feel you've earned is the point system. Assign value points to each item on your Want List then pay yourself points each time you perform the behavior or reach an objective. Points are effective because you get them immediately and can cash them in later for a wide variety of wants.

Returning again to the issue of discipline, it's easy to say, "Yes, I will do this for fifteen minutes, three times a day." That's fine and good. But the bottom line is you must do it. There's no way around it. If you don't perform the small step you won't acquire the skill. The "Self-contract" (see Chapter 5) can help with this. Write the objective down, specify what want you will satisfy when you complete the objective, sign, and date it. Indicate how long the contract will be in force. And, when possible, have a friend witness and sign it, too. Use peer pressure to help move you in the direction you have chosen to go.

SHAPE SKILLS

Imagine yourself an artist, sculpting a human form. The face would have eyes, nose, and a mouth—but not immediately. To create these you would chisel a rough, round shape for the head, then slowly shape it into finer and finer detail. Follow this shaping principle when acquiring any new skill. Begin with a step that roughly represents the final behavior. Proceed with successive approximations of the skill you ultimately desire. This is important. Employing this principle separates those successful in developing their potential from those who try but fail. For each approximation, set a precise behavior objective to guide you. Slowly increase precision after each succeeding objective.

You can fine-tune any of the three components of the objective: what, when, and how much. Tuning "how much" means requiring more of the new behavior, doing it longer, or doing a better job at it. Let's look at Hank. He had been told many times that he was cold and distant with co-workers. He felt alienated from the others and was rarely included in any social activities. Through self-observation he saw that most of his conversations were technical and contained a lot of technical jargon. With the aid of a communications workshop and several self-help books, he pinpointed the kinds of questions he asked as the first target of change. Rather than asking his typical fact-eliciting questions, Hank wanted to learn the skill of eliciting feelings. Beginning skill training with his officemate, Gordon, made reaching the first objective easy: "Each day for a week I will ask Gordon at least one feeling question."

After successfully reaching this objective, Hank applied the shaping principle to the how-much component by requiring more feeling questions. His second objective was identical to the first except that he required three feeling questions instead of one each day. Having met this objective he again increased the number of feeling questions he planned to ask Gordon. Next, Hank fine-tuned the "when" portion of the objective. Again, he began working with the person he felt most comfortable with—Gordon—and slowly shaped when he asked feeling questions. When he achieved a high frequency of feeling questions with Gordon, he moved to Rhonda, an attractive woman in the office whom he sometimes felt uncomfortable with. After meeting a series of objectives for asking Rhonda feeling questions, he again increased the difficulty of the situation by moving to Manuel, around whom he almost always felt uncomfortable.

If you were learning a sport, such as skiing, you'd begin with simple movements. As you mastered the basics you would increase the complexity of the behavior being learned. The instructor might ask you, for example, to ski across the hill keeping your knees bent and your uphill ski forward. After mastering this step, the next step might be to add a turn at the end of the transverse. By slowly increasing the complexity of the behavior, you would soon be skiing down the slope from side to side.

FIND A PRACTICE LAB

Hank wanted to be able to initiate warm, friendly conversations with people he hardly knew, not just with those in his office. This would be a valuable skill for his business trips as well as in his social life. To accomplish this goal he selected Henry's, a neighborhood tavern frequented by people from his office complex. Henry's was his "practice lab." In Henry's Hank slowly increased the complexity (what) of the behavior he was teaching himself. At first glance this may look like a long, laborious process that takes time and work. On the other hand, those who have refined their social skills did so over years and years of informal training.

HANK'S SKILL-BUILDING PLAN

Objective 1. Three times this week I will go into Henry's and purchase a bag of peanuts to go.

Objective 2. Three times this week I will purchase a beer and sit for at least a half hour.

Objective 3. Three times this week I will sit in Henry's and smile at at least three people I notice looking at me.

Objective 4. Three times this week I will sit in Henry's for at least a half hour, and look at at least one person I find interesting long enough to catch their eye, and then I will smile at him or her.

Objective 5. Three times this week I will sit at the bar at Henry's for at least a half hour and ask the person next to me at least one feeling question.

Just as you should direct yourself when practicing in your imagination on your mental stage, it's helpful to self-direct when first practicing in real life. For example, Hank might think to himself, "Sit down.

Take a deep breath and relax. Good. Just be calm now. Yes, breathing feels good. Here comes the waitress. Order a beer. Now look around and see who's looking my way. Oh, there's someone over there. Just relax and smile. Be natural. That was number one. It was easy. Look around and see who else is looking this way." In this way Hank directed himself through each step.

Self-directing may seem artificial but it helps. You probably carry on continuous internal dialogues anyway. With self-directing you can be harnessed into the service of your objective. Not only is it easier to stay on target but self-directing also blocks out destructive negative-talk. Practicing a new complex skill usually feels unnatural at first. Expect this. By self-directing you can get over your initial resistance much more rapidly. Ease yourself in by talking to yourself. It's okay. But don't be abrasive like some dictatorial teachers you have suffered. Direct yourself in a helpful manner. Be positive and guide yourself gently. Most important, acknowledge what you do right.

EVALUATE GAINS

Evaluation is two-fold. Are you accomplishing your objectives? If the answer is yes, then score a big plus for your ability to develop a plan of action and carry it through. If you're not achieving your objectives there are three troubleshooting points. Is there a powerful win following the behavior? A win is needed to reinforce the learning. Wins encourage you to repeat the behavior again in the future. If you have objectives that require carrying out the behavior a certain number of times and you are missing the target, you may not be supplying a powerful win. When practicing make sure to provide a win each time you carry out the practice step. If you have been providing a win with poor results, then experiment with other wins. Find one that has an impact.

When you don't perform the behavior take a good look at the prompt point. Have you provided something to remind you to perform? New behaviors don't come naturally. You must provide an artificial cue, something to prompt you to do it. If you didn't write out a self-contract, experiment with doing so. Then remember to direct yourself through the behavior.

The final troubleshooting point is the behavior itself. People tend to demand too much of themselves. Perhaps you are requiring a step that's too big. Don't expect to go from practicing your serve at the backboard to playing a hot game with the area pro in one step. Attempting large steps set you up to fail. Build in success by breaking the troublesome step down into smaller steps. Use the shaping principle.

Often you will move rapidly through your objectives in the beginning but have difficulty keeping up the pace. When you fail to achieve an objective, you have probably required too much of yourself. Go back and re-examine the steps. The principles of inertia apply to learning. Once your progress stops it takes an extra force to get it going again. The best thing to do when you reach a plateau is to slow down and ask much less of yourself.

The bottom line, however, is whether or not you have made progress toward your goal. By counting how often the behavior or outcome occurs before, during, and after you implement your change plan, and comparing these frequencies (see Chapter 5), you can tell if your skill-building program has been successful. Jeff, for example, could compare the number of sales before and after he began asking for sales. Molly might rate how thoroughly her directives were followed. Hank might count the number of times people in his office seek him out for casual conversation. If your data comparison reveals an improvement in the skill you are working on, then you can conclude your skill-building program is effective.

When there has been little progress toward the outcome you are seeking, even though you are succeeding in your small steps, stop and troubleshoot. Go back and take another look. Reanalyze the chain of behaviors. Perhaps there's a broken link you overlooked. If you're stumped and can't find the link, you might consult an expert who knows how to achieve the goal you are seeking. A couple of hours of his or her time should be sufficient to identify the behavior chain.

The primary reason people have trouble with skill building is that they speed through the steps without doing each one carefully. This impatience is most often at the root of the problem.

MAINTAIN YOUR GAINS

New behaviors are learned most rapidly when they are followed by a powerful win each time you perform them. But they are maintained most effectively when the behavior is followed by a win only sometimes. Use this principle in your skill building. When first practicing the behavior on your mental stage and in your work situation, indulge yourself with wins from your Want List (or with points) each time you perform the behavior. As you do it more frequently, wean yourself. Go to your Want List only sometimes. Many skills are self-maintaining. The behavior brings its own reward. Jeff's asking for sales, for example, is maintained by the sales themselves. Molly's using a new style of giving directives is maintained by her employees carrying out the directives. Hank's asking feeling questions and initiating interactions in social places is maintained by the positive responses he gets. And don't forget the power of your own pats on the back. Self-acknowledgement is something that's always available. Develop the habit of focusing on what you do well and acknowledging it. Too often we do just the opposite and dwell on what we do poorly. Such negativity has a dampening effect on learning.

The greater your ability to teach yourself new skills, the greater your personal power. You can't predict what skills the future will demand. The workplace is changing too fast for that. Now a days job security depends upon knowing how to acquire needed skills. When you have a method for learning new skills you can take on new situations with less apprehension and a greater sense of control. Even when changes are forced upon you, you will have confidence that you can handle it. This skill-acquisition ability translates directly into personal power. Other people will quickly sense your power to rise to new challenges and will make more opportunities available to you because they will be confident that you will perform well.

CHAPTER 8

DEVELOP SOCIAL SUPPORT

THE FOURTH PATH TO PERSONAL POWER

No man is an island.
—John Donne

$\mathcal{S}$upportive relationships build personal power. We are more resilient, accomplish more, and feel worthwhile when we have close supportive relationships. Social support acts as a buffer against stress and burnout. We can tolerate a greater degree of stress when we have supportive relationships. In fact, research shows that people with close emotional and social ties are physically and mentally healthier, spend less time in the hospital, and live longer. Curiously, this finding holds for relationships with pets as well. And in recent years people suffering from schizophrenia and depression have been encouraged to get pets because of their uplifting effect. A sense of community at work can modulate the stress of both boring and high-pressure jobs. It you've developed firm relationships at work, these can be rallied in times of crisis to help you get over the hump.

Close friends and good relationships with co-workers and family reaffirm your competence and self-worth. Supportive people can help you handle difficult situations by listening to your problems and giving feedback. You can turn to this support system for acknowledgement of your efforts and for condolences when things don't work out the way you'd hoped. They can encourage you to tackle challenges, learn new skills, accomplish goals. And friends can divert your attention from the negative when you seem stuck and help you develop a new outlook.

Supportive relationships do more than buffer the effects of stress and build your sense of self-worth. Allies can help you get your job done. It's a rare person who can get a job done without calling upon the cooperation of other people. For one thing, few jobs involve stand-alone activities. Most jobs involve getting input of some sort from others in order to do your part. You may be waiting for invoices to be processed so that you can ship orders, for example. Co-workers can help—or hinder—your accomplishing your objectives. For example, co-workers can share information you need to perform well; or they can withhold that information, making your job harder. When you have allies who you can count on to help you get things done, you feel more in control—even in very difficult situations. Your personal power grows because you can call on certain people to effect certain change.

SOCIAL WORKPLACE

The workplace is a social environment. Succeeding on the job requires more than just accomplishing tasks. It is a rare person who can complete his or her work responsibilities independently of other people. Most work is a complicated intermeshing of many activities and functions. We pick up where others have left off, we rely on others for important information. Others must meet their deadlines so that we can meet ours. We work in collaboration in teams, that can come together and disband. We lead, we follow. At every turn we must cultivate cooperation. Success in almost every job means building productive relationships.

You can improve your effectiveness at work by taking time to build a network of allies. Allies are not necessarily buddies or people you would pick as personal friends. Allies are people who have some priorities in common with you and can be counted upon to be helpful in certain situations. Allies can give you needed information, connect you with the right person, and open doors to valuable resources. Some alliances spring up naturally. You and someone at the next desk may have certain common problems dealing with a critical supervisor, for example.

> You may feel shy or uncertain about calling on sources of support. But do it. Support makes a job more fun and less difficult and often is the difference between success and discouragement. Ask for help if you need it, want it, feel stuck, are curious about how someone else would handle your situation, or have tried to make changes with little success on your own. Don't wait until you are in a crisis.
>
> Asking for or receiving help does not mean that you hand your problem over to someone else to solve. Social support is no substitute for having a strong sense of self-efficacy. The best support enhances your sense of mastery.
>
> **Lyle Miller & Alma Smith**
> *The Stress Solution*

Effective people—people who get things done—work through allies. They have relationships with people who have information and resources they need, or who can open doors, or connect them with people who can help. We've all seen movies about the private-eye who gets the low down on the criminal by calling upon a friend in the police department to run a check on him. The broader one's network of allies, the more opportunities for accomplishment. You will increase your personal power—your ability to make things happen—by cultivating friendly, helpful relationships throughout your company, community, and industry. As management expert Keshavan Nair said, to get things done it is important to "have friends in low places." These allies can provide invaluable information about what is really happening in certain areas of the company. They can be a valuable conduit of influence. Nurture the alliance and these allies will increase the chances for success of your plans and policies because they will convince their peers of the rightness of your actions.

ALLIES BUILD YOUR VALUE

People with a network of allies throughout the company get things done. If you're getting your job done and are an integral part of helping other people get their jobs done, you're more valuable to the company. When you're part of several networks around the office, you become perceived as indispensable. When it comes time for layoffs you'll be viewed as too valuable to lose. And if you should face down-sizing or decide you want to move on, your network of allies is the best avenue to a new job. They will know you and will want to direct you toward available opportunities.

> ...making personal contacts can critically influence career success. Succeeding at school is merely a start. To succeed in the real world, you need more than ability—you need contacts.
>
> Cynthia Chin-Lee
> *It's Who You Know*
> *Career Strategies for Making Effective Personal Contacts*

HOW TO CULTIVATE ALLIES

Allies don't just appear, you must cultivate them. This requires caring attentiveness to the process. There are several approaches to making and keeping allies.

NETWORK

Pick potential allies on the basis of the information and resources they have access to rather than their position. Sometimes people in seemingly low positions have useful information. Security officers have information on the comings and goings of people, for example. Secretaries have information on the preferences of their bosses. Mailroom clerks usually know the cheapest way to ship various things.

Information Is Power

The currency of networking is information. Dr. Bettie Youngs who wrote the book *Is Your Net Working?* draws the analogy with the "old boys" network, "the grapevine," and "the buddy system." She defines networking as a method of making links from the people you know to the people they know. "Hi, Sally Martin suggested I call you. She thought you might be able to give me a referral to a good graphic artist." Use networking contacts to exchange information, advice, referrals, and support.

> **NETWORKING IS LIKE GARDENING**
> Effective networks must be created and cultivated and followed up. They don't simply happen; you can't purchase, beg, steal or borrow one. You have to establish one yourself, then care for it continuously and consistently like tending a garden.
> **Anne Boe & Bettie Youngs**
> *Is Your Net Working?*

Consider a project you're working on or an objective you wish to meet. What information do you need? What resources? Think of people you know who might have the information or resources or who might know someone who does. Make sure to think broadly about who you know. For example, the clerk in the mailroom might be able to help you get a report out to a client quickly. The butcher at your corner market might be able to refer you to a caterer for a company luncheon.

COMMUNICATE GOODWILL

People are sensitive to the receptivity of others, especially when first meeting. Your receptivity—the degree to which you will respond in a friendly way to approaches from others—is subtly communicated. If you look at the floor when arriving in the morning and go straight to

your desk without saying, "Good morning" to co-workers, you've communicated, "I'm not friendly. If you speak to me I may be unfriendly."

Goodwill is communicated through social rituals. The ones we're most aware of are ritual greetings. "Good morning! How are you this morning?" We all understand that this is a goodwill greeting and not an actual request for information on your well-being. When a person enters a group situation, such as in the example above, of when you walk straight to your desk without saying "Hello" or "Good morning," people wonder "What's bothering her?" or will conclude "He's unfriendly."

Communicate goodwill to people around you by using ritual greetings. Make sure that you say "Hi" or "Good morning" in an upbeat voice and communicate friendliness in your nonverbal gestures. The objective is to invite people to speak to you rather than to turn them away. You can do this nonverbally, especially by smiling. Eye contact but not staring is important. An open posture, leaning forward, and touching a person's shoulder or arm communicates receptivity.

A show of goodwill invites people to speak to you and promotes a comfortable ambiance when interacting with you. It sets the stage for developing a congenial association that could become a beneficial alliance.

SHOW INTEREST IN OTHERS

The most powerful resource you have for building social relationships is your attention. When you pay attention to others they feel good about themselves and about you. Showing interest is easy. All you have to do is to ask questions. Find out how others feel about community issues. Ask about hobbies. Be curious about what others want to accomplish.

> **Attention to the concerns of others creates obligations. Show concern for what is important to the people in your organization. They will respond with concern for what is important to you.**
>
> Keshavan Nair
> *Beyond Winning*

When asking questions use open-ended questions that draw people out. Open questions begin with words like "what," "where," "how," "when," and "who." A question like "What did you think of it?" shows interest and encourages the person to elaborate upon what was being said. Preferably, questions should be short. The following questions are powerful and versatile. You can ask one in response to most things another person might say.

■ POWERFUL QUESTIONS FOR SHOWING INTEREST ■ AND GETTING INFORMATION

What happened?

What did you do?

How did you feel?

What's your opinion?

What do you suggest?

What's an example?

What do you mean?

You'll be amazed how many places you can ask these questions and how effective they are in drawing people out and communicating your interest.

Bill: What a day!

Bob: *What happened?*

Bill: Oh, it was crisis management all day.

Bob: Yeah? *What happened?*

Bill: This one woman just had a fit over the warranty.

Bob: *What did she do?*

Bill: She yelled and threatened and was damned unreasonable.

Bob: *What did you do?*

Bill: I listened until she ran out of steam.

Bob: Then *what happened?*

Bill: She finally calmed down and I asked her what would correct the situation.

Bob: *What did she do?*

Bill: She said I could understand what an inconvenience it was for her.

Bob: *What did you do?*

Bill: I told her I understood and that's all it took. She hung up!

Bob: *How did you feel?*

Bill: Relief and pride.

Bob: *What do you mean?*

Bill: I mean, I felt I did a damned good job with a difficult person.

Practice asking these simple, but powerful questions. You might write them on a file card that you can carry in your pocket and pull out to review just before you converse with someone. Before you know it, showing interest by asking open questions will become second nature. And you'll be amazed at how having these questions on the tip of your tongue makes it easier to listen and really focus attention on what the other person is saying. You don't get distracted by thinking up your next question. One of the three questions—"What happened?" "What did you do?" and "What did you feel?—" work in almost all situations. And a second benefit will be the increased quality of information you'll gather. Try it.

INVITE OTHERS

Another way to show interest is by including others. At parties and informal gatherings invite others to join your conversation. "Joyce, here, has had some experience with that client too. What do you think his agenda is, Joyce?" Draw people out and set the stage to get attention from others. Help them to open up and feel included.

Don't wait to be invited. Instead take the initiative and invite others to do things with you. Look for small ways to invite others. You can invite a co-worker to walk to a meeting with you, for example. Ask co-workers to join you for lunch. Look through the paper for interesting events and ask a friend to accompany you. People love to be invited out.

BE A TEAMPLAYER

Being a teamplayer means working cooperatively to accomplish the group's purpose. Often this involves passing the ball rather than grabbing it and running for the touchdown yourself. Instead of trying to stand out as the performer, being a teamplayer often means setting other people up so they can make the shot. This means thinking beyond your function and job responsibilities to the goals of the larger group and ways that you can be helpful to others. When another person makes the basket and the team advances because you've passed the ball, everyone wins. You become an important player upon whom others depend.

When you help others accomplish their goals, they are inclined to want to help you, too. Helping doesn't take a lot of effort. Sometimes it is as easy as sharing information while introducing people to each other. Get outside of yourself and think about what you could do to help someone else succeed. Even if nothing else comes of it, helping feels good.

When people get caught in the burnout cycle they tend to withdraw and not to have enough energy to extend themselves to others. They stop giving information, stop being helpful. This in turn closes the person to support of others. Eventually other people withdraw from the person and stop being helpful. You can see the cycle of isolation that sets in.

GIVE INFORMATION

Information is power. Information is needed to get things done. With information, you can encourage money-saving activities and prevent problems. Be generous with your information. Information is the currency of cultivating allies. Give it freely to people who could benefit from it. If someone performs better as a result of information from you, that person will be inclined to help you sometime in the future when you ask a favor.

Be alert for small ways that you can help people around you to succeed by offering them access to information resources you have. It doesn't take a lot of time or effort. It's more a style of operating, of being generous and outgoing with your information or of being tight and stingy.

ASK FOR ADVICE

When you ask others for advice, they are flattered. They feel important. And they become committed to you. They want to see you succeed. By seeking advice you can identify and clear away barriers and resistance to your projects. Identify who will be affected by your work and what you want to accomplish. Approach these people and ask them what problems and barriers they foresee. Then ask them for advice on handling them. This a powerful method for gaining support and heading problems off at the pass. Not only can you make plans for getting around barriers and correcting problems, but people who may have resisted what you wanted to accomplish become supporters when you seek their feedback and endeavor to find ways to satisfy their concerns.

A production manager could ask advice from the sales manager to get information on what the customers want, for example. Not only is this sort of information invaluable in the production stage, but it is dynamic. The sales staff will be more supportive and committed to selling the product because they were consulted in the formative stages. Additionally, they can show the customers how their concerns were addressed.

MAKE OTHERS WINNERS

Making others feel like winners is easy. All you have to do is notice what a person is doing well and comment on it. It only takes a minute. A powerful way of giving credit is to speak positively of something someone did to another person in front of that person. For example, in Janice's presence you might say, "Here's an excellent report on the climatic conditions in the area that Janice prepared for me. The background information is quite thorough and the conclusions are provocative." When you give credit in this manner, not only is the person's self-esteem enhanced, but they become one of your supporters. Additionally, people who've observed you giving credit generally will be predisposed to be positive to you, especially when the person you've given credit to is an ally of theirs.

Consider who has contributed to your work. This may be people on your staff who have performed well, for example. It may be people who have helped by giving you important information. Look for opportunities to acknowledge these people. Take a look at co-workers and other people you interface with. What have they done right? How have they assisted you, even in small ways? Take the time to give people credit for performing. It doesn't have to be a star performance. Give people credit for good performance, for being a teamplayer, for being helpful. Make a list of people who you rely upon to get your work done. For each, identify things they have done well and ways that they have helped you—even if it is part of their job description. Make a point of giving these people credit. While it takes only a few seconds, the potential gains are tremendous. Not only will you gain their cooperation but you help them beat burnout. Everyone wants to feel that others notice and appreciate their contributions. Be generous with your acknowledgement.

SHOW BELONGING

When you belong to a group or a community, people feel they have something in common with you and feel free to talk with you even though they may not know you initially. The fact that you are a member of the group or club means that you belong and you're "one of us." Belonging to a certain degree means being accepted.

Actively act in such a way to show that you do belong to this group. Begin by acting "as if" you do belong. Groups usually have certain characteristics or you could call them rituals and styles. These can be in their style of language. People may speak with particular intonations, use slang or speak with a drawl or accent. What they talk about and how they say it may be particular to the group. People may use nicknames, relay stories about group members, tell inside jokes, and use words like "we", "us," or special references like "me and the boys." Sometimes community members wear particular styles of clothing like Brooks Brothers suits, the grunge look, or cowboy style. Sports icons are common. For example, you could show belonging if people in your office are 49er fans and you wear a 49er tee-shirt during the Superbowl. People in the group may have certain grooming habits like wearing beards or certain hairstyles, for example. There also may be gestures and body language that are common among people in the group.

When you look like you belong it is easier for people to talk with you because you have something in common. Finding ways to show belonging begins by observing people in the group or community you want to belong to. Notice what they talk about. What is the style of dress? What do people do? What do they have in common that identifies them as members of the group? You might keep notes. How can you incorporate language or dress style to show belonging?

WAYS TO SHOW BELONGING

Language style	Slang, intonations, drawls, accents Wordspronouns "we," "us," inside jokes, nicknames, stories about the group
Gestures	Handshakes, hugs, body language, salutes like raised fist, peace symbol, thumbs up
Clothing	Sports icons like hats, tee-shirts, political ribbons and buttons, dress style like Brooks Brothers, grunge look, cowboy
Grooming	Hairstyles like Ivy League, tiny pigtails, braids; beards and the "Don Johnson" look, make-up, fancy fingernails

---

DEVELOPMENT A BROAD RELATIONSHIP FOUNDATION

It's important to have supportive relationships at work and to feel belonging rather than alienation. It's equally important to have a broad relationship foundation should one of the main pillars—work or family—show cracks. The hangout is one such cornerstone.

FIND A HANGOUT

People most commonly divide their lives between family and job. There are hidden losses. Parts of you die of attrition, while other facets never have a chance to develop. With all your eggs invested in these two baskets, it doesn't take much to throw both out of kilter. The hangout is a third pillar, a respite from both work and home. Typically some informal spot like an espresso house or a neighborhood-type tavern, the hangout is removed from the cares of the office and home. The TV sitcom "Cheers" is an example of such a hangout. Its story is set in a neighborhood bar where regulars and visitors created a sense of community.

The main activity is "hanging out." There are no goals to be met, no statuses to be maintained. You can relax, enjoy a convivial atmosphere, and have an opportunity to meet people of diverse backgrounds. This third place provides an emotional resource vitally important during burnout. You meet people who—whether just passing through or regulars—come together on an equal basis. Hangouts help subdue feelings of alienation and isolation. Regulars can develop a sense of wholeness, belonging, and community. It's a place to gain acknowledgement as a different person—a third person—not a worker, not a spouse.

SEPARATE HOME AND WORK

Some people's lives at home and work are so intertwined that they even live in "company ghettos" with all of their friends being from the company and most social activities being company-related. The danger lies in the enormous amount of power the company acquires when you have all of your eggs in one basket. What happens to that basket is very important. You become vulnerable, more susceptible to pressures to conform. There can be far-reaching ramifications seeping into every part of your life until eventually you look like a "company clone." If a problem develops at work, you have a double problem: A threat to your job and the possibility of losing your social support system as well.

There are a number of advantages in keeping your work and personal life separate. Having two (or more) support systems, you are stronger. Keeping these two foundations distant from one another forms a more stable base, and provides you with a unique perspective on both.

■ **Sandra's story:**
In 1969 I was a teacher in an Army Education Center where almost everyone on staff was an Army person.

Having spent my formative years in a military lifestyle, I quickly developed a good rapport with the staff and I liked my job very much. But, as in any situation, there were subtle pressures to conform. There was an unstated "approved" lifestyle, one that I did not care to live! Peer pressure is powerful and can slowly mold you into something you did not choose, you know.

At the time that I had this job I lived in a Haight-Ashbury "hippy commune." On the surface the hippy movement endorsed freedom and encouraged doing your own thing. Nothing could have been further from the truth. The same pressures operated among the flower children as everywhere else. There were pressures to conform to certain norms and values—very strong pressures. Some I found compatible, others I didn't.

Each morning I woke up in my hippy commune, climbed into my car, and drove to my other world, the Army base. I felt completely at home and relaxed in both worlds and each insulated me from the other.

I remember one day in particular. Another teacher commented, "Sandra, you are so loose, you make me nervous." Ironically, later that day, my boyfriend, who resembled a lion with his mane of long blond hair and thick yellow-red beard, said in irritation, "Sandra, you are so uptight, you squeak."

It was a curious contrast. I knew that each, within their own frame of reference, was absolutely right and I had to agree with them both. But rather than being boxed in by their opinion, I was free to choose whichever version of me I wanted at the moment. As my boyfriend berated me for my uptightness, I simply thought back to what the teacher at work had said that morning. Recalling the other teacher's words, I had support, someone to refute my boyfriend's allegation that I was so uptight!"

While this double lifestyle doesn't agree with everyone, Sandra found it enabled her to function in a high-pressure situation: the Army. As a side benefit she was able to develop more facets of herself: "I have many more selves and a wide range of available options."

MAKE A PLAN FOR BUILDING SOCIAL SUPPORT

Start building your social support system today. Don't put it off. Make a list of possible things you can do and decide upon one specific action to build your relationship with a friend, family member, co-worker, or in your professional organization. Then make a commitment with yourself to take action.

Use a self-contract. Write down exactly what you are going to do and when you will do it. And remember to give yourself a "win" for following through. You deserve all the wins you can get. When you have a strong social support system and helpful allies your personal power grows. It is easier to get things done when other people cooperate. Friends and family bring work problems into perspective. Allies expand your sphere of influence and help buffer you from burnout.

CHAPTER 9

TAILOR THE JOB
TO FIT YOU
THE FIFTH PATH TO PERSONAL POWER

*W*hen motivation wanes and work becomes a task or even drudgery, the burnout victim begins to question why he or she tolerates it. The paycheck is usually the only reason found—or more accurately stated, not losing the paycheck propels him or her out of bed in the morning and into the commute traffic each day. In time, the arrangement seems less and less equitable. The price is simply too much. The money doesn't compensate for the damage done to the already waning spirit. Often the weary worker sees a bigger paycheck as the solution. But a raise is a short-term high. A week or two later, work feels much the same as it did before. A raise with no other change is probably not going to significantly influence your motivation. Jane, for example, insisted that if she's paid more her job will become more "meaningful." But her focus is short-sighted; she hasn't analyzed the root problem or attempted to make working more satisfying. Chances are, even if Jane did convince her boss that she deserved a raise, she would have the same complaint in a couple of months, perhaps sooner.

Almost every job has some leeway for tailoring the way it is performed. Generally speaking, changes that result in an increased sense of potency have a beneficial effect. Potency is the feeling of "I can do." Of course, in your own particular situation you should pinpoint precisely what you need so that you can mesh the work with your personal workstyle. Tailoring a job is a creative process; there are no pat formulas. The following are tactics to consider. With a little from each you might be able to fashion your own best fit.

Take time to consider the situation. Pinpointing motivation extinguishers and how you respond to them is important. Don't succumb to the urge to seek a salve rather than a solution. Consider the problem in terms of what you can do rather than lamenting over the problem and convincing yourself that you are helpless.

TAILOR THE JOB

For many the word "work" often calls up images of routinized labor, with the worker going through the day lockstep. This is not always the case. Many people work in vaguely defined situations and their daily goals are even more obscure. Functioning in such a directional vacuum can be extremely frustrating. When people are paid to do a job, they want to know what is expected of them. No doubt the system would run better if everyone knew exactly what their function was and the necessary steps were for completing it. But expounding on the failings of the supervisor or the company does little to improve your plight and may, in fact, foster a sense of helplessness. Worse yet, expecting others to do something blinds you to a hidden source of personal power.

New professionals just coming out of graduate training programs often find themselves in just such a predicament. The school environment left behind was highly structured with lots of little achievement markers and acknowledgements along the way. Having grown accustomed to such support they are often ill-prepared to work in the real world. Tucked away and forgotten in a little cubicle, the graduate has no one to turn to for direction and without the structure, often feels confused and frustrated. With seasoning, some begin to see an ambiguous situation as an opportunity. Sue, the social worker we met earlier, was just one such person. She was on her own and she eventually realized if she was going to survive working she had to set her own goals and manage herself. Taking this step was a breakthrough. She no longer viewed ambiguity as a threat but as an opportunity for autonomy. More significantly, she was less dependent on the external world to fuel her motivation.

IDENTIFY HOW YOU FIT IN

How your job fits into the overall organizational goals often remains a mystery. It's easy to wonder how your pecking away diligently at your work has any impact on anything at all. One way to find out and to lay the ground work for setting productive goals is to go through the following analytical steps. Begin by looking at your organization as a total entity and ask the question, "What is the organization's essential output or goal?" In Sue's case, the agency's ultimate goal was to meet client emergency needs: providing food, shelter, and counseling. Following the same logic used in identifying behavior chains (see Chapter 6), proceed backward from the organization's overall output to departmental outputs and then from departmental outputs to your output.

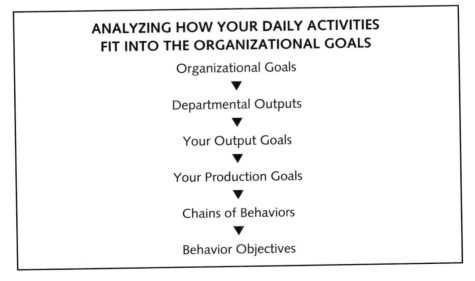

**ANALYZING HOW YOUR DAILY ACTIVITIES
FIT INTO THE ORGANIZATIONAL GOALS**

Organizational Goals
▼
Departmental Outputs
▼
Your Output Goals
▼
Your Production Goals
▼
Chains of Behaviors
▼
Behavior Objectives

SET GOALS

Sue's unit's goal was directing the client to the appropriate service group within the agency. Sue contributed to the unit output by providing a description of the client's problem. Once she identified her output, she began working on unrooting the behavior chains needed to make an accurate description of the nature and scope of the client problem. One link in the chain was to establish rapport with the client who was more likely to discuss a problem if he or she felt comfortable. Having identified establishing rapport as a vital link to her ultimate output, Sue proceeded to pinpoint the specific behaviors involved. One of these was to ask "feeling questions." Sue established a skill building program for increasing the number of feeling questions she asked during each intake interview.

Goal setting provides the if portion of the if-then formula, and self-acknowledgement is the then portion. If I reach my goal, then I will acknowledge myself.

Even in well-defined situations, setting goals is helpful. Establishing a goal is satisfying because it yields a sense of potency. There are always ways you can motivate yourself with goal setting. When you set a goal, you take command and define a target. You know which way to shoot and have a yardstick to measure improvement. The act of setting a goal alone enhances personal power. Goal setting is a particularly valuable survival skill in unresponsive environments, for you can extract a positive response through feedback on your progress. In other words, you create a response from outside. Feedback is the longitude and latitude or where you stand, relative to a particular standard or goal. Because it is a reflection of you, your goal has personal meaning. Therefore, even a boring job can be meaningful by working toward a goal. Goal setting is an eternal source of personal power; once you know how to use it, it can never be taken from you.

By combining goal setting and self-acknowledgement, you have everything necessary for self-motivation. Remember, the if-then principle is vital for a sense of potency. Through goal setting and self-acknowledgement you can create an if-then climate in any environment.

ACKNOWLEDGE YOURSELF

Even in unresponsive and hostile environments you have an inexhaustable source of powerful wins. You can give yourself acknowledgement and rewards from your list. Unfortunately, few people know how to use these self-rewards. Most people engage in negative-talk, a powerful punitive means of self-control. On the other hand, surprisingly few use self-acknowledgement. Thus, for most of us this self-renewing source of power remains dormant. Instead, we remain dependent on acknowledgement from others.

MANAGE TASKS

Another powerful win or positive pay-off is the opportunity to engage in an activity you enjoy. For example, as a child your mother knew your preferences, and may have said"When you finish practicing the violin, you can go play ball." In this case, the opportunity to play ball became a kind of reward for practicing the violin. Most of us understand this principle and use it intuitively to manage ourselves. Research has demonstrated that the opportunity to engage in a "preferred activity" can be used as a reward for completing an "unpreferred activity." Preferred refers to the likelihood of your engaging in the activity. For example, when you walk into your office in the morning suppose you are most likely to open your mail and least likely to dictate a report. Opening mail would be considered a preferred activity while dictating a report is an unpreferred one.

Within this principle lies a key to using work to motivate work. For example, consider the following study of how salesmen sequenced their sales calls. In the first stage of the study, the salesmen were told to call on both old customers and prospects. They could use any sequence they pre-

ferred. As you might expect, the number of calls to old customers, which often resulted in easy sales, far exceeded the number of calls to prospective customers, who required persistence and persuasiveness to score a sale. Making old calls was a preferred activity. That is, of the two types of calls, the salesmen were more likely to make old calls. In the second stage of the study, the salesmen were told they should make five old calls only after having made a sale to a new customer. They were required to actually make a sale, not just a phone call. Predictably, the number of new calls made increased dramatically. This is similar to what occurred when your mother said, "Eat your peas, then you can have more meat." Being able to eat more meat-part of the meal motivated you to eat the peas. An unexpected result in this study was that not only did the number of new calls go up, but the number of old calls went up as well. The salesmen made more calls in both categories. In the third stage, they were told they could once again make calls in any order they chose. Calls of both types dropped. Calls to prospects dropped to zero, and calls to old customers dropped to a level below that in the first stage of the study.

Break your work up into segments, and sequence it so that those activities you perform frequently or "prefer" follow doing the tasks you tend to put off.

Let's look at how Gina employed this same strategy. She hated filing and consequently left it to last. She did do a little filing each day, but the number of papers she grudgingly stuck in folders did not compare to what accumulated in the "To Be Filed" basket. She dreaded filing, yet knew she had to do it. She felt confident that if she could just get the filing out of the way with a minimum of pain, her outlook would improve.

Using task management, Gina identified photocopying as a preferred activity. Although the photocopying itself was rather boring, it provided a break in the routine and an opportunity to chat with whomever happened to be in the production room. So she tended to do photocopying right away. Gina made an agreement with herself to do a specific amount of filing before she did any photocopying. The desire to get through the filing and onto the photocopying provided the motivation to file. A secondary gain was an increase in personal power as she overcame a burdensome chore. By managing tasks, Gina worked more efficiently and was less vulnerable to the boring and routine aspects of her work. Her focus switched from dreading to accomplishing.

Cam also used this strategy. He enjoyed studying and learning, which was fortunate, because continuing his professional growth meant he had to keep abreast of the latest developments. Unfortunately, it was becoming increasingly difficult for him to do what he called "later work"— which was work that had no immediate pay-off but was important at some later time. Not only was he not keeping up with the stacks of journals at home and in his office but he was also feeling deprived and unhappy about it. This discontentment was creating quite a problem for him. His situation was becoming punitive and negative. He felt trapped in what he called "now work"—processing papers, writing routine reports, and sitting in meetings. His day was consumed in satisfying the immediate demands of his job. While he met these daily demands and deadlines with ease, he had less and less time for his "later work" such as going to professional conferences, reading journal articles, working on proposals for new projects, or creative contemplations. These were overrun by the daily priorities of the "now" activities.

Cam solved this problem with task management. He saw that working on the daily papers and reports were preferred activities, while "later" activities were dormant. He set up a schedule that made working on one daily project (a "now" activity) contingent upon doing a little "later" work. For example, he required that he spend 20 minutes reading one journal article before he could work on a particular "now" report. Although it was a step removed, the deadline attached to the "now" work provided a deadline for doing the "later" work as well. With this formula Cam reclaimed the energy dissipated in working to avoid, and invested it in working to gain. An increase in personal power resulted.

MANAGE TIME

The constant phone interruptions also challenged Cam's patience.

All one had to do was dial his number to get an immediate audience with him, whether he liked it or not. No sooner would he get into a task than the phone would ring. What he needed was a block of time free from the phone. To create such a block Cam had to manage time. He told his secretary to hold all his calls between 9 and 11 A.M. At ll:00 he returned the calls. This arrangment worked well. By deciding how much time would be devoted to what activity, Cam was able to concentrate on one task at a time without distraction. He produced more and did it effectively because he had more production time.

Ralph had a similar problem grasping elusive time. What began as a little harmless chit-chat with his officemate had escalated into time-gobbling rap sessions. He wasn't getting anything done. Ralph and his officemate worked out the following plan: An hour in the morning, from 10 to 11, and an hour in the afternoon, from 2 to 3, were designated as "quiet time." During these periods they agreed to be quiet. If either was restless and wanted to talk, he would go elsewhere for a responsive ear. At the end of the hour they shared coffee and conversation. Managing time created time, Ralph got a lot more done, and he enjoyed his officemate and the breaks more, too.

SET PRIORITIES

It is easy to fall into the trap of working on the next thing that comes by, which is sometimes called "crisis management" rather than working on what's really important to accomplishing your job. By setting priorities and sticking to them you can be more effective. Setting priorities is particularly important when you have too much work and too little time in which to do it. Under these circumstances there will be many times when you simply must leave certain things undone. This is okay and most employers will accept it so long as what you don't do is relatively unimportant to accomplishing your major purpose. It is easy however, to spend a lot of time doing routine things and then find that all of your time has been used up before you get to things that are important. Chances are that the really important things you must do are also more difficult. So it is easy to procrastinate and then find you don't have time to get to them. Setting priorities can help you to keep your eye on the ball and to get the important parts of your job done within the time allotted.

YOU WERE HIRED TO SOLVE A PROBLEM

You were not hired to do a job; you were hired to solve a problem. Jobs are created because the organization has a problem. For example, a couple may be running a mail-order business out of their home. Initially, they do all of the work themselves. As the business grows various problems crop up. The phones may ring so frequently that they cannot adequately take the calls and still process the orders. Likewise, the number of orders may increase to the point that they cannot process all of the orders quickly enough themselves. Delayed orders result in customer complaints. How to handle the phone calls and process the excess orders are problems. So the couple creates a job that involves answering the phone and processing orders. The job was created to solve a problem. The newly hired employee's purpose is to provide a solution to this problem.

Identify Your Purpose

The first step is to identify the problem you were hired to solve. Sometimes it is obvious as in the example of the mail order business. Other times it will be more difficult. One way to identify the problem is to imagine what would happen if no one were dealing with the problem. That is, try to picture what would happen if the problem went unsolved. Make sure that you focus on the problem to be solved and not the tasks that you or others have carried out in order to solve the problem. For example, the problem that a receptionist in a law office is hired to solve is not answering phones. Answering phones, per se, is not a problem. A few of the problems a receptionist solves are unanswered calls, people walking into attorney's offices unannounced, people calling with questions and interrupting the attorneys while they are with clients. The receptionist solves these problems by answering calls, screening calls, routing calls to the appropriate party, greeting clients, keeping clients in the waiting area, announcing clients, and so forth.

Once you've identified the core problem or problems you are hired to solve you have identified your purpose in the company. This helps you to have a basis against which to set priorities. Here's how it works. When you know your purpose, which is the problem you have been hired to solve, then you know what you are to accomplish. Activities that have a big impact upon solving the problem are more important and should have a higher priority than those that have a lesser impact.

Identify Tasks and Activities

List your tasks and activities at work. If you have difficulty remembering them, just close your eyes and *see* yourself at your work space doing what you do at work. Alternatively, for several days you could jot down things you do as you come to them during your work day. Make sure that you include everything you do such as answering the phone, completing forms, meeting with co-workers.

Rate Impact

Using a scale from 1 to 10, with 0 being "no impact" and 10 being "great impact," rate the impact that each activity has upon your solving the problem you were hired to solve.

Assign Priorities

Use the impact ratings to assign priorities to each task or activity. Assign an "A" priority for tasks and activities with impact ratings over 7; "B" priority for impact ratings from 4 to 6; and "C" priority for impact ratings below 3.

Schedule Activities

Use your priority ratings to schedule your day. Start with "A" tasks and activities. Try scheduling them directly on your calender. Leave "C" priorities until last and, whenever possible, delegate them. Consider what would happen if you simply did not do the "C" activities at all. If the consequences are minimal, you might consider dropping the activity from your workload. In many cases you can do this without asking permission. After all, when you've analyzed your purpose and are accomplishing that purpose you are doing your job. If questioned, you have a solid basis for having dropped the activity.

ALTER JOB FOCUS

Few jobs are clearly defined. While this can be a problem, it is also an opportunity. Take advantage of its ambiguity and shape the job according to what you enjoy doing and what best capitalizes on your skills and interests. First, look around for needs and ways you can provide a service. When you see a problem within your department, write it down, mull it over, and consider how you can convert it into an opportunity. Always focus on this question: "How can I provide a

service?" Simultaneously review all of your activities. There must be some you enjoy more than others. Expand and make more important those parts of your job you enjoy most. You can accomplish this by simply spending more time on these parts. When you discover a service you can provide by engaging in an activity you enjoy, move on it! And make the services you provide visible. Be alert to ways of highlighting what you do, the needs you fill. In this way you can mold the job into one that is more interesting. It will evolve with you, and you'll receive more acknowledgement for your efforts because you have pointed them out. Don't wait passively for the world to notice what you're doing. Most people are so caught up in their own activities that they simply don't see you. Wave a flag; toot your horn.

EXPAND THE JOB

Jobs are not static, they are elastic and change. Jobs can be stretched. Jobs are alive. They grow and evolve. You can make your job stretch and grow to fit you better. The best way to expand your job is to identify "unattached problems." These are problems that have not been assigned to any specific person. Since these problems are not assigned and don't fall within anyone's domain, they are free for you to take. Take possession of unattached problems that you feel you can solve and that interest you. In most cases this strategy doesn't require asking permission and you can obtain formal authorization after the fact. Depending upon how important the problem is to the company, you might be able to use it to obtain an upgraded job title, add support staff or services, or possibly even get a raise.

Always be alert for unattached problems. In rapidly changing environments unattached problems are plentiful. This is true of both down-sizing and expanding companies. It's a good idea to keep a list of the unattached problems you discover. When you have several such problems, consider each one at a time and ask the following two questions. First, "Can I solve this problem?" If you can answer yes, then this problem is a good candidate for you to assume. The second question is "Does solving this problem interest me?" If it does interest you and you can solve the problem, then you should seriously consider taking on the problem as yours.

Years ago when I worked as a social worker in the San Francisco County men's jail I used this principle to expand my job in ways that I found more satisfying. I met with inmates in the jail twice a week to discuss their various problems that included rescuing possessions from hotels, writing pleading letters to judges, arranging for a room after their release, getting meal tickets from social services, providing a razor in order to shave before a job interview.

There was no central referral service or hot line for these people. Consequently, I often had to research the available services which took a lot of time. I discovered that services were often referred to in newspaper articles and announcements. So each morning I skimmed the local papers. When I noticed a service that might be useful, I wrote all the details on a file card. Soon I had a rather large file of resources. I felt much more competent when a recently released inmate came to my office and I could filp through my files to a service that might help him. Instead of feeling helpless and frustrated when facing the serious problems that the men brought to me, I felt powerful. There was something I could do!

Soon a curious thing happened. Service providers in other agencies heard through the grapevine about my resource file and began calling me for referrals. In talking with these people, I realized that there were service providers in several agencies working with the same client population. The problem was that we were all disconnected and rein-venting the wheel. So I took the initiative and invited several of these people to my office to discuss how we could work together. The meeting was helpful so we began meeting monthly. I never asked my supervisor for permission to keep a referral file or to meet with the other service providers. It was an unattached problem and I grabbed it and ran with it. Eventually, I moved on to another job elsewhere. Guess what? Keeping the referral file and holding the meetings was presented as part of the defined job to the new case worker. By uncovering and taking an unattached problem, I had expanded the job.

INCREASE DIVERSITY

Variety—working on tasks that vary—can refuel energy. Many people find that when they do the same thing over and over that they lose interest. Without interest it becomes difficult to perform well and quality declines. Diversity can renew interest, even when the various tasks taken individually may each be rather routine.

DESPECIALIZE

One way to increase diversity is to despecialize, to become more of a generalist. A generalist does a variety of things rather than specializing in one activity. No matter what your job or station in life there are always ways to despecialize. Antonio, for example, was a research consultant specializing in statistical analysis. While he found it fascinating, it didn't satisfy him. It wasn't enough. Having been through several phases of indifference, he knew his lack of interest was a danger signal. Then the yardman who maintained Antonio's rental units quit. Antonio had to fill in until he could find someone reliable. Halfway through repairing and painting a picket fence, Antonio sensed a change. A feeling of aliveness was returning. From that point on Antonio spent a little time each week building fences, planting roses, clipping hedges, and spraying bugs. By "despecializing" he found a balance between his mental and physical needs. Doing one or the other of his tasks provided not just an escape but also nourishment.

Murphy, a big city cop, is another example. His idealism had motivated him to join the force two years earlier. He was a compassionate man who felt for others and believed he could alleviate some human suffering through police work. But most of his encounters with citizens were in negative circumstances. They were criminals (or suspected criminals) and he was the bearer of bad news. With alarm, Murphy felt himself changing. His idealism began to dim and his compassion became dull. He began to despair. While he still felt police work was right for him and he wanted to keep working, he recognized he had to have some balance if he were to continue. His solution was to accept a part-time job delivering flowers on weekends. His encounters with people during deliveries were very different from those on the beat. He was the bearer of beauty. Even when the situation was a sorrowful one, his arrival was associated with sympathy and remembrance. His positive image of himself—as well as his confidence in his fellow human beings—was reaffirmed.

Here's how Sue, the social worker, despecialized. Doing intake interviews almost exclusively was becoming an emotional drain. The clients began to blend together, and Sue felt herself getting dull. Over lunch she discovered Ruth, the woman who handled client processing, was also experiencing what Sue called "sameness drain." Ruth was bleary-eyed from paper work, and Sue was drained from people work. They laughed over the image of waiting for clients to glide by their desks on a conveyor belt. The idea of trading jobs once a week seemed worth a try. They didn't race into the plan immediately. Over many lunches and dinners, Ruth and Sue tutored one another. Both felt good about the results—a close friendship, a broader skill base, and renewed enthusiasm.

WORK PART-TIME

Part-timing is another way to create diversity. Most week days James was the lunch cook in an uptown restaurant. His evenings were divided between working in a bookstore with a coffeeshop serving cake and cappuccino in the evenings, and later working as a waiter in a singles bar until midnight. Any one of these jobs would have become dull in short order, but the diversity of the three-way combo maintained his interest. All told James worked about 40 hours a week, made about the same amount of money as if he had worked a full-time job, and had a schedule that allowed him a three-day weekend every week.

PURSUE HOBBIES

Traditionally hobbies have served the purpose of refueling creativity and enthusiasm. The hobby (or avocation) provides an outlet for expression of those selves that are hidden at work. Pursuing a hobby usually takes you into worlds far away from work. You meet new people, different people. It reminds you that your work situation is not the whole world. Also, as you excel in your hobby you get acknowledgement from others that can help ward off the "starvation" experienced at work.

Sometimes a hobby can even evolve into a new vocation. Roy, for example, was in the training department of a large West Coast police department. He often entertained others in the department and the rookies during training with his cartoon caricatures. His pen won him popularity and livened up many dull classes. One day a crisis arose and Roy was right there with a service to offer. The witness to a particularly grisly crime shook his head to all the mugshots. A talented artist was needed to translate the victim's vague remembrance into an image. Because of the nature of the crime, the police department didn't want to risk a leakage to the press by using the newspaper's artist. Roy's drawing was accurate. The criminal was apprehended, and Roy had taken his first step to becoming a nationally known police artist.

SPEAK UP

Some job modification strategies require the support of your supervisor. When contemplating the possibilities of a more dramatic overhaul keep in mind that your relationship with the organization is contractual. You have agreed to perform a certain service in exchange for a specified amount of pay and benefits. But aside from the salary, length of work week, the extent of benefits, and general tasks not much else is actually specified in most work contracts. As with any contract, unstated issues are open to interpretation and negotiation by both parties. Too many people give their employers more than they have contracted, so work contracts need to be periodically clarified and renegotiated. Remember, no person or company remains static: People change, companies change. What may have been a good arrangement two years ago may no longer be optimal. It might be necessary for you to talk with your supervisor about what's dampening your motivation and suggest steps that could turn it around. This requires self-confidence and assertiveness. Don't just dump a bunch of vague complaints on your boss. Putting him or her on the defensive is not a winning approach. But more importantly, by expecting your boss to solve the problem, you proclaim yourself helpless. It would be better to pinpoint the problem by describing what is happening to your work spirit and suggest possible solutions.

Keep in mind that one of your boss's major job functions is to get work done through people. Constructive speaking up is not the same as complaining or confronting; it is giving the supervisor valuable feedback. It's important for both you and the organization that you speak up and do so effectively. Suffering in silence leads to a loss for both of you. If you feel hesitant or uncomfortable doing this, you may need a skill-building program to help develop your assertiveness skills.

> Some time ago, my wife was invited to serve as chairman of a committee in a community endeavor. She has a number of truly important things she was trying to work on, and she really didn't want to do it. But she felt pressured into it and finally agreed.
>
> The she called one of her dear friends to ask if she would serve on her committee. Her friend listened for a long time and then said, "Sandra, that sounds like a wonderful project, a really worthy undertaking. I appreciate so much your inviting me to be a part of it. I feel honored by it. For a number of reasons, I won't be participating myself, but I want you to know how much I appreciate your invitation."
>
> Sandra was ready for anything but a pleasant "no." She turned to me and sighed, "I wish I'd said that."
>
> Stephen R. Covey
> *The 7 Habits of Highly Effective People*

SET LIMITS

Unchecked, jobs can get out of control, creeping into every corner of your life, demanding more and more from you. Forgotten is the work contract. Sometimes it's because of continual crises; other times it's a succession of critical projects or perhaps even an overzealous supervisor who believes that working late each night is a sign of motivation and, hence, promotability. Whatever the reason, know your limits. What are the limits of your obligations and responsibilities? Have you agreed to these in the work contract? What are your needs outside of work for other activities? When you have answered these and other questions, it becomes time to make your limits known. This doesn't have to be a confrontation. But it is important to speak up and let your supervisor know you have fulfilled your obligations and you have other needs. Explain that when you work more, the organization gets less. Once you have set your limits, keep them. And limits can be applied to more than work hours. You might have set a limit on the number of committees you serve on, for example.

REDISTRIBUTE JOB RESPONSIBILTIES

Like people, jobs evolve. Consider Clem. He hopped into the saddle of a university computer center and did a superb job of picking up the pieces from the chaos left by his predecessor. He also unveiled an unusual talent for motivating people in the process. Consequently his

programs were a success and the center expanded. Demand for computer services mushroomed, and without realizing it Clem's job was mushrooming, too. His responsibilities had multiplied enormously until he could no longer juggle all the projects and departments under his direction. Overlooking the possibility that his job had outgrown what anyone could realistically manage, Clem felt like a failure. As he saw it, the only solution was to bow out before anyone realized he'd lost his touch. Clem told the residing dean he planned to resign. Fortunately for Clem and the center, the dean convinced him to delay acting until a compensation specialist could take a close look at his responsibilities. Upper management was startled when the analyst recommended three jobs be carved out of Clem's responsibilities. Clem had been covering three full-time jobs.

IS RESIGNATION NECESSARY?

[Look for] opportunities for transfer to tasks more suited to your skills, capabilities, and interests in your current employment. Your employer has a vested interest in retaining you for many reasons. The knowledge you have about the organization, its services, products, procedures, and style are costly to impart to a new employee, in addition to the recruitment expenses of the search for another person if you should leave.

You should think very carefully before resigning. A carefully prepared presentation to people with the authority to arrange job-content changes, transfers, or promotions should be considered. They will expect you to have prepared a sound case for your request. The higher the people within the organization with whom you discuss your situation, the more authority exists to change tasks within jobs, create new positions, or arrange transfers. The essential components of your strategy for change within your current job include selecting who to talk to, seeking a time when privacy can be assured, and thoroughly rehearsing the presentation of your request.

In the process of discussing your career with them you may learn more about alternative opportunities within the organization than you knew before. You may secure a commitment to facilitating your reassignment and thus avoid the strain and hazards of a search for a different employer.

Paul Stevens
Stop Postponing the Rest of Your Life

TAKE A SABBATICAL

A sabbatical, or leave of absence, from your responsibilities to assume a dramatically different one has been a tradition in academia and is becoming more common in the corporate world as well. It is a half-step between staying in your job and getting a new one. You can take on different responsibilities, sometimes in a different part of the country, for an extended period of time, and return at the end of the sabbatical period to your former position. In larger corporations, with all their levels and divisions, sabbaticals are a feasible solution to the recharging of drained motivational batteries. Sabbaticals have the added advantage of providing a vehicle for expanding employees' capabilities, a big plus for the company and the employees. If you are an "essential component," many companies will consider granting you a leave of absence if they think they can eventually get you back.

This was a tactic Ron used. He had been branch manager of a savings-and-loan company for over five years. Under his leadership his branch outperformed the others on almost every index. But the job was beginning to get to him. On his thirty-sixth birthday he was keenly aware of the passing of his youth. Age itself was not a concern, but he was disturbed by his increasing awareness of "paths not taken." Whether it was a "passage crisis" or something else, Ron didn't know. He did know he needed a change and a dramatic one. It was either quit or take a leave of absence. The organization opted for the leave of absence. They hoped to keep him on board until his retirement. Ron, knowing that his old position was on hold, did something he always wanted to do. He became a kindergarten teacher in a troubled inner-city school. While the other teachers seemed overwhelmed with despair, for Ron the challenge was invigorating. Ron's enthusiasm was contagious and many of the teachers began to show flickers of life. Rejuvenated, Ron returned to his post at the savings and loan. He had a new perspective on the economic problems faced by the inner-city residents and was determined to seek a solution. The savings and loan reaped a double gain: They used Ron's leave of absence to train a manager for a new branch and retained one of their star performers.

TAILOR YOUR JOB

Virtually every job has some leeway to tailor it to fit the person doing the work. Often routines of the job are shaped more by the last person doing it than by the actual task. Yet, people forget that jobs are malleable. Instead, they implement the job in the same style as the last person. When that style doesn't fit, it is like trying to squeeze the round peg into the square hole. A job that doesn't fit can be abrasive to your motivation. Don't try to turn yourself into a pretzel. Tailor the job to fit you instead. In the process you will increase your personal power because you will feel in command of your work and you will probably do a better job.

CHAPTER 10

CHANGE JOBS
THE SIXTH PATH TO PERSONAL POWER

Does the path have a good heart?
If it does, the path is good. If it doesn't, it is of no use.
Both paths lead nowhere; but one has a heart, the other doesn't.
One makes for a joyful journey;
as long as you follow it, you are one with it.
The other will make you curse your life.
One makes you strong; the other weakens you.
—Don Juan
The Teachings of Don Juan

No amount of modification can force a "good fit" with certain jobs. After enough saddle sores you may decide the only way to save your spirit is to get out. This option is always available, but most burnout victims contemplate it with longing and fear. The decision is toughest when your job has benefits you enjoy such as prestige, a big salary, or country-club membership. But the real question is: How much are you paying? How many of your precious moments are you spending to have the privilege of sitting around the club pool? Don Juan expressed it more profoundly when he asked, "Does the path have a good heart?"

Think of your career and the kind of work you do. How did you acquire the skills that enable you to do this work? How did you happen to develop these over other skills? How did you get on your current path? Who picked it for you? Answers like "I don't know" or "It just happened" suggest complacently following whatever path you found before you. Complacent decision making leaves you ill-prepared to confront the challenge of burnout. Paradoxically, the despairing burnout victim is actually closer to finding a path than is the nonconsious decision-maker. But the burnout victim's decision making is impaired by constricted vision. All perceived alternatives are rejected as looking equally bleak. Feeling helpless, hope that a good path can be found falters. In this weakened spiritual condition the burnout victim faces what could be the most important challenge of his or her life: finding a path with a heart.

FIND A PATH WITH A HEART

What paths are before you right now? You can continue with no change, make modifications in your present job, get a new job doing the same work elsewhere, or change what you do entirely. Which will yield a joyful journey? One reliable test is the quality of your moment-by-moment encounters. If your journey satisfies your needs, clearly the path is good for you. In contrast, those that inhibit progress, deny your needs, or negate you will extinguish your spirit. Such paths should be avoided. The successful quest begins with self-knowledge. Who are you, and who do you want to become? Many of your moments are spent working. Encounters in these moments shape whom you become. How often have you heard, "Hi, I'm John. I'm a butcher (baker, candlestickmaker). What do you do?" Don't deceive yourself into believing you can separate your work from your life. You cannot.

JOB FIT

Good job fit is one of the most important factors influencing success. When there is a good "fit" between you and your job—which includes the company, co-workers, and so forth—you are more likely to like what you are doing and to be successful. A good fit means that what you are doing and the company philosophy are compatible with your basic values, that you get along well with others, and that you have the skills needed to do the work. When you resonate in this way with your job, other people tend to go the extra mile to help you. Succeeding is easy. Working is usually fun because you like what you are doing and the people you work with.

> I began to experience a great longing to change my life. The thought of letting go of what I had . . . was truly terrifying. . . . Then one day, as I drove to work . . . a startling thought entered my head. It was as clear a thought as if someone was speaking to me: "Do what you love, the money will follow." At that very moment, I knew I had to, and would, take a leap of faith. I knew I had to, and would, step out, cut myself loose from all those things that seemed to bind me. I knew I would start doing what I most enjoyed: writing, working with industry (instead of public education), and living in the country instead of in the city.
>
> That decision transformed my life. Since that day, I have gradually expanded my role as an educator and as an organizational pychologist. I have added a depth and a complexity to my work which I had always hoped I could—a dimension my intellect thirsted for, but which self-doubt made me believe could not be mine.
>
> Paradoxically, I have also simplified my life. I have relocated to a quiet rural community where I wanted to live. I am working on projects and with people that hold keen creative interest for me. All my material needs are met. I did what I love, and the money did follow.
>
> Marsha Sinetar
> *Do What You Love: The Money Will Follow*

But many people do not have a good job fit. They may not have rapport with others in the workplace. Perhaps it is that their values and lifestyles differ too much. When people see you as different from themselves, they tend to hold back. Getting the cooperation and information you need to perform well is harder. If you don't like the work, then working is a chore and it is harder to learn what you need to succeed. When you are in a job that doesn't fit you well, it is easy to get into a vicious cycle of poor performance. People tend to withhold, making it harder to perform. When you perform less well, then your self-confidence suffers, which sets you up to have more difficulties performing.

VALUES

Strange as it may seem, many, perhaps most, people don't know what would be a good job fit. And they don't know how to find out. The answer begins with you. You begin by identifying your values—what really matters to you. It is easy to talk about values in the abstract but when it comes to stating one's values most people discover that it can be quite difficult.

"Values" is a catch-all phrase for those things we feel are worthwhile. Values are what really matter, what gives us meaning. Values come from the heart because they have to do with how we feel about things. When work engages our values, we have a sense of meaning and feel we're doing something important and worthwhile. In contrast, work that involves doing things we don't care about leaves us feeling empty. Worse yet is work that violates our values. The path with a heart is the path that engages our values. Everyone is not the same and people don't value the same things. A path that has a heart for me, may leave you feeling empty. So the first step in finding a good fit is to clarify your values. When you identify what is important to you—what gives you meaning—then you know what to look for in a job.

What You Love Doing

One way to uncover values is to examine things you love doing. Here's how it works. Take out a piece of paper and quickly write down

fifteen or twenty things you love doing. Doing this quickly is helpful because you want to tap into feelings and stay away from what you think you "should" or "shouldn't" love doing.

Once you have your list, read it over and check the five or six things you love doing the most. Examine these first. This is what to do. Imagine doing one of the things you love doing and ask yourself, "What do I love about this?" When you get an answer, ask yourself again, "What do I really love about this?" Keep probing each answer. For example, Ralph loved riding his bike with friends on the weekend. An outsider might have assumed that physical exercise was what Ralph loved. But when he asked, "What do I love about this?" he answered, "Striving toward a goal with friends." Asking what he loved about this, Ralph answered, "The feeling of esprit de corps."

The objective is to work your way to the root value. For Ralph, it might be taking on a challenge with a team, for example. Repeat this exercise with each item on the list of things you love doing. The process is a little like the young child who asks daddy, "Why?" and then asks "Why?" to each explanation given.

Make sure to jot down notes from each answer to the question, "What do I really love about doing this?" After you've gone through the process with several things that you love doing, you can review the notes looking for patterns. These patterns will provide a picture of what is important to you.

YOUR IDEAL JOB

There is an old saying: If you don't know where you want to go, you probably won't get there. The same is true in your work. If you don't know what your ideal job would be, then you probably won't get it. If you're going to get your ideal job you must determine what it would be. One way to go about identifying your ideal job is to begin with what it is not. Start by identifying situations in your current job that bother you. From these bothersome situations you can begin to specify what conditions would exist in your ideal job.

IDENTIFY BOTHERSOME SITUATIONS

Close your eyes and recall a typical day at work. Review it in your mind and notice what situations tend to make you feel frustrated or helpless. List these on a piece of paper. Now bring to mind a particularly distressing day and review it in your mind to identify what about it was bothersome. Record these situations on the list. The more specific you are in describing the bothersome situations, the better. Turn back to the inventory called "What Is the Burnout Potential of Your Job?" (page 31) in Chapter 3 and list each item you rated as a 6 or higher.

Look for Bothersome Patterns

After you have identified several bothersome situations, read over the list several times. Group the bothersome aspect of each situation into categories. Use the following categories:

Management	i.e., lack of rewards, vague directions, favoritism, criticism
Co-Workers	i.e., conflicts, politicking, cliques, rejection
Type of Work	i.e., writing reports, detail, helping people
Environment	i.e., noise, poor lighting, crowded, fast-paced
Other	i.e., specify what

Read over your list of bothersome situations again. Pay particular attention to the categories that predominated. Close your eyes and review each situation on your mental stage. What patterns can you see? List reoccurring patterns you discover on a new sheet of paper.

CREATE A PICTURE OF YOUR IDEAL JOB

Set aside some time and find a quiet spot where you won't be disturbed. Make yourself comfortable. Relax by breathing deeply, tensing and relaxing the muscles or with any other method you prefer. With your eyes closed, mentally review one of the bothersome patterns you identified. Study the bothersome aspect of the situation. After you've thoroughly reviewed the bothersome pattern, envision a work situation in which this pattern did not occur. What would happen instead? What specific ways would the job be different? Play around with it in your imagination until you find an alternative you like. This is an "ideal scenario." Repeat the exercise with each bothersome pattern. Write a brief description of the ideal scenarios next to the respective bothersome patterns.

Envision Your Ideal Job

After you've studied each bothersome situation and imagined alternative scenarios you are ready to make a first stab at envisioning your ideal job. Review the ideal scenarios. Then, once again relax by breathing deeply or with another method. Imagine a work situation that includes several of the ideal scenarios you identified. Try to actually *see* the ideal work place. What is the environment like? Is it inside or outside? What sounds are there? What is the light like? How many other people work there? What are co-workers like? Do you socialize with them? Where? Doing what? Do you have a boss? What is his or her supervisory style? What do you do? What are your work hours like? How do you get to and from work? What do you do in your spare time? What rewards do you get in this job? How do other people treat you? The more complete the picture of your ideal job, the better.

On a blank piece of paper write "My Ideal Job" at the top. Write a description of the job you pictured. Add as many details as you can imagine. Picture yourself in your ideal job again. Notice what you missed, then add these details to your description. Don't try to do this in one sitting. Begin with the sketch. Project yourself into the ideal job. Notice how it feels. Add details. See the situation, the other people involved, and what you are doing. Edit as much as you like. Continue shaping the sketch until you fashion an "ideal job." This may require many sessions. Come back to it many times over a week or two. Keep adding features to your ideal job.

IDENTIFY BARRIERS TO YOUR IDEAL JOB

What keeps you from being in your ideal job right now? Look carefully at this and be specific. On a new piece of paper create two columns. Write "Barriers" at the top of one column and "Challenges" at the top of the second column. Under "Barriers" list everything standing between where you are now and your ideal job.

Taking the barriers one at a time, determine what you must do to remove the barrier and write this in the "Challenges" column. Don't be "realistic." Just write down what it would take to get around the barrier. Pay particular attention to what you are thinking as you do this exercise. If you hear yourself saying a lot of reasons why you "can't," then list "negative thinking" as one of the barriers. Overcoming negative thinking is one of the greatest barriers of all!

You can move toward your ideal job but don't expect to reach it immediately. Choose a challenge and make a plan of action for meeting the challenge. Then work on doing so in small steps. Make sure that you give yourself "wins" for success. Each day you will be a little closer to your ideal job. As you overcome the barriers, you will feel more in control of your work and your life because each day you will be taking action to prevent burnout.

IDENTIFY AVAILABLE ALTERNATIVE JOBS

When considering a job change, most people simply head for the want ads in the newspaper or make an appointment with a headhunter. This is not the most fruitful approach. The competition for advertised jobs is fantastic. Big-city newspapers have thousands of readers. More importantly, it is unlikely that a listed job will be uniquely suited to you, a match to your ideal job. Accepting a mass-advertised job means you must fit yourself into its mold. There is a strong possibility that it will not be a good fit with who you really are. Seek a mold that fits you. Better yet, create your own.

Now that you have a pretty good image of the ideal job you are seeking, it is time to begin a broad sweep of possibilities. Don't restrict yourself to any particular field or allow bias or stereotypes to narrow the scope of your investigation. Open yourself to all possibilities. Broaden your vision. Look around and see what's actually out there. Save being critical and narrowing down options until you know what's possible. It's foolish to limit your scope. You may believe you know all that is available; but new fields and specialities are born all the time. For example, two bright forecasts are "energy management" and "Black cosmetic specialists." There are many opportunities out there.

People are at work everywhere. Select anyone at all and project yourself into this person. Compare what you discover to the blueprint for your ideal job. Ask people about their work. People love to talk about their work. As they paint a picture, project yourself into it. See yourself doing what they do.

If one field beckons, follow it. Find out everything you can about it. Talk to anyone who knows anything about it. Ask if you can visit their office, plant, or studio and see what they do. Don't be shy. Most people enjoy such show-and-tell. Go to the library. Ask the reference librarian to direct you to the occupational directories that describe thousands of jobs along with their future projections, skills, training required, and working conditions.

> Add the numbers, and it's hard to find a field that's growing as fast as consulting. At last count there were 450,000 consultants in the United States, and they were multiplying at the rate of 16 percent a year.
>
> A profitable growth industry—right?
>
> Not necessarily. For many people who have left corporate careers involuntarily, "consulting" is nothing but a polite way to spell UNEMPLOYMENT. There's nothing necessarily profitable about hanging out a shingle as a consultant.
>
> But with good skills and careful planning, many mid-career professionals have established profitable consulting practices that have continued for the rest of their lives. Others have filled what might have been wasted time, meeting expenses while building bridges to new employers. In either case, serving a tour of duty as a consultant can be a worthwhile career move, if it's a strategy based on careful planning.
>
> William A. Charland, Jr.
> *Career Shifting: Starting Over in a Changing Economy*

It's curious how people resist looking into the future in a purposeful way. What prompts the resistance varies, but the end result is the same: Deprived of the power of foresight they plod along the path—

perhaps disgruntled, perhaps complacent—and exercise little control, remaining vulnerable. With this approach finding one's ideal job is chancy at best. Joel is a good example.

■ Joel's story:

We met shortly after he started with the county as a public defender. Over a three-year period I watched him sink into disillusionment. Each time we spoke he related a horror story worse than before.

Listening to Joel recount the latest outrage during a chance meeting in the stacks of a local bookstore, it became obvious he was beginning to seriously doubt that justice existed; yet he was complacent, entertaining no alternatives, making no plans. Unable to resist, I asked what strategy he planned for getting out. He looked at me blankly. Joel simply did not think that way. When I prompted him a bit, attempting to discover his secret dream, he relayed all the reasons why it wasn't possible to think about it at this time. He still had his college loans to pay off. That would take another two years. And then, of course, there was a good retirement plan, and who could match the pay? He reminded me that he had briefly (part time for six months) been with a private law firm that hadn't worked out. So that possibility was exhausted.

"Certainly," I thought, "there must be a secret dream." I persisted. Joel claimed there was none. It was as if using his imagination was taboo unless the action pictured was immediately possible and very probable. That he might have to stay in his job for two more years until he paid off his loans meant it would be two years before imagining alternatives would be permitted. But how much of Joel's spirit will remain in two years? And what of his health, his idealism, and his concern for his clients? How much of that will be intact after the moratorium?

Sometimes people resist because of attachments. They are attached to what they have been doing. They literally cannot imagine themselves doing anything different and refuse to even try. Looking on time spent as an investment, they throw good time after bad. I have seen people on a meager path who never look down the other fork of the road, never wonder what might be around the bend, never even see another path because they are gazing steadily at their feet. If the path you are on now is heartless, then it behooves you to take a look around and see where else you could be.

HOW TO TRANSFER SKILLS

Many people dream of getting into something else. But many professionals, for example, seem to believe that change requires abandoning their speciality forever and joining the pool of unskilled labor. It's either stay here in the hustle-bustle of the big city or back to the farm. They seem blind to the possibility that many of their skills are transferable.

■ Ian's story:

Ian had a tenured faculty position in one of the world's outstanding medical-training facilities. His academic career had been successful by any standard. He had conducted significant research, written a respected text, and was popular among the interns as a lecturer. By his early forties he had won all the trophies on this path. All that remained was to shoot for the big time—the Nobel Prize. But frankly, he just didn't have the energy, and he secretly suspected that even if he won this most prestigious acknowledgement he wouldn't be any happier. Ian dreamed of "doing something else." Yet he never got more specific because as soon as his mind pursued the possibilities he once again saw himself the son of the immigrant struggling up from the bottom. Ian believed if he walked out of the medical center he would leave behind his skills and wisdom.

*No longer would he be respected and envied. A commoner
again, he'd be one of the unnoticed masses. Ian didn't see
that while microbiology was his speciality, his skills were
transferable to thousands of applications. When Ian as-
sessed his skills and began to consider the infinite ways they
could be applied, he no longer felt hopelessly trapped but
was overwhelmed with possibilities instead.*

Analyze your skills with the objective of seeing how they can be
transferred; more often than not you'll find that retraining is not
necessary.

■ **Consider Gil's example:**

*Gil had been an engineer for over fifteen years. He loved
his work but he had difficulty working with the other
engineers. "As far as I'm concerned the people-thing is most
important. The work was fine but I had a group of people
involved in their own games. They couldn't or wouldn't
communicate. It was hell. I was constantly coming up
against a brick wall. Finally, it got to the point where I
couldn't take it anymore. I was burned out. I quit, dropped
out of life, and became a hermit for eight months. Eventually I realized no matter how far into the mountains I went
people would still find me, so I came out of the mountains."*

*Subsequently Gil became involved in political activity
and through a group of friends he ended up volunteering
his services at Legal Aid. "I discovered I could still use my
skills. As a scientist I solved problems. Once I got over being
attached to my identity as a scientist, I saw that I could
apply these same sophisticated skills to legal problems."
Then a crisis arose. The agency needed a legal assistant to
do research and prepare cases for the attorneys. The crisis
paid off for Gil. He stepped into the job and stayed there for
four years. He then set up a free-lance consulting practice
specializing in legal research and eventually developed a*

*large clientele of lawyers. He never went back to school,
never took a single course. Yet Gil now functions as an
independent and highly paid professional in a new field.*

What Gil's example illustrates is that most skills are transferable. Both scientists and lawyers must solve problems. Skills such as being able to write clearly, communicate effectively, deliver a persuasive presentation, and solve problems are transferable to a wide range of fields. Often the barrier is only in your mind. Gil advises: "When you make a change like this, the best thing to do is to pretend you've gone to a foreign country, a new culture. Recognize that all the rules have changed. What you used to do or used to be doesn't matter here. Assess what it is that you can do; then look around and find a need for it. " This is good advice.

Don't allow yourself to be limited by the idea that you must have training. Most employers are interested in whether or not you can perform the service they need and perform it well. How you acquired the skill is unimportant. What is important is what you can do. A college degree is only one way of acquiring a skill and only one way of certifying that you have it. The most effective way is to demonstrate your skill: Demonstration speaks louder than degrees.

ANALYZE YOUR TRANSFERABLE SKILLS

Probably most of the skills you use in your current job can be transferred to a variety of careers. But don't expect a prospective employer to do the translating for you. It is vitally important that you take the time before approaching an employer for a job to analyze your skills and how they might be transferred.

Start by making a list of your skills. Sometimes it is easier to start with the technical skills, like ability to repair a particular kind of equipment or run a particular machine. Then focus on your "soft" skills, like ability to make decisions, ability to analyze problems, ability to argue a point, and so forth. Make sure to include your people skills such as ability to draw people out, ability to make people feel comfortable, ability to get others' cooperation, and so forth. Don't forget basic skills like ability to read, to drive a car, and write a letter. Really push yourself to list the things that you can do. All too often people will list five to eight skills, mostly technical, and then insist that that is all that they can do. Nonsense! When you take the time to think about it you'll discover that you have dozens of useful skills. In fact, just this exercise of listing your skills is empowering when you stop to take a real look at all of the things that you can do.

Next comes the challenging step. One by one brainstorm how you might be able to employ each skill in the field under consideration. For example, a social worker might transfer "counseling" into "job interviewing" and "facilitating employee behavior change," a lawyer might translate "writing briefs" into "analyitical writing ability" or "ability to write concise reports." It's helpful to find someone versed in the field you are considering and ask that person to go over your skills and suggest ways that they can be transferred.

> It's a fact of life. For the rest of our careers, you and I will be working in the midst of an economic revolution. . . . The best strategy I know for directing the course of our careers these days is to focus on our skills. Skills are our best bridge to the new economy, as well as to the talents that lie within us. . . .
>
> *A career is a continuing education.* The bottomline benefit in most jobs is what we learn, not what we earn.
>
> William A. Charland, Jr.
> *Career Shifting: Starting Over in a Changing Economy*

RESEARCH

Eventually you'll want to get out of your imagination and into the world to see what's actually available and to check it out. When you've drawn up a pretty good blueprint of your ideal job, it's time to look for real possibilities.

The first step is to find the person who has the power to hire you for your ideal job. If the job doesn't exist, then you must find the person who can create it. Skeptical? Don't be. This is not as hard as it seems. Even if you don't know who this person is or where to look (which is probably the case), he or she can be tracked down rather rapidly. A study of how people network revealed that the average number of acquaintance links between you and any other person in the United States is 5.5. In other words, you'll need a referral chain of approximately five to six people to locate your man (or woman). Joe refers you to Sam, then Sam refers you to Cheryl, which would be a two-link referral chain. If you're restricting your search to your current locale, the number of links will probably be fewer than five. It's a small world, and you're closer to the person who can hire you for your ideal job than you realize.

It takes six or fewer referral links to find the person who can hire you for your ideal job.

The first referral is to be found among acquaintances. Think of everyone you know and identify those people who might know someone who knows the person you seek. If you ever wanted to be a detective or an investigative reporter, now's your chance. Call these friends, explain what you are doing, describe your ideal job, and ask if they know someone who might be able to help you. If they do—and someone will probably have some lead—get a name and ask if you can say they suggested you call. Very soon you will be meeting with a person who can hire you for your ideal job. Most people know someone and are happy to give you his or her name. People feel good when they can be helpful, especially when it's as easy as giving you a name. In addition to immediate acquaintances, you can make initial contacts at the "watering hole." Traditionally people hang out with others in their profession or from their company. Locate these enclaves. They can be bars or tennis courts, health spas or private clubs.

Association directories, available in most libraries, are another source of leads. Research these and then call up the person who is likely to be the decision-maker. Explain that you are not looking for a job but are researching the available alternatives to make a decision later on and request an appointment. More often than not you will get it. If not, ask for a referral. You will almost always get a referral because people don't like to say no. If someone must say no, it is easier if they can give you something. When you get a referral, call number two and say number one suggested you call. After a couple of calls you'll usually get an appointment.

There are several important things on the agenda for this meeting. First, check the match between what your contact says is available (or possible) and the blueprint for your ideal job. Be assertive and probe. Ask your host if you can go on a tour or speak with other employees. If possible, purchase a beverage in the cafeteria and linger. Notice the ambiance. How does it compare to what you want? Keep all your receptors open. Notice what it feels like to be in this place. Ask questions. Gather as much information as you can. If it looks like a potentially good fit, then move to your second objective: Uncover the "hook." How can you hook this guy or gal? What need does he or she have that you fulfill? What service can you offer? Look for problems you can solve. People are hired to solve a problem. It doesn't have to be huge problem like balancing the company budget. Make sure it's a problem for the decision-maker. Get into his or her shoes and look for manageable problems you can solve. Again, before leaving the interview make sure to get at least one referral. Send a thank-you note. (You might consider sending the secretary who helped you get the interview a thank-you note, too. This could be helpful in the future.) Through this process of interviewing and asking for a referral you will rapidly zero in on the very job you are seeking.

It's not at all uncommon during field research to receive a job offer. But it is not advisable, however, to accept the offer immediately. Don't be foolish and rush through the exploratory stage. Resist grabbing the first offer. Better to indicate that you will seriously consider the offer when you get to the point of making a decision. In the process your attractiveness is likely to go up. The allure of hard-to-get is not restricted to lovers, you know.

DECIDE

Making a decision is always a big bug-a-boo. Implicit in having to choose one alternative over the other is the threat of losing. The basic operating system is nondiscriminating when it comes to threats. As soon as the appraisal "threat" is entered, the fight-flight or stress response is triggered. You go on alert. Often people handle decision stress by procrastinating, pushing the decision off onto somebody else, and other methods of avoidance. You should expect a tendency to avoid. It's natural but not conducive to making a good decision. Good decisions require tolerating a certain degree of stress: thinking about potential losses, being uncertain, and possibly confused. You must be able to go through the stress and come out the other side rather than avoiding it by making a snap decision, or just complacently accepting what's given to you. Using the relaxation techniques discussed in Chapter 6 will help you manage the stress your decision generates.

Considerations

The first step in weighing the alternatives is to identify all the considerations of which there are two types: actual changes and opinions. Changes include income adjustments, moving, differences in the work itself, new schedules, and so forth. Opinions are feelings about the changes. One error many make is to overlook how the changes might impact others. Neglecting to consider how your decision will influence important others—including your family, friends, colleagues—and their feelings about it, leaves you vulnerable to unforeseen losses and quick decision reversals. To avoid this, list all the ways your decision will mean changes for the other people touched by your decisions. Make sure you list all the pertinent considerations and spend considerable time thinking about each one.

Don't weigh the considerations intellectually; instead, use your mental stage once again. For each consideration, project yourself into the future and pretend the change is reality. For example, suppose one alternative requires moving to a different area. On your stage project yourself into that new place. See yourself living in this new community. Make it as real as possible. Include the weather, visualize your home or office, and doing the things you would be doing. Now, notice exactly how you respond to this. What do you feel and think? How do you feel about the weather? Do you suddenly realize that long winter months mean being homebound, a lot of snow shoveling, and difficult driving? How do you respond to this?

Get down off the stage and reflect on what you observed. Decide whether or not your response was positive or negative. Rate the strength of your reaction. Was shoveling snow mildly negative or extremely negative or did you enjoy the stinging feeling of the cold snow flakes on your cheeks? Go through this process for each item on the list. Don't try to remember your ratings. Write them down for later.

Balancing Alternatives

It's easiest to compare only two alternatives at once. The objective is to determine which alternative has the largest number of gains and the smallest number of losses. The easiest way to do this is to simply lay the alternatives side by side and take a look. Sometimes one alternative will completely outweigh the other, making the decision between the two easy; other times it will be much harder. You may have to recycle through the consideration stage a few times. When you finally select one as most advantageous, repeat the balancing process with all possible pairs among your alternatives.

STRESS INNOCULATION

Any alternative you choose will involve some losses, and they often come before the gains. For example, you may decide to leave the company in favor of becoming an independent consultant. Being a consultant may promise a number of positive gains, but they take time to actualize. The immediate consequence of leaving the company is a dramatic cut in income and a lot of apprehension. You have to be able to go through this period of loss to get to the gains. Of course, changes of any type, especially those that are negative, are stressful. You must adapt, develop a new routine. Sometimes it's only a minor disruption and adjustment; other times it may be more serious. In some cases the stress may be so extreme it will prompt you to make a quick reversal in your decision or to take some other foolish action. Of course, you want to prevent this.

Stress innoculation is helpful in handling inevitable losses. It works much like a vaccination. The doctor injects you with weakened germ cells, then your body responds to this physical threat by developing antibodies to ward off the hostile invaders. These antibodies are then on hand and ready for any future toxic invasion. Stress innoculation is similar. By exposing yourself briefly in your imagination to the stressful situation, you will be more able to cope with it when the actual situation occurs.

Innoculation can be done on your mental stage. Step onto your stage and project yourself into the future to a time when you would be experiencing the loss. *See* yourself in the negative situation. For example, if you had to move to a new community, see yourself feeling alone and isolated on a weekend evening without friends. Allow yourself to experience the negative emotions that accompany this lonely weekend evening. You will probably feel the fight-flight kicking in and your tension level increasing. This is okay. Just allow yourself to *experience* how it feels for a few minutes. The next step is important: After you have rehearsed the loss and experienced the increased stress, *see* yourself taking some action to handle the problem. Notice as you take the coping action that your tension level goes down. You might want to get on your stage to analyze exactly what this action could be and develop a possible plan for handling the situation. Try out each plan on your stage until you find the one that works. Once you have developed your "coping fantasy," innoculate yourself periodically by imagining yourself in the loss situation, allowing your plan to cope with what is happening, and notice your stress level reducing. By using this procedure you will experience a lesser degree of stress when you are in the real situation, and you will know what actions to take. You will be prepared. This will enable you to feel in command, which will further reduce your stress level. With this simple procedure you'll have increased your personal power and be able to perform more effectively than if you didn't use this anticipatory procedure.

MAKE A PLAN AND ACT

Write down everything standing between where you are now and reaching the goal you have decided on. For each item on the list determine whether or not it is under your control to change it. Examine each barrier and challenge the assessment that you cannot change it. For example, after working as a lunch cook for about a year James decided he wanted to go to chef school and become a professional. He lamented that the tuition alone was $7,000. He saw this as an impossible barrier. "How can I get that money? I barely make ends meet as it is. I can't save." His friend proved to be a good one and challenged James's limitation. "Look, James, you're trained as an electronics technician. I know you don't like the work but it pays—and good. If you really wanted to get that money all you'd have to do is to work for one year building semiconductors and you have $7,000 and more!" But James did not want to hear this: He equated difficulty with impossibility. Thinking in terms of the impossible leaves you helpless. Think in terms of the possible and don't worry about the probable.

Determine the minimum change necessary to achieve the goal you have settled on. Go back to the list you made of your skills. Take these skills and rearrange them in every combination you can conjure up to draw a map from where you are now to where you want to be. Be careful of the tendency to shave down the goal, to make it "more realistic." What you may not realize is that if you are determined and committed to what you want you have a good chance of getting it.

■ Consider a famous example:

Early in her career, Dr. Joyce Brothers was living on a student's income with her medical-resident husband and young child. She reports that at the time her husband was earning $50 a month and she earned nothing. Her passionate desire was to have enough money to buy a Cadillac. She decided she would work to get one. At the time the television quiz show "The $64,000 Question" was the rage. She and her husband analyzed each contestant on the show to *uncover the formula for being selected as a contestant. She then used this formula to make herself into an attractive candidate. She became an expert on boxing, which was incongruous with being a petite blond psychologist. She says, "I ate, drank, and slept boxing. I even borrowed a series of films on the great fights of the century and rented a projector so that I could run them at home." She had her doubts but persisted. Ultimately not only was she selected to be on the show, but won the big prize! A highly improbable way of getting a Cadillac!*

Brothers says this about the effort: "This was a watershed experience for me, the first time I had gone all out, giving up everything else in my life to get what I wanted. And it changed the whole direction of my life. I knew what it was to work and work hard, but I had never worked so intensely before, never had this kind of total commitment. I had pushed my energies and my brain and my emotions to the limit, to the point where it hurt—and it paid off."

Make a plan for reaching your goal, too. Use your imagination; don't limit yourself. Consider every way you can imagine to achieve what you want. Look at what skills you have and then make your plan. When you have made a plan and have determined your path it's time to go to work. Work as hard as you would for "the company." Many people will go all out for a job, yet when it comes to themselves and their own goals, they work half-heartedly. You owe it to yourself to give it your best shot. Chances are you'll hit the bull's eye. The hard part is not the reaching, but the deciding what the goal is. All that is required to get where you want to go is hard work and determination. Remember this: You could be working just as hard for something you don't want, and don't even like.

Of course, there will be a price you must pay. Any change requires giving up something. If you have done a good job balancing your alternatives you should know what the price is. Use the stress-innoculation procedure until you can see yourself paying the price without feeling anxious and uptight. Then pay the price and get it out of the way as soon as you can. The important thing is to get on your path and move toward your goal.

INTERVIEWS

If your decision includes a job change you will have to confront interviews. The people you met during your field research are the obvious place to start. Call those people who have the power to hire you for your ideal job (or one close to your ideal) and say you have reached a decision about what you want to do and request an interview. Chances are you will have to seek no further. But just because you've already met the person don't go in cold and try to "wing it." It is important that you prepare.

Any time you go to an interview make sure you meet with the decision-maker, the person who has the power to hire you. Otherwise it is a waste of time. Personnel departments typically cannot hire; their function is to screen out or reject. Avoid them. Get to the decision-maker. Your objective is to persuade this person that you want the job and to show that you can do it. This means you need to do some advanced research. You may have done this earlier when researching your path. If this is the case, great! The most important thing is to unroot the decision-maker's problem or need. Don't concern yourself with the larger company's need. Instead, look for a service you can provide the decision-maker. Look for a problem that needs solving; then demonstrate that you can do it. Don't worry about the limitations of whether or not a job exists. If it doesn't, the decision-maker can create it. In other words, if you have unrooted a genuine need you might be able to invent your own job. This is ideal because when no vacancy exists you have no competition. Whether there is an actual job existing already or you're proposing one, you need to demonstrate your skills to do it.

RESUMES

Most people were taught in high school to prepare a resume that lists work experience from the most recent backward in time. This form is convenient for the system, but it is neither the only nor the best form to use to present yourself. It highlights gaps in your work history and can obscure what you actually do have to offer. And it's dull. You don't stand out. Keep in mind that the purpose of the resume is to get you an interview. You don't need to have all the dates you ever worked and other specifics written down. If the decision-maker is interested, he or she can get that information later.

The rule of thumb with the resume and the interview is to demonstrate your skills. Whenever possible make the resume an example of what you can do.

■ **Consider how Ann did this:**

Ann grabbed the attention of the news service and won an immediate offer with her resume. She presented her work history as a news story and had it printed in the same typeface on long strips of the kind of paper used by the service. At first glance her resume looked like it had actually come over the "wire." She used language common in the newswire stories like "Take One, Take Two" preceding descriptions of her skills. "North Eastern Action" was followed by descriptions of jobs she held in stations in Northern New York and the descriptions themselves sounded like the newswire stories.

Ann's calling card was modeled on the FCC license required of all radio personnel on the air. She had worked in radio for over twenty years. The card was a miniature of the license down to the color and typeface with one notable exception: Instead of "Federal Communications Commission" her card said "Famous Creative Communicator." Needless to say, when her resume came across the desk of the decision-maker at the news service it immediately caught his eye and overshadowed all the others. The resume was a sample of Ann's creative abilities and demonstrated in its language and form that she had a good understanding of what the newswire did.

In like manner, Jackson was a graphic artist who presented his resume as an example of his graphic-art work. He used spacing, bold lines, and graphic bullits to draw attention to information he wanted transmitted. Just looking at the resume showed the type of work Jackson could produce.

Not all job histories are conducive to these creative forms. Don't let that deter you. Throw down preconceptions and limitations and see what you can come up with. Even when you use a standard resume layout, the "functional" resume is probably the best. Here the information is divided into skills or functions you have performed rather than a time-line of jobs. Sort the skills into categories such as "supervision" or "coordination." Use these general functions as the main topical headings.

THE JOB INTERVIEW

There are many very good resources on interviews to maximize your chances of getting the job offer. It would be a good idea for you to study some of these. In general, follow this guiding principle: Think of some way to *demonstrate* what you can do for the person who has the power to hire you. You might bring examples of your work to the interview. Remember, show and tell. Many people do this as a matter of course. Artists, for example, always show a portfolio. Sidney kept a loose-leaf notebook with information about himself. He religiously added all his performance reviews. If something appeared in the com-

pany newspaper report on his projects, he added it. And once in a while his name appeared in the community paper. "If your name appears in the paper, people assume you must be good. Of course, this is not really the case, but it makes a good impression," said Sidney. Bringing a sample of what you have done to the interview is persuasive and makes an impact.

Prepare your presentation in advance. Convert tasks into skills. Show how the skills you acquired in the past can be used in this new context. Don't wait for the interviewer to make this connection. Always emphasize the service you have to offer. Words like "responsibility," "accomplishment," and "contribution" have more impact than "tasks" and "duties." Investigate the position and tailor your presentation so that you look like the perfect candidate.

Switching to a new line of work or a new career is a big change and not one to do glibly. Yet you should always hold it as a real possibility. Just considering it can refuel your spirit. At the very least it reminds you that you do have options. You are not trapped and helpless. In previous times, people often remained in one line of work until retirement. Things are different now. If you began work at age 25 and worked even to 65 (and we could question if one should "retire" at such a young age); that's 40 years—plenty of time for two full careers. Many people are pursuing this direction. Mid-life career changes are becoming common. It's a way to have a second start on life. Don't close your opinions and limit yourself. Look around and see what is possible.

> **We can find a way of life that is meaningful and purposeful, a way of life that *makes your heart sing,* a way of bliss.**
> **Hal Zina Bennett & Susan J. Sparrow**
> ***Follow Your Bliss***

CHAPTER 11

THINK POWERFULLY
THE SEVENTH PATH TO PERSONAL POWER

*Freedom is more often lost by false assumptions
than by power of one's enemies.*
—Harry Browne
*How I Found Freedom
in an Unfree World*

*A*ctualizing your potential generates personal power, and personal power, in turn, encourages self-actualization. Personal power sustains the spirit, making it immune to burnout. To most of us, power implies actively taking command in the situation. Certainly all avenues explored so far have advocated active command. Learning how to run the basic operating system in order to relax is an example of actively taking command. Identifying skill deficits and arranging encounters with the world to teach yourself the needed skills is a way to gaining personal power through activity. Modifying your job by managing tasks and time or getting out altogether and switching to something new are also active attacks on burnout. Active command is a proven avenue to personal power. Because it is the most familiar it is easy to conclude it is the only path to personal power. There are times when active command can be futile and even detrimental.

WHERE'S THE STRAWBERRY?

Consider the following story:

A DELICIOUS STRAWBERRY

A man traveling through a remote area encountered a hungry tiger. The tiger chased him to a precipice where the man climbed down a vine hanging down the side of the cliff. Halfway down he noticed that below him were two more hungry tigers, licking their chops in anticipation. Then the man looked up to see two mice chewing at the vine upon which his destiny hung. Turning his attention to the cliff beside him the man saw a strawberry plant with one luscious, perfectly ripe strawberry hanging out of a crag. He picked the berry, popped it into his mouth, and said, "Ah, delicious!"

Inspired by Paul Reps
Zen Flesh, Zen Bones

The man seems a helpless victim of doom, about to become lunch to the hungry tigers. Yet, he enjoys the moment and in so doing increases his personal power. He completely actualizes himself in the situation, but not through an active mode. Rather he surrenders to the moment and accepts what is. This path to personal power is foreign and often frightening to the Western man or woman. The man's fate is certain. Soon the tigers will eat him. A terrifying thought to say the least. One that would certainly prompt fight or flight. But there is no escape, and fighting will only hasten his demise. So he enjoys the strawberry, instead. What he pays attention to and how he thinks about it is the secret to the man's ability to function in this dreadful situation.

THE POWER OF THOUGHTS

We think almost continuously when we're awake and most of the time when we sleep. The way in which we think exerts a tremendous influence on how we feel and act. Try the following exercise.

THE QUIET-MIND EXPERIMENT

Take a deep breath. Stop all thoughts. Simply allow your mind to be quiet. Do this for two minutes.

What happened when you tried the experiment? If you're like most people, thoughts clamored into your mind from nowhere. Few people are able to quiet the mind for more than a couple of seconds. The important point is that there are thoughts in your mind at all times, even when asleep. Sometimes you're aware of them but more often you're not. For most people, thinking occurs in words and images. The mystics call it "the chatter." What you think about and how you think about it has a tremendous impact on how you feel about yourself, about your work, and how you act. The following exercise will illustrate this.

BUMMER EXPERIMENT NO. 1

Bring to mind a minor "bummer," a somewhat unpleasant situation or encounter from the past. Imagine being in the situation and relive it. Make it as vivid as possible. Continue to think about the bummer for about sixty seconds. Notice what you experience.

Before reading on, take a couple of deep breaths and relax. Put the bummer aside and turn your attention to your pleasant fantasy. Enjoy the warm pleasant feeling of relaxation. Remember, this is an exercise where you are experimenting with different thoughts and studying their effects upon you physically and emotionally.

Think about what you experienced when reliving the bummer. How did you feel? Most people who try this experiment experience changes like quickening breath, increase in heart rate, tightness in the stomach, and other signs of activation. In other words, thinking about the bummer triggered the stress response.

If you think back to the actual situation, you will probably notice that the sensations you experienced when thinking about the bummer are similar to those experienced in the real situation. This is what most people report, and it's important because it illustrates our paradoxical nature. On the one hand, the mind is more complex than the most sophisticated computer ever developed. At the same time, the body is easily deceived. We respond to thoughts in the mind as if what we are thinking about is *actually happening*. That is, the body responds to thinking about the bummer in the same way as when actually experiencing it. You probably noticed the response in a mere thirty to sixty seconds.

FOCUSING

The man in the story can trick his body into being calm if he doesn't think about the tigers who are certain to eat him. By focusing his thoughts solely on the strawberry and how delicious it tastes, he remains calm and experiences pleasure. Herein lies a key to personal power, especially if you feel trapped in impossible or unpleasant situations. You do not have to be a victim of the situation. By managing your thoughts and directing your attention, you can control how you feel and how you respond. And you can increase the quality of your moments, to live your life more fully.

WORDS

It's through the constant chatter of words that you carry frustrations from work home with you. Consider the following story.

TWO MONKS

Two monks were meditating as they walked along a muddy road. They came across a beautiful young woman trying to cross the road without getting her shoes muddy. Without saying a word, the first monk picked up the woman, carried her across the road and set her down.

The monks resumed walking without talking. When they reached their destination the second monk said, "Why did you pick up that woman this morning? You know women are dangerous." The first monk replied, "I left her on the side of the road. Are you still carrying her?"

Inspired by Paul Reps
Zen Flesh, Zen Bones

Words not only provide a vehicle for communicating information, but they also trigger emotional and physiological responses, both positive and negative. This is the secret behind the effectiveness of the "pleasant fantasy" in relaxing you. The same principle applies here. When you simply think about the bummer, each word (or image) in that thought triggers the feelings you experienced in the original situation. When you worry, anxious words in your mind keep you in a state of stress. Most people have very poor thought habits and indulge in negative, helpless thinking that keeps them in a state of constant turmoil and stress.

The ease with which words can trigger the stress response seems like a flaw in the human system. Take a closer look and you'll see this is a survival system. Survival is every organism's one priority. Without realizing it we are all continually appraising information gathered through our senses. This appraisal involves a basic yes/no question: "Is there a threat?"

Have you ever had this experience? You are sitting by a fire, feeling good, and reading a book. Suddenly you notice something out of the corner of your eye and instantly fly out of the chair. In mid-flight you realize that it is not the large hairy spider descending from the ceiling on a web, but merely the movement of the curtain behind you. Virtually everyone has had this kind of experience. What it demonstrates is that even when you are safe and secure in your home and relaxed, there is a part of you that is alert and on guard looking for threats. If a threat is detected you can mobilize and flee faster than your conscious mind can think.

The workings of this guardian mechanism are subtle, fast, and complicated. All kinds of things, including words, can come to indicate a threat. In fact, negative thinking and worrying can register as threats and result in chronic stress.

USING HELPFUL THOUGHTS

Most of us pay some lip service to the philosophy of positive thinking. Thinking "every day and every way, I'm getting better, better, and better" is a good thing to do, but sometimes such global statements are not very convincing when caught in the throes of negativity.

If you study them you'll discover that most worrying and negative thinking makes you feel helpless. This is why I call it "helpless thinking." If you engage in a lot of helpless thinking you will soon believe what you are saying to yourself and will become particularly susceptible to burnout. In fact, it is a vicious cycle because as people fall victim to burnout they tend to engage in more and more helpless thinking, which accellerates the process. When you keep telling yourself that you are helpless it makes it very difficult to turn

around the situation and beat job burnout. Consequently, it is vitally important to tune into your thinking and take corrective action if you hear yourself thinking in helpless ways.

What you need to do is to substitute a helpful thought for the helpless one. For example, berating yourself for thinking "Oh, I blew it!" is guaranteed to result in stress. In contrast, you will experience a greater sense of control—personal power—if you think, "I made a mistake, but I can learn from my mistakes." Both thoughts are "accurate" descriptions, but the first one is a helpless thought that generates feelings of helplessness while the second way of thinking is powerful because it focuses on what you can do.

If a project you're working on bombs miserably, thinking "I've failed" is helpless because it emphasizes your failure, whereas thinking "It didn't work out" is more helpful because the failure is attributed to "it." While both thoughts may be equally valid, the first tends to register as "threat" and trigger guilt and anxiety, whereas the second will prompt you to develop a plan of action. The first is a helpless thought; the second is a helpful thought.

IDENTIFYING HELPFUL THOUGHTS

Negative thinking is tenacious. It can take on a life of its own to become an entrenched habit that is difficult to dislodge. Fortunately, you can rework thinking habits. It's a good idea to start off with just one area of helpless thinking rather than to attempt to change all demoralizing thoughts simultaneously. For example, you may begin with helpless thoughts relating to George, someone you always have difficulty dealing with. Once you have some success changing thoughts related to George, you can take on another batch.

Write Down Your Helpless Thoughts

You need to know exactly what you're thinking. It's fairly simple. Each time you catch yourself thinking a negative thought, jot it down word for word. Do this for four or five days. When you record a helpless thought, write down the *exact* words.

If you really want to be scientific, which is a good idea, simultaneously count the number of helpless thoughts you think to use as a basis to evaluate your success in cutting down on helpless thoughts. After you try some of the techniques for increasing helpful thinking you can count your helpless thoughts again to determine empirically if you've improved. You can count helpless thoughts by making a hatch mark on a file card each time you think one. Another method is to put twenty or thirty pennies in one pocket and each time you think a helpless thought, move a penny to another pocket. Then, after a certain amount of time, count the pennies in the second pocket.

When you read over your thought list you'll probably notice some kinds of helpless thoughts reoccur over and over. These are the important ones. Perhaps you can identify what prompted them. If you can, jot the prompt down. It'll help you later.

Get a packet of ordinary 3 x 5 file cards. Transfer the helpless thoughts from your list onto the file cards, with one on each card. Leave the backs of the cards blank. When you feel relaxed and objective take these cards one by one and reinterpret each helpless thought into a helpful one and write it on the back of the file card. There are several examples in the following table. You should end up with a packet of "flash cards," with a helpless thought on one side and a helpful one on the other.

HELPLESS THOUGHTS	HELPFUL THOUGHTS
"If I say 'no,' he'll be disappointed."	"I can't meet everyone's expectations."
"I have so much to do I'll have to work all weekend."	"I can set priorities and work on important things first."
"It's an important session and I'm going to blow it."	"I can make a plan to control myself."
"I made a big mistake!"	"I can learn from my mistakes without dwelling on them."
"I was a fool to say anything."	"I spoke up, that's what's important."
"I'm a failure and going nowhere."	"I am reliable and do a good job."
"I've always been high-strung. I can't change."	"That's just a bad habit. I can learn new and better responses."
"I can't relax."	"If I breathe deeply I'll relax a little."
"I really blew it this time!"	"That's in the past. Next time I can . . ."
"My boss is a lousy supervisor! She never says what she really wants."	"This is my chance to practice expressing concerns without alienating."
"I'm sorry that. . . ."	"I regret that . . . ."

■ Consider Jackie, who realized that constantly saying, "I'm sorry" made her feel inadequate and lowered her self-esteem. By rewriting this habitual apology she felt better about herself and increased her personal power.

It started out as a smart aleck remark from a boss. He said, "I never apologize. It shows weakness!" So I took that and carefully watched myself each time I said "I'm sorry". And damn if it didn't work. I can say "Excuse me", "Pardon me", "Regretfully", or even "Oop's" and it takes away those feelings of my own inadequacy—a big, big job stress.

PROMPT HELPFUL THOUGHTS

Your helpful thought is unlikely to spontaneously occur; something must remind or prompt you to think the helpful thought. One way to do this is by following the "preferred activity" principle. Find an activity you do frequently that you feel either neutral or positive about. Examples include going to the photocopy machine, making telephone calls, and getting a cup of coffee. Call this a "preferred activity."

Use the urge to engage in the preferred activity as a signal to remind you to read a helpful thought. For example, you might place your file cards next to the phone. Each time you need to make a phone call, use this as a signal to remind you to read and think the helpful thought on the first card. Then put the card on the bottom of the stack and place the phone call. In other words, the preferred activity (in the example it's making a phone call) becomes a signal that prompts you to read the helpful thought. Then you make the call, which serves as a kind of reward for thinking the helpful thought. In this way helpful thoughts will be more available in your mind when you need them. The next step involves substituting a helpful thought for the helpless one in real situations.

THOUGHT STOPPING

As soon as you notice yourself worrying, stop the helpless thought and substitute a helpful one. To do this you must know how to stop the thought. Try this experiment

---

BUMMER EXPERIMENT NO. 2

Bring to mind a mildly unpleasant situation. Silently talk to yourself about the bummer. When you feel yourself getting worked up, yell "Stop!" silently to yourself. Notice what happens. Then switch your attention back to this book.

What happened right after you yelled "Stop!"? Did your thoughts about the bummer stop—if only for a moment? This demonstrates the essence of thought stopping. It's a technique that is simple to do but difficult to master. Usually after yelling "Stop!" the thought stops but only momentarily. Yelling "Stop!" is commanding yourself to quiet your mind. As you have seen, this is practically impossible (without years of training, anyway). The command empties the mind for a moment but it immediately fills back up with the most available thoughts—the worries.

Don't despair. The mind is paradoxical. While it has sophisticated computer-like capabilities, the mind can think only one thought at a time. This means if you quickly fill the void following "Stop!" with a helpful thought, you can crowd out the helpless one. This is the reason for writing down and practicing helpful thoughts. "Stop!" creates a break in worrying, but you don't have time to compose a helpful thought on the spot. Instead, have one ready and rehearsed because you'll have only a moment to make the substitution. Even then you'll probably discover that keeping your attention on the helpful thought will be difficult and you'll tend to drift back into helpless thinking.

THE MIND IS LIKE A WILD ELEPHANT

The mind is like a wild elephant that you must master. In mastering a wild elephant you begin by chaining it. But when first chained the elephant rears up on its hind legs, throws its trunk back, and roars. It flaps its ears, slaps its tail, and runs away.

If you are a good elephant trainer you don't scold the elephant, but simply grab the chain and pull it back. The elephant will try to run away again and again. When this happens you must pull it back. Again and again the elephant will rebel and again and again you must pull it back.

Eventually, the elephant will be tamed when it learns that you are its master. Then you will have great power because you can climb up on the elephant and ride it fast and far. When the elephant learns who is the master, it will no longer have to wear its chain.

Like any habit, persistent practice is required to dislodge the helpless thinking. In the beginning you will probably find that your mind will rebel, like a wild elephant, and run back to helpless thoughts. Instead of criticizing yourself, just yell "Stop!" (silently) and pull your mind back to the helpful thought. You may have to use thought stopping several times in a row, but with practice it will become easier and easier.

THOUGHT STOPPING

1. Notice the helpless thought.
2. Interrupt by silently yelling "Stop!"
3. Think a helpful thought

SELF-DIRECTING

Following directions is helpful in the first stages of learning anything complicated. When learning to ski, for example, it's helpful if your instructor observes and directs your attempts. She may call to you, "Now, shift your weight. Good, you've got it." You may have noticed that it helps to talk to yourself when you are learning to do something complicated. This is called self-directing.

Like learning tennis or skiing, learning to think in a new way is a complex skill, one made easier by following directions. Talk to yourself. Determine in advance what you are going to do and then direct yourself in a helpful way through the various performance steps. With thought stopping, for example, *tell yourself* to yell "Stop!" Immediately after yelling "Stop!" *tell yourself* to think the helpful thought. Guide yourself through the thought and acknowledge yourself each time. Acknowledge noticing the bummer thought and yelling "Stop!" Acknowledge thinking a helpful thought even if you do slip back into helpless thinking. Notice what you have done well and point it out in a positive manner, as any good instructor would.

PRACTICE ON YOUR MENTAL STAGE

Helpless thinking is as difficult to unroot as crabgrass; therefore, everything you do to fight it is worth the effort. Go back to the data you collected and look for those situations that prompt helpless thinking. Select an easy to moderately difficult situation. For example, suppose seeing George prompts you to think, "I can't say 'No,' he'll be furious!" In preparing for your next encounter with George, know exactly what helpful thought you'll substitute. In your imagination go to your mental stage, set the props for the encounter with George, and step on the stage. See and feel yourself interacting with him. Hear the helpless thought in your mind. Direct yourself to yell "Stop!" Tell yourself to substitute the helpful thought. Tell yourself to notice feeling calm and in command. Tell yourself to acknowledge yourself for carrying out your plan. Remember to talk yourself through each step. The more difficult the situation and the more entrenched the helpless thought, the more you should rehearse on your stage.

ILLUSIONS

An unending stream of images, sounds, and other data from the senses are synthesized, translated into words, and appraised for threat potential. Of course no two events are precisely alike, but some are similar enough that we use the same words to describe them. In this translation process, similarities weigh heavier than differences. Because of this, something is lost as raw data of the senses become words in your head. Rarely are these associations challenged. It's become an automatic process. We respond to what we tell ourselves is out there rather than to reality itself. We live in an illusion, mistaking the words and categories to which we have assigned the sensory data for the event itself. This goes on so rapidly that it is usually unnoticed. Accepting your thought about an event becomes synonymous with the event itself. You may think such things as "You made me angry!" or "He hurt me." But when you slow down the workings of your mind and closely observe what goes on you'll see that you respond to the appraisal of the event rather than the actual event itself. For example, "You said I was bad (event). That is a cruel and hurtful thing to do (appraisal). I'm hurt (response)." Stated another way, your mind gathers the data from its senses, converts it into a word prompt, appraises it by asking "Is there a threat? Yes or no?" It then responds to the appraisal of the event, not the actual event. We respond to our own thoughts about the situation rather than to the situation itself.

APPRAISALS CLOUD VISION

The appraisal is not random but is based on past experience. The appraisal is a statement of what we expect. The more we encounter certain data, the less we pay attention to it. We give it brief notice, recognizing similarity to previous events, and then make a prediction. This is the appraisal. Then we respond to the appraisal and not to the event.

■ LOOKING WITH EARs ■

E = Event
A = Appraisal
R = Response

We may completely overlook valid but contradictory information. As a result of paying less attention to sensory data and relying heavily on expectations from the past, appraisals are ultimately based on selective perception because valuable information is blocked out. We simply don't see it because of what we expect to see, even though the information is there to be gathered.

When we look at the world with EARs we don't see the world as it is; we see what we hear. This is an illusion. We can change what we "see" by changing our appraisal of the situation.

THE APPRAISAL PROCESS AND BURNOUT

As noted earlier our prime objective is survival, so our senses are always scanning the world and bringing in data that we subject to the appraisal: "Is there a threat?" Without realizing it, we constantly monitor the events in our world. Remember, threat appraisals activate the basic operating system and trigger the stress response.

The process does not stop here, however. There is a second appraisal: "Am I powerful? Do I have the power to stop the threat?" We respond based upon these two appraisals. The basic operating system flips into fight/flight in response to threat potential. Mood and behavior are a direct response to the appraisal of having personal power.

EXPECTATIONS

At the heart of the appraisal is an expectation, an outcome prediction based on past experience. Expectations are easy to recognize by the "shoulds" and "shouldn'ts." "He should be able to set a clear goal." "She should be more reasonable." "He shouldn't talk to me that way." "The company should be fair." Statements containing "should" or "shouldn't" are demands. They demand that the world conform to your expectations. Krishnamurti, a great Eastern philosopher, would say that you are attached to what you expect, clinging to a "should." He says that attachments lead to suffering. You suffer when you demand that the world conform to what you expect and refuse to accept what actually is.

When you engage in thinking based on expectations and "shoulds"—and we all do it—you are setting yourself up for suffering. Always implicit in an attachment is potential loss. If the expectation is not fulfilled—if your "shoulds" are not met—you suffer a loss. Even when things are going well, exactly as you desire, if you become attached and demand that it all continue, the threat of loss is present. Remember, a loss or a potential loss is always a threat. The stress response kicks in when faced with a threat. To repeat, when you are attached to something, believing things should be the way you want, a potential threat exists.

Letting Go of Attachments

"Should" thinking is the way most of us think. But it's not the only way to appraise events. You can change your EARs by altering the way in which you appraise events. The key is to change your appraisals by reinterpreting the data.

> # ■ CHANGE YOUR EARs ■
>
> Change expectations to preferences
> Change "shoulds" to "wants"

Any appraisal based upon an expectation or a "should" has the potential for causing a problem. You can get around this by substituting preferences for expectations. An unfulfilled preference is not a loss and causes no suffering. It is something you'd like but don't demand. You are unattached. If the preference is actualized you win and have more of what you want in your life. Unfulfilled expectations and "shoulds," on the other hand, tend to be seen as catastrophes and personal affronts. We respond to them as threats, which activates the basic operating system, triggering the stress response.

With practice we can change our appraisals of events. The first principle is to think in terms of preferences, instead of expectations. Suppose, for example, a friend is late. If we think, "She is late again and

TOP
BANANA

she *shouldn't* make me wait!" we will probably respond emotionally. Instead we could think, "She is late. I prefer that she be on time but she is not because she is a poor time manager." In the first instance, we "expect" the friend to be on time and appraised the lateness as a violation of social etiquette. Then we respond with hurt and anger to being treated improperly. In the second instance, we appraise the situation as not having a preference met, and not as an example of mistreatment. Here we respond more directly to the event, the friend's lateness. Without the emotions interfering, we can concentrate on the best course of action.

IS THAT SO?

A concerned brother demanded that his pregnant sister tell him the father's name. "It was the Old Man on the hill," she lied. Furious, the brother stomped up the hill to the Old Man's house. "Look what you've done to my sister you evil Old Man!" he yelled. "Is that so?" the Old Man replied.

Time went by. After the birth the brother stomped up the hill with the baby. "This baby is your doing. You must take it!" "Is that so?" the Old Man replied.

The Old Man fed and cared for the baby. As it grew he came to love the child who brought much joy into his lonely life. But the girl grew remorseful and confessed her lie to her brother.

Shamefaced he climbed the hill again. "Old Man," he said, "I am sorry that I wrongly accused you. Now I'm taking the baby back to its mother where it belongs." And the Old Man replied, "Is that so?"

Is That So?

Most of us would probably respond differently if we were wrongly accused. We'd probably say things like, "No, I am wrongly accused. I shouldn't be wrongly accused and it is terrible that I am!" Chances are we'd respond by getting very upset. When the Old Man says, "Is that so?" he is neither agreeing with the brother's rendition of events nor is he saying that he likes the situation. Asking "Is that so? Are those the facts?

Is that what she said?" doesn't tend to trigger an emotional response. Without the negative emotions, the Old Man suffers less and is more clearheaded. There is nothing to stop him from getting his lawyer to fight the situation.

The next time you are given bad news, try asking "Is that so?" instead of insisting "This is terrible!" or "He shouldn't do that to me!" It's a powerful response. Try it.

USE POTENT LANGUAGE

Another way to change appraisal is to use potent language, language that emphasizes personal power. Redefine the data coming into your senses in a way that makes you feel potent. This is tricky but with practice you can learn to do it.

Aleksandr I. Solzhenitsyn describes how seeing adversity as a teacher helped him survive years in one of the worst Russian prison camps:

HOW TO FACE DIFFICULTIES

"How to face difficulties?" he declared again. "In the realm of the unknown, difficulties must be viewed as a hidden treasure! Usually, the more difficult, the better. It's not as valuable if your difficulties stem from your own inner struggle. But when difficulties arise out of increasing objective resistance, that's marvelous!

"The most rewarding path of investigation is: 'the greatest external resistance in the presence of the least internal resistance.' Failures must be considered the cue for further application of effort and concentration of willpower. And if substantial efforts have already been made, the failures are all the more joyous. It means that our crowbar has struck the iron box containing the treasure. Overcoming increased difficulties is all the more valuable because in failure the growth of the person performing the task takes place in proportion to the difficulty encountered!"

Aleksandr I. Solzhenitsyn
The First Circle

The essential key is to look for ways in which you can control the situation, ways in which you have a choice or can assume responsibility. If things don't turn out as you desire, for example, instead of saying to yourself, "This is a disaster and I'm helpless," it's more helpful to say to yourself, "This is a challenge and I will find a way to overcome it." Rather than "I'm ruined," think, "This is a new beginning, rebirth." The more difficult the situation, the more crucial the appraisal. For example, prisoners of war who survived often viewed the brutal guards they had to endure as their teachers. When adversity is seen as an opportunity to learn you feel more in control. "This is a lesson, a test. I am not helpless. I can do something—I can develop my skills to deal with this difficulty."

If this tactic can help prisoners endure twenty-five years of hard labor and demeaning treatment, it can help you handle problems in your work situation. You'll be surprised at how effective it is to change your view of the problem. Think back to the man on the vine. He did not succumb to helpless thinking; rather, he focused on what he could control—enjoying the strawberry.

CHAPTER 12

DEVELOP
DETACHED CONCERN
THE EIGHTH PATH TO PERSONAL POWER

The way you spend your days
is the way you spend your life.
—Barbara Sher
Wishcraft
How to Get What You Really *Want*

Let's look back over where we've been before exploring the most powerful path to personal power. A sense of helplessness triggers the burnout cycle. Feeling emotionally and professionally impotent, motivation dwindles, which leads to poor performance, decreased self-confidence, increased conflicts, and chronic stress—all of which cycle back to further dampen motivation. Immobilization is the result. The burnout victim is physically able to work and enjoy doing so. It's not a matter of ability to perform. Interest is gone, enjoyment is empty, life is drudgery. The burnout victim is inoperable—a sophisticated computer unplugged, with the energy source turned off. Burnout is a malaise of the spirit.

The burnout cycle is painful and there seems to be no escape. The burnout victim anticipates a bleak future. One of the differences between people who prevent burnout and those who succumb to it is in the moment of despair. The survivor finds a third way. Burnout need not lead to failure or a destroyed, wasted life. It can be a challenging lesson. Those who accept the challenge find an opportunity to actualize a richer, fuller life.

Like the man on the vine, surrender. Stop demanding that the world be different from what it is. Instead, accept the situation and look inward. "What do I want? Who am I?" Within these questions lies a lifeline. Seeking teaches you how to engage your energy source. You will learn how to plug into an internal source of power and regain access to vast stores of ability and knowledge.

THE WAY OUT OF BURNOUT

The third way, the way out of burnout can be found by seeking inward. This is often thought of as mysticism, which many believe requires leaving your profession, experimenting with drugs, dressing in baggy white or orange clothing, going to an ashram to find a guru, living a spartan life, eating macrobiotic foods, walking around with a blissful expression, and speaking in an esoteric, cosmic vocabulary. Such external changes mean nothing at all. They do not bring about a mystical experience. Detached concern has little to do with these sorts of things; it is something else entirely.

BE LIKE A MIRROR

Detached concern is best introduced by metaphor. Imagine, for a moment, gazing into a mirror. When you are in front of it, the mirror reflects your image. This is that nature of mirrors—they reflect whatever passes before them. When you move aside, the mirror stops reflecting your image. When you step aside the mirror does not say, "No, it's not fair that you leave. I'll keep reflecting you." The mirror is detached and does not "cling" to images. The mirror is not concerned with the past or future but only with what is in front of it at the moment. This is not indifference or withdrawal; rather it is a total commitment to the activity at hand, reflecting an image.

MOTHER TERESA

An example of detached concern is provided by Nobel prize winner, Mother Teresa of Calcutta. To the inquiry, "It must be dreadful working with these sick children and then so many die anyway. How can you stand their dying?" Mother Teresa is reputed to have answered, "We love them while they're here." Like the mirror, she reflects a total commitment to what she is doing in the moment, namely nursing a sick child who may die in a matter of hours. She does not concern herself with worrying about the future or being attached to a child who may have died yesterday.

A MAN OF KNOWLEDGE SEES

This is how Don Juan explains detachment to Carlos, his apprentice:

You should know by now that a man of knowledge lives by acting, not by thinking about acting, nor by thinking about what he will think when he is finished acting. A man of knowledge chooses a path with a heart and follows it; and then he *sees* and knows. He knows that his life will be over altogether too soon; he knows that he, as well as everybody else, is not going anywhere; he knows, because he *sees*, that nothing is more important than anything else. . . . Thus a man of knowledge endeavors, and sweats, and puffs, and if one looks at him he is just like any ordinary man, except that the folly in his life is under control. Nothing being more important than anything else, a man of knowledge chooses any act, and acts it out as if it matters to him. His controlled folly makes him say that what he does matters and makes him act as if it did, and yet he knows that it doesn't; so when he fulfills his acts he retreats in peace, and whether his acts were good or bad, or worked or didn't, is in no way a part of his concern.

Carlos Castaneda
A Separate Reality: Further Conversations with Don Juan

WHAT IS DETACHED CONCERN?

Detached concern involves focusing all efforts into what you are doing at the moment, yet remaining unattached to the outcome. While positive outcomes are, of course, preferred, attention is given to the effort itself and not what follows. This does not reduce interest, however. On the contrary, this expression of personal power is noted by more commitment. Energy is not wasted on regretting, doubting, or grieving for the past or worrying about the next moment.

PRACTICE GOOD SPORTSMANSHIP

The idea of detached concern is difficult for most Westerners to grasp. One parallel in our world is sportsmanship. A good sport is expected to play to win (concerned), but not to insist upon winning (detached). Athletes who swear and kick the lockers when they lose are considered to be poor sports. We believe that it is more important to be a good sport than it is to win.

Good sportsmanship and detached concern teach us that how you shoot the arrow is more important than hitting the target. Whether you are a chief executive or a newly hired clerk, a social worker or a paper pusher, immerse yourself in the moment, focus your attention on what you are doing, and let go of the outcome, good or bad. Events will not always be to your liking and you will not always win. Don't demand that you win. Instead, concentrate on playing a good game. Let losing teach you how to shoot the arrow next time. Don't cling to losing, either. Like the

monk walking along the muddy road, leave negative situations on the side of the road.

In short, detached concern is a state of being actively involved, more responsible, and committed to an action of the moment—yet unattached to the outcome. Interestingly enough, you'll find that acceptance of what is and focusing on the now bring calmness, greater ability to concentrate, and increased possibilities for deriving nurturing sustenance from your encounters with the world.

BE YIELDING

Each day during the winter, snow fell on two trees in a field. The firm limbs of the big oak tree supported the snow until the branches, no longer able to bear the weight, broke and fell. Next to the oak tree, a pine tree also accumulated snow, but its limbs were supple, not rigid. They bent to the ground and let the snow slide off, then returned to their original position. The pine tree survived the winter, the oak did not. Like water flowing downstream, flow around the rocks in life. Be flexible. Don't be attached to a particular notion of the way things ought to be. Look for alternative and creative ways to reach your goals.

SHIFT YOUR VIEWPOINT

Philosopher Alan Watts once said, "Problems that remain persistently insolvable should always be suspected as questions asked in the wrong way." Do you trap yourself into damned-if-you-do, damned-if-you-don't situations by the way you look at things?

LAUGH A LOT

When you catch yourself taking things too seriously, laugh. Think of the "cosmic chuckle" and of the absurdity of it all. Satirize your distress. Imagine yourself in a Charlie Chaplin script. Pretend you are a stand-up comedian and that the disastrous situation is material for your next gig. As a discipline, practice finding humor in disaster. You'll save your sanity, your health, and your perspective.

WASH QUICKLY

[Sarge, my prison guard] pulled open the door . . . and said, "Whass!"

I stepped onto the wet, slimy floor. It was littered with rotting bandages and bits of garbage. . . . A huge black rat ambled out the drain hole at the base of the back wall.

"Whass!" He pointed to the rusty pipe. . . . "Whass queegly!" And the door slammed behind me.

Okay, Sarge. I'll whass queegly. . . . As I undressed, the big rat kept poking his nose back in, impatient that I was still there.

The water was cold but the shower felt good. . . . There was a sliver of soap on the algae-covered slab across from the shower. I lathered my body briskly. I realized it had been almost three months now since I had showered [before my capture].

I thought back . . . and realized I just hadn't been as tough as I thought I was. I hadn't done as well as I should [in resisting torture]. I was disappointed, devastated. . . . The cold water had become even more tolerable now, and I let it run over my neck and shoulders as I held the pipe with both hands, head lowered in pensive dejection.

Finally I raised my head. And there at eye level on the wall in front of me, scratched indelibly by some other American who'd been there before me, were the words "Smile, you're on *Candid Camera!*"

I couldn't not smile. . . . I laughed out loud, enjoying not only the pure humor and incongruity of the situation, but also appreciating the beautiful guy who had mustered the moxie to rise above his own dejection and frustration and pain and guilt to inscribe a line of encouragement to those who would come after him. He couldn't have known how many scared and broken GIs would . . . see his impudent reminder that they weren't alone, and pull themselves together to face whatever life's candid camera might have in store.

Capt. Gerald Coffee
Beyond Survival

EARS ARE THE BARRIER

The constant chatter in your mind stands in the way of detached concern. Words, symbols, and images, through years of associations, are powerful in triggering emotional reactions. Impressions come in through the senses and are translated instantaneously, usually outside of your awareness, into abstract symbols or words. This happens so fast and so continuously that most people mistake the abstractions for the world. The result is that you live most of your life in an illusion, buffered from reality by appraisals of the data coming in through your senses. Whenever this mechanism is in operation, which is most of the time, you operate on something akin to the seven-second delay. The appraisal process, no matter how rapidly it occurs, puts a space between you and the experience. In other words, you usually live in the past or the future, not in the moment itself. Your life is consumed by trivial monologues that keep you in a state of constant unrest. Ceaseless worrying about office politics and impossible aspects of your job, for example, consumes the vital moments of your life. Through this internal chatter, you carry these stressors with you everywhere you go. Remember the story about the monk who carried the woman across the muddy road and how the second monk upset himself by worrying about it all day. As these psychological toxins grow you become cut off from experiences themselves, unable to derive pleasure or substance from your daily routine because you don't connect with the real world at all.

Detached concern requires eliminating the appraisal process altogether. As you saw in the quiet-mind experiment in the last chapter, it is exceedingly difficult to turn off self-talk, but don't despair; with practice and determination you can do so.

The key to turning off internal monologue lies in the paradox of acceptance. By observing and accepting your thoughts you can quiet the chatter. Self-observation is most important. By looking you eventually come to know yourself. Look. Accept. Don't attempt to change. See who you are. This leads to self-mastery, the eternal source of personal power.

THE APPRAISAL MODE LADDER

There are, many parts of yourself to look at and many ways of looking. The appraisal mode ladder provides a lens for looking at how you interpret sensory data. The most primitive appraisal occurs in the associative mode.

Associative Mode

When you think the word "black," what is the first association that comes to mind? Most people say "white." What do you associate with "boy"? "Girl" is probably the first association. This is essentially what occurs during associative appraisal. Something simply comes to you, just pops into your mind. Associations can be so fast that you're not aware of them at all. There's no chance of self-control until you know your associations. Try the following simple "looking exercise" for seeing learned associations.

THE MULTIPETALED FLOWER

1. Relax yourself with the method you prefer.
2. Imagine the center of a flower without petals.
3. Place a word that represents the object of your study in the center of the flower.
4. Focus on the word and notice what thoughts come to you.
5. Note the association, whether you understand it or not. Make the association into a petal and tack it to the flower.
6. Return your attention to the word in the center of the flower and repeat the process for several minutes.

Don't struggle to find an association. Assume a passive stance and wait until something comes into your mind. Long-forgotten programmed associations will begin to surface. Simply observe each association and, like Pin the Tail on the Donkey, tack the petals of association onto the flower. Always bring your attention back to the word in the center of the flower. Don't be seduced into tangents by tantalizing associations.

Even if you do this exercise for only two or three minutes, you will probably find it illuminating. Why not try it now? Just so you have a better feel for what we're talking about here. A good word to start with is "work." Relax yourself and imagine the word "work" in the center of the flower. Notice what comes to you. Try this for about two minutes. What were your petals? Was there anything you didn't expect? That puzzled you? Don't judge yourself by these associations or try to change them. Just look at them. You now know a little more about yourself and your basic programming. Many find it helpful to jot down the associations discovered in a personal journal.

This exercise is helpful in exploring barriers. For example, you could place a word representing a troublesome decision, or the name of a person you have difficulty communicating with, in the center of the flower. Associations that come provide valuable insights and needed information for determining a course of action.

Fixed-View Mode

Much as the name implies, fixed-view appraisal yields a single interpretation of a particular situation or configuration of events. When operating in this mode, the possibility of another interpretation is never considered. Without any contrast whatsoever you believe your appraisal to be completely synonymous with reality. A dangerous assumption! Fixed-viewers intellectually buy the concept of EARs (that we respond to appraisals of events and not the events themselves), but see rewriting the appraisals as lying or a distortion. They assume there is but one "correct" interpretation that cannot be improved upon.

Fixed-mode thinking can be problematic. People who think this way believe that the way they see the world is the one and only way; anyone who doesn't share their view is clearly wrong. Not only does this create the potential for conflicts and breaks in communication, but the person is buffered from the real world and doesn't see the buffer. With each fixed-view appraisal, you forfeit a little personal power. When you believe your view is the only real one, you overlook the appraisal and thereby lose a way to alter your responses. You have given over power to the appraisal and to the knee-jerk reaction upon which the appraisal is based. When your view is one of helplessness and frustration, feeling boxed in and caught in a double bind or an unfulfilling world, you are headed for burnout. This is a stumbling point for many burnout victims. By clinging to powerless appraisals they aid and abet their own burnout. Here is a story about fixed-view thinking:

> **A CUP OF TEA**
>
> A professor visited a Zen master who invited him to tea. The master poured the tea into the professor's cup. When the cup was full he continued pouring the tea until it overflowed onto the table.
>
> Shocked, the professor exclaimed, "It's overflowing. It's full— no more will go in!"
>
> "Like this cup," the master said, "you are full of your own opinions. How can I show you Zen unless you first empty your cup?"
>
> Inspired by Paul Reps
> *Zen Flesh, Zen Bones*

Your ability to learn and to adapt is a source of personal power. Fixed-view appraisals make learning difficult if not impossible. Assuming you already know what is going on and what it means you do not look. Quality of learning is directly proportionate to the quality of feedback you receive from experience. By not looking at the incoming data, you are cut off from the feedback needed to learn. Consequently you continue clinging to a fixed-view even if it is no longer applicable. The fixed-view becomes a self-imposed trap.

Multiview Mode

Making the transition from the fixed-view to the multiview is rarely easy. You must believe there are many equally viable ways of viewing any particular event. The fixed-view is attractive because it gives the sense that everything fits into place very neatly. All challenges and contradictions have been carefully screened out or categorized. There is no contrast, no contradiction, nothing to remind you that this view of things is but one of many possibilities. You've got to break the habitual

mind-sets that blind and prevent you from seeing the world. The multiview mode brings power because it offers a choice. When you have a choice you're not helpless.

A handy tool for breaking mind-set is the paradox. Ambiguity and contradiction befuddle fixed thinking. Look at the sketch. What was the first thing you saw? You probably saw a rabbit. As you continue studying this sketch you'll see an ambiguity and then a duck emerging. Notice how your attentiveness and curiosity increased as you looked at the picture. Perhaps there's even a third entity in the sketch. Philosophers have appreciated the transcendental qualities of the paradox for centuries.

Stories with a paradoxical twist are used to aid students of Zen and Sufism to see in a different way. And in fact, we in the West have also had a tradition of learning from stories. Think of the fairy tales you grew up with and the parables Jesus told. Try one for yourself. Consider the following Zen story.

THE SOUND OF ONE HAND

The student listened intently as the master clapped his hands and said, "This is the sound of two hands when clapped together. What is the sound of one hand clapping?

The student went to his room to consider the puzzle. During his contemplation he heard someone playing a flute. "Ah, I have it!" he thought. But when he played a flute for the master, he said, "No, no, that is the sound of a flute being played." As the student contemplated the question again, he heard some water dripping. "I have it now," he thought, and went to show the master. "That is the sound of dripping water, not the sound of one hand," said the master.

Again the student contemplated. He heard the sighing of the wind, but the master rejected that sound. Then he heard the cry of a bird, but the master rejected that sound as well. For almost a year he pondered what the sound might be. When the student at last let go he heard the soundless sound of one hand clapping.

Inspired by Paul Reps
Zen Flesh, Zen Bones

It is contradictory to ask someone to demonstrate the sound of one hand clapping. Within the normal frame of reference one hand can't clap. So what can that sound be? In pondering such a paradox, you can break out of a fixed-view. Solving the riddle requires stepping outside your mind-set and looking at the question in a different way. The more you're able to do this, the more personal power you have. It enables you to be the master of your appraisals rather than a slave to them. Try this Sufi story.

A YOUNG MAN'S SEARCH

A young man was searching for knowledge which he thought he could find through experience. He wanted to know what was beyond the ordinary life. He went into the world, experienced many things, and went many places.

One day he arrived at a cave of an ancient sage who sat with a crystal in front of him. The young man was intrigued, as he gazed into the crystal. He was amazed by what he saw. There were things he'd never even heard of or even imagined possible. The young man asked the master, "I do not want to be a spectator. I must experience these wonders myself."

"Step inside." the sage said as he invited the young man to step into the crystal. Filled with wonder, the young man found he could, indeed, walk into any of the scenes he had seen in the crystal

After a short while the young man stepped out of the crystal again. The sage handed him a hammer and the young man smashed the crystal and walked away without saying a word.

Inspired by Idries Shah
The Magic Monastery

The story entices and tickles the mind, encouraging you to try on one interpretation after another. Within the paradox lies a key for surviving the organization and preventing job burnout. After an intensive study of the distribution of burnout symptoms within the organization, Abraham Zelnick and his group of Harvard Graduate Business School scientists drew this conclusion: "Bureaucratic practices set limits to the assertion of power by individuals in the organization, but the possession of power in organizations reduces the harmful consequences of bureaucracy to the individual. Therefore survival in bureaucracies falls to those individuals who know how to negotiate a double-bind situation, while advancement in bureaucracies falls to those individuals who can *make an opportunity out of a paradox.*" (Italics mine.)

The man dangling on the vine above the hungry tigers was in a damned-if-you-do, damned-if-you-don't situation. By focusing his attention on the strawberry and altering his appraisal of the sit uation, he was able to negotiate the double bind and regain his power. Exercising your mind with stories such as these develops the ability to make opportunities out of paradoxes. At first it is simply a mental exercise. But the stories act as a catalyst. As your skill increases you'll be able to transfer what you've learned to the frustrating ambiguities and contradictions at work. You'll be able to make multiview appraisals, rather than being stuck in the fixed-view mode that the organization promotes. But these skills and abilities do not come instantaneously. They require much practice and contemplation.

Look for the Third Way

Most of us tend to think in dichotomies. The moment is pleasurable or painful. When it's painful we attempt to fight it or flee from it. Too often these two options are of little help. By developing your ability to make multiviewed appraisals you can find a third way: not fighting, not fleeing, but the way of acceptance, surrender. Surrender is not typically equated with mastery or power, yet surrender can be a powerful response. Consider the sailboat. The boat skims along the top of the water not by fighting but by surrendering and going with the wind. A third-way appraisal helps in any difficult, unpleasant situation. Consider the frustration to be your teacher. If your boss, for example, is vague and ambiguous when telling you what to do, accept this person as he is. He is your teacher and this is an opportunity to learn to work in a vague and ambiguous situation. When you pass this lesson your boss will no longer be a problem for you, nor will vagueness and ambiguity.

Detached Concern

Detached concern is a mode of nonappraisal. The thinking mind is silent. Without your meddling thoughts you respond directly to your senses. There are no criticisms; no congratulations, no judgment, no warning, no thinking at all. There is awareness only. Without thoughts to continually drag you into the past or the future, you can be truly in the moment.

Tim Gallwey, the Inner Game specialist, refers to this state as being "out of your mind." This does not mean out of control, however. In fact, when operating in this mode your abilities are synchronized and fin-tuned, and you function at your best.

> #### SKIING OUT OF YOUR MIND
> . . . your busy, chattering mind stops altogether and you enter into a world that is pure experience. You are calm, quiet, im-mersed in your activity. There is no separation between action and awareness, thinking and doing. You are in total harmony with yourself and your surroundings, and all else—time, space, past, and future—pales before the present moment. . . . "The usual mental struggle—trying to do everything right, worrying about how we look or about falling and failing—is forgotten. Enjoyment is so intense that we don't even think of making a mistake—and we don't. The thinking mind is in a state of rest; awareness is at a peak. For a time, self-imposed limitations are forgotten; we are skiing unconsciously."
>
> Tim Gallwey
> *Inner Skiing*

Performing while "out of your mind" is what Gallwey calls the "breakthrough mode" because when you get out of your mind you make physical, creative, and spiritual breakthroughs. Without the diversion of your internal conversations and inquisitions you can tune in completely. There is no barrier between you and the world. Whether you are skiing, delivering a speech, working at a drafting table, or raking the lawn, when you're "out of your mind" you feel plugged in and energized. You and the task merge into one. You perform at your peak and the experience refuels you. You're not in a state of nothingness simply because the thoughts have ceased. Thinking has been replaced by awareness. You are alive and aware of being alive. What you are doing is less important than that you are doing.

Detached concern is a higher level of consciousness that can take a lifetime to evolve. Some call it the "master game" and believe it to be the only game in life worth playing. What you do is unimportant. It's how you go about doing it that counts. It doesn't matter if you are a housewife, a civil engineer, an artist, or a politician. What you do is only the canvas on which you paint that beautiful picture. Learning to achieve this sublime state of being, this continual state of being turned-on is the path with a heart. It feeds and nurtures you.

Directions can be stated in two deceptively simple words: Just look. Awareness is the higher self. Thinking interferes with awareness. By throwing up a smoke screen of speculations and interpretations, awareness is dimmed. Most of us feel frightened by the idea of not thinking. Awareness is infinitely superior to thinking, but letting go of thinking is scary. We believe that without the thinker—the self that continually talks to you—we will be helplessly out of control. But reviewing those moments of peak functioning—the breakthroughs—you'll notice that you were out of your mind and not thinking. In other words, with your thinker turned off you performed without analyzing. Who was in command when you were out of your mind? This is the question that muses the sages. The self that was in command is your higher self. Many people do not realize this self exists. The language of this self is awareness, not words. Try the following simple awareness exercise.

SIMPLE AWARENESS

1. Close your eyes
2. Notice your sensations. Feel the surface beneath you. Notice your clothes touching your skin. Notice the sounds around you. Don't dwell on their meaning, just notice how they sound. Notice these sensations and let them be.
3. Notice your feelings. What is your mood? Do nothing about these feelings. Simply be aware of them and let them be.
4. Notice your thoughts. What are you thinking about? Notice the tone. Don't change the thoughts, just be aware of them.
5. How does it feel to be you right now? Notice who is noticing.

The alert feeling this exercise induces is awareness. By simply observing, you tune in. Achieving higher consciousness cannot be done by force. The mind will rebel, you will have a mutiny. Most people have given their thinker far too much power. The only way to control the mind is to tune into it and tame it. Just look and discover who you are. Become aware of your basic operating system, of your movements, of your feelings, of your thoughts. Through observation you will eventually tame your selves and become your own master.

To reach higher consciousness you must understand that there is a you beyond your thinker. Consciousness evolves through a series of developmental steps. For ex-ample, the child in the womb is literally one with its mother. They separate at birth, but this separation is not immediately obvious to the child. One of the first steps in developing consciousness is the concept of "I" or ego. The child becomes aware that it is separate from

the mother and from the world. It is a separate being. There is self and not-self.

A story from my childhood illustrates how I was instrumental in one infant's first rite of passage. Like all babies he wrapped his tiny but amazingly strong fingers around anything within reach and inserted it into his mouth, biting as hard as he could. Having suffered a couple of painful bites, and using a six-year-old's logic, I thought it would be clever to make him experience his own bite. I placed the large toe of his tiny foot into his mouth. And like an automatic reflex he bit his toe as hard as he could. His wailing was evidence of the severity of the bite. I was never able to trick him into biting his toe again, however, because he had learned that his foot was self and my finger was not-self.

Virtually everyone makes it through the first step of separating one self from the world, but far fewer attain the awareness of the self beyond thinking, feeling, moving, and sensing.

HIGHER AND LOWER SELVES

You have four lower selves. There is the instinctual self—the basic operator who maintains heartbeat, respiration, and other vital functions. There is the moving self, who takes care of getting you where you want to go. There's the feeling self, who tells you what you want. And there's the thinking self, who analyzes, interprets, decides, and directs. When allowed to take command, the higher self orchestrates the actions of the four lower selves. There are many exercises you can use to stretch and strengthen your abilities and guide you in connecting with your higher self. Interestingly, they all have one central activity: looking.

> If we wish to control and manage our resistant nature, then a simple, excellent way to do so is to observe it objectively and without judgment when it shows up in our day-to-day choices. I stress the importance of non-judgmental observation, because the general rule regarding our inner workings is that anything we can detachedly observe, we can eventually control.
>
> Marsha Sinetar
> *Do What You Love*
> *The Money Will Follow*

WATCHING YOUR INSTINCTUAL SELF

By simply watching heartbeat, skin temperature, breathing, or muscle tension, you can gain control over these vital functions. In biofeedback, you notice particular sensations, like temperature in your hand, and associate that with the feedback sound. In the muscle-tensing exercise, for example, you observe tension and relaxation and compare these two sensations. In other words, mastery over tension is achieved by watching, not controlling or trying to control. Similarly, you can learn to slow the rhythm of your breathing by focusing your awareness on your breath. Exhale very slowly. Then inhale gently. Hold the breath momentarily and slowly breathe out again. Use a slow regular quiet effort. Don't strain. Imagine slowing your breathing rhythm down to the point where if a feather were held before your nose it wouldn't move. Simply be aware of your breathing.

WATCHING TENSION WHILE YOU ACT

This exercise is done while walking in a steady pace. Slowly count to ten while gradually tensing your body all over. Constrict the muscles in your calves and thighs, clench the hands and feet, and grit the teeth. At the count of ten you should be as tense as you can possibly be and still be able to move. Now while slowly releasing the tension count backward from ten to one. Let your body go limp. You should be at the count of one when your body is at its most relaxed point but still moving. Increase tension a notch or two until you feel just right. This is your optimal level for performance. You're not so loose that you can't function, but not so tight that movement is restricted.

WATCHING YOUR FEELING SELF

The feeling self is the most difficult to study because it overlaps and interacts with the other selves. The feeling self is the great motivator, and only with motivation will you have the power to achieve anything real. With emotional involvement words are transformed into deeds, theory into action. The "theater of selves" provides an ideal arena for watching emotions.

THE THEATER OF SELVES

While remaining completely relaxed project your self onto your mental stage and imagine reenacting an encounter or event. Make no changes; do not criticize or evaluate. Dispassionately watch the self acting. How does he or she feel? Just notice the emotion with a nonjudgmental, observant attitude. As you perfect this exercise, carry it into the theater of your daily life. If you must evaluate, limit it to simple ratings of the feeling. When observing anger, for example, let ten represent the most angry you can imagine feeling and let one represent the complete absence of anger. As you observe angry feelings, rate them from one to ten. Don't try to change the feeling; just become aware of it. Strive as far as possible to separate the sense of "I" from the physical sensations being studied.

When you become somewhat skilled in watching yourself "act" in the theatre of selves you'll make a curious discovery. By observing and at the same time not identifying with the sensations, they will change little by little without your directly trying to change them.

WATCHING YOUR THINKING SELF

Use the multipetaled flower exercise described earlier in this chapter to watch associations. When you become proficient at that exercise, move to the "Who am I?" exercise. This involves a series of structured questions and answers. Begin with the question "Who am I?" Note what answer comes and then challenge the answer. After each challenge ask another question.

WHO AM I?

Question: "Who am I?"

Answer: "I am John." Challenge: "No, John is a name I call myself."

Question: "Who is the I called John?"

Answer: "I am an engineer." Challenge: "No, engineering is the work I do."

Question: "Who is the I who works as an engineer?"

Answer: "I am tired." Challenge: "No, tiredness is a feeling I experience."

Question: "Who is the I who feels tired?"

"Who am I?" is a rigorous exercise. At times no answer may come. Notice and accept the silence. With practice you will eventually discover the I who is the "higher self." As a variation try the "Who am I?" exercise while observing yourself reenacting an encounter on your mental stage. After noticing how you feel, ask, "Who is the I who feels angry (sad, happy, alone, etc.)?"

Watch yourself during your daily routine. Stop and observe what you are doing, feeling, sensing, or thinking. In a detached, impartial, impersonal manner, ask, "Who is doing this? Who is feeling this? Who is sensing these things? Who is thinking these thoughts?" Wait and see what answers come to you. Through this process you will see your mechanical responses to external stimuli. One result of these practices is that your attitude toward people, things, and events will tend to gradually change.

Using Teaching Stories

Earlier in this chapter we experimented with using the paradoxical Zen stories to break through fixed-view thinking. Teaching stories can help you look at your thinking as well. The moral of the story is unimportant here. This is not a "religious" experience. What is important is looking at how your mind works and looking at what comes into your mind. These associations will reveal your programming. Follow the directions for the multipetaled flower but substitute a teaching story for the flower. There are lots of teaching stories available, so don't restrict yourself to Zen stories. Fairy tales are fun to use and evoke interesting associations. Psychologist Eric Berne, founder of Transactional Analysis, believed that your favorite fairy tale is a mirror of your life's "script." For example, if *The Ugly Duckling* is a favorite, you might enact it in your imagination, and notice what associations come into your mind. There are lots of teaching stories to choose from: Bible stories, Greek myths, and ethnic tales are a few.

Using Symbol Cards

We do not think in words alone. In fact, much of our thinking is in images or pictures. Drawing a map in your head when you get directions over the phone is an example of thinking in images. When you "know" what you think but you can't put it into words is another example. The reason it is difficult to put knowing into words is that these two types of thinking take place in different parts of the brain. Word thinking occurs in the left side of the brain and image thinking in the right side. Left-side thinking includes words, deductive logic, lower mathematics, and rote memory. Right-side thinking is more difficult to describe and to think about because describing involves words. What you experience when you listen to music is right-side thinking. Many of the experiments you have tried while reading this book involved right-side thinking. Other examples of right-side thinking include: looking at a painting, inductive logic, "ah-ha" experiences or "flashes" of insight.

Try an experiment. Call forth an image of a bird. What did you do to bring the image into your mind? Probably you cannot answer that question. Yet, you can bring the bird into your mind any time you choose. It is difficult to discuss how the mind works, but it is fascinating to watch it.

Like words, images are learned. Again, call forth a bird. What associations came to you? Perhaps the word "free" came into your mind. More likely, other images came to mind: maybe a tree, maybe clouds, maybe a nest. Some people "hear" an image like a bird singing. Each of these associated images is filled with vast amounts of information—all in images. Images often prompt emotional responses. Some images elicit pleasurable feelings. For example, we usually feel good when imaging a Christmas tree or a birthday present. Other images can trigger negative emotions such as fear, anxiety, or anger. These feelings then prompt us to act. Because this all occurs without the use of words it is often called "unconscious."

Like word-programs, we can look at our image-programs. Psychologist Carl Jung believed all people share certain image-programs. He called these the "collective unconscious." We also have our own unique image-programs. Jung painted pictures of these universal images, or symbols, as they are often called. By looking at the symbol and noticing what associations came to mind, he studied his own programming.

We can do the same thing by looking at symbol cards. Available in most large bookstores and some toy stores are tarot cards. These cards contain pictures of universal human dilemmas: "The Hanged Man" swinging in indecision or "The Sun" bringing a new beginning are examples. When you look at these pictures, associations come to mind. You can use the symbol cards to discover your associations and as a result you will know more about what controls you. In essence, it's a way of looking into your unconscious.

Many of you know that these symbol cards are sometimes used to "tell fortunes." What actually happens is that the fortune-teller encourages you to talk about the pictures. As you do you tell your own fortune. The process is very similar to what psychologists do with "projective tests"—the ink blots or the TAT pictures. The symbol cards are another tool for looking at how you think and what you think.

WATCHING YOUR ACTING SELF

By practicing "intentional" doing you can generalize detached concern into your daily life and capture the magic of the moment. Intentional doing is doing one activity with complete attention. The activity can be anything you choose.

> In walking, just walk; in sitting, just sit; and above all don't wobble.
>
> Saying of Yun-men

INTENTIONAL DOING

Determine what you are going to do and why. Set definite limits—how long, to what degree, to what quality. Clearly visualize the process before beginning. Picture the tools, material, the forces involved. Begin doing the activity you choose to practice with and just notice yourself doing it. If you become distracted, stop all activity. Return to the starting point, redefine the intention, and start over again. Strive to keep an inner silence and practice simple awareness of what you are doing so that you can receive impressions simply and directly, bypassing thoughts.

TIE YOUR SHOE LACES IMPECCABLY

One day Carlos and Don Juan were walking through a steep ravine. As Don Juan paused to tie his shoe, a huge boulder broke loose from the rock wall and came crashing down to the floor of the canyon, landing just about where the two would have been had they not paused. Carlos gasped, "Had we not stopped, the boulder would most certainly have crushed us to death!"

"Suppose," speculated Don Juan, "on some other day, in some other ravine, I stopped to tie my shoe lace just as another boulder broke loose precisely above us. That time had we continued walking we would have saved ourselves."

Perplexed, Carlos asked, "What can one do?"

"My only possible freedom is found in tying my shoe laces impeccably," replied Don Juan. In other words, the only solution to the dilemma of fate is to perform every act consciously, impeccably.

Carlos Castaneda
The Second Ring of Power

CONNECTING WITH YOUR HIGHER SELF

Simple awareness or "just looking" plugs you into your "higher self"! The body changes shape and size, and the mind changes outlook, but the I of consciousness persists from birth to death unchanged. To know oneself is to find that point of consciousness from which observations of these changing moods takes place. Thinking is a power that may bind you or set you free. But one result of just looking is that eventually you'll be able to get out of your personal self. Awareness makes all experience fresh. As you perfect these skills, you will know where you are going, what you are doing, and why you are doing it. The secret lies in remaining unattached to the results of your activities and measuring success and failure in terms of inner awareness rather than outward achievement.

BUILDING A MENTAL RETREAT

Unfortunately, all too often a moment of mental quiet is looked upon as a moment wasted. We persuade ourselves that we do not have a half hour to spend sitting quietly. Energy invested in seeking will come back to you tenfold. With your increasing power you will be able to calm yourself in difficult situations, focus attention into intense concentration, rally abilities to perform at your peak, and pull from within new, creative combinations of your knowledge and experience.

The mental retreat is a personal place constructed to your own specifications. It is your place, made for you, where you can regroup and refuel. The mental retreat provides an unending power source available any time, any place. In building the retreat, most important is that it works for you. Modify the guidelines presented here to meet your unique needs. The retreat is helpful because it is one that is easy to be in any time, any place. You do not have to be passive or go to a secluded place to use the retreat. You can be active. Project the retreat around you so that what you are doing is in the center of the retreat. As you are doing something—leading a board meeting, driving on the freeway, writing a report—look at what you are doing. Notice your lower selves: what you feel, what you think, how you move, what you sense. Remember to watch only and not to judge, criticize, or even compliment. The more you do this, the more benefits you will reap. By watching yourself while "doing" you can find contentment in any situation. Even in the worst conditions you'll find a path through the shadow of death. The more you use your mental retreat in this way, the more your ability to concentrate on what you are doing will increase. So, you can expect the quality of your work to improve. And finally, you will be living each moment fully. But these are not things you can whip out a credit card and buy. You must work for them. It is a life-long process.

Guidelines

When you wake up in the morning, your first responsibility is to confront your self. Yet, most people neglect doing this in favor of ruminating over the latest hassle. We tend to give activities and problems priority rather than tuning into the energy source, which can fuel activities and solve problems. Visiting your mental retreat is a helpful habit. Make it a normal part of your daily life. The best results are achieved by daily practice. Don't demand grandiose commitments of yourself. Start out small and develop a habit that you can expand on. Once you learn how to use it, you can enter your mental retreat any time, any place because you carry it with you.

When first visiting the retreat, it's easiest if you're comfortable. An easy body posture helps to put the mind at ease. It's best if you sit up rather than recline on your back. Choose a time when you will not be disturbed and when digestion is at rest. When learning to use the retreat use the same quiet spot or room every day if possible. Select a comfortable spot to sit. Develop a habit in small steps. You might begin with only ten minutes. Don't rush into it. When this feels natural, extend the time gradually to a half hour or more. Morning is a good time because it sets the tone for the day. Early evening is also a good time because it helps you to unwind from the day and provides a pleasant transition into evening. Just before sleeping is a good time, too, because it helps you relax and prepare for a restful sleep.

The first visits to the mental retreat are the hardest. You will be bombarded with intruding thoughts and discarded memories. Expect these. Totally irrelevant thoughts will drift into your head in the middle of an exercise. As soon as you become aware of the distraction, notice it, dismiss it, and begin at the point where you left off. It is difficult to concentrate for fifteen minutes or more. Persist. The side benefits of using your mental retreat include the development of intellectual discipline and the power of concentration that you can carry into all facets of your work.

Visiting your mental retreat will energize you, but it won't remove struggle from your life. Struggle is part of the dance of life. Struggle provides resistance against which you exercise your selves, both higher and lower. And as you develop your abilities, the struggles will only become more difficult because the magnitude of the struggle is proportionate to the extent of your abilities. Interspersed among the struggles is joy. Even in the dreariest of situations, there's always a crag in the cliff where a strawberry grows. You must look to see it. Let expectations and attachments go. Accept the joys of the moment. For even struggle is doing and when you're aware, there's always joy in doing. When you can kiss this joy you will have the key to preventing burnout.

> **KISS THE JOY AS IT FLIES**
>
> **He who takes to himself a joy**
> **Doth the winged life destroy,**
> **But he who kisses the joy as it flies**
> **Lives in eternity's sunrise.**
>
>   **William Blake**

CHAPTER 13

WHAT MANAGERS CAN DO TO PREVENT BURNOUT

*A*bsenteeism, on-the-job accidents, drug and alcohol use, conflict, substandard performance, and other signs of worker malaise are everywhere. A World Labor Report of the United Nation's International Labor Organization estimated that stress-related diseases such as ulcers, high blood pressure, and heart attacks cost the U.S. economy $200 billion a year in absenteeism, compensation claims, and medical expenses. The problem is not restricted to the United States. The report called job stress a "global phenomenon." For example, in a French survey, 64 percent of nurses and 61 percent of teachers complained of stressful working conditions. Stress claims by government employees in Australia increased 90 percent in three years in the early 1990s. The U.N. agency report claimed job stress is a worldwide plague that afflicts British miners and Swedish waitresses just as it burns out Japanese school teachers and American executives.

While everyone is not a manager in an official sense, we all manage other people. We manage our co-workers, partners, spouses, children, and friends. We can do this in a way that encourages cooperation, or in ways that undermine it. At the same time, our co-workers, partners, spouses, children, and friends are managing us. So we should all be concerned with interacting with others in such a way as to encourage enthusiasm and feelings of empowerment.

Traditional methods of leading and motivating people no longer seem to be working. Job burnout is a motivational problem that can occur in any situation in which people feel they cannot win and feel helpless to change it. The results of the U.N. study pointed to lack of control as a key factor in the high stress levels they observed. Skills lie dormant while interest in working wanes. Work becomes a chore.

COMMON BURNOUT SITUATIONS

The critical boss is the manager who constantly ignores good work and progress toward goals and concentrates solely on errors and areas that need improvement instead. In a short time employees feel that it's useless to attempt to please this boss and stop trying.

Feeling respected by others and having work acknowledged is a primary source of self-respect for most working people. When good work goes unrecognized, self-esteem diminishes and employees lose interest.

Not knowing how one fits into the organization can lead to a feeling that one's work is irrelevant. Recognition for work seen as meaningless has little motivational clout. Rather than feeling like a vital part of a team effort, the employee feels like a cog in an unsympathetic system.

Incompatible demands create a no-win situation. Line workers, for example, are often expected to produce both quality and quantity. Meeting such mutually exclusive demands is rarely possible because succeeding at one usually means failing at the other. Similarly, operations managers may see production goals as incompatible with complying with governmental equal opportunity regulations and environmental protection requirements, for example. Employees whose jobs place them on the boundary between departments can also face double-bind or damned-if-you-do, damned-if-you-don't situations. These situations exist because the priorities of different departments such as marketing and manufacturing rarely coincide.

Ambiguous goals make success difficult. Employees who misunderstand what is expected of them often direct their efforts toward the wrong goal or in the wrong way, resulting in failure and discouragement. Clearly such a situation, if not corrected, impairs motivation and will be reflected in a drop in productivity. When employees don't have enough information to set priorities and to make decisions they stand a small chance of accomplishing goals or of producing quality work.

No room for growth can create a feeling of being trapped. Monetary rewards and job security are necessary but rarely sufficient to sustain motivation. When employees feel there is no challenge in their work or that there is nothing to strive for and nowhere to go, they become bored and disgruntled.

Bureaucracy itself can place insurmountable barriers to accomplishing output goals with outdated rules and excessive paperwork. Absence of job impact eliminates a powerful motivator. When employees have little to say about the conditions or nature of their work they soon feel powerless. As a result the company loses their employees' commitment or enthusiasm.

Another problem is job fit. There is greater potential for stress when the fit between person and job is poor. The U.N. Labor report said, "When demands are being made which do not match a person's current abilities or needs or expectations, the poor fit causes them to come under greater stress." In the current unstable economy where downsizing has become a household word and countless people are being laid off, many people are in poorly fitting jobs. They feel that they are lucky to have a job, even if it doesn't fit them well.

FEW REWARDS

In the burnout situations described above when workers don't get an expected payoff or reward they feel powerless and ineffectual. Feeling like helpless victims, the work becomes extremely stressful. If the double-bind situation continues unresolved, the employees experience chronic stress. The resulting interpersonal irritations, alcohol or drug use, medical and home-life problems, and performance decline add to feelings of powerlessness and futility. Earlier chapters have described the vicious cycle and how, if left unchecked, it can damage ability to work.

Also discussed are specific steps individuals can take to protect their motivation and renew their enthusiasm for working.

LACK OF CONTROL

Most of us understand intuitively that there must be a reward or payoff for performing. If there is no reward workers will not continue to put out quality work. This is common sense as well as a scientifically verified fact.

Less understood is the importance of a feeling of control over work. To sustain performance workers must seek a cause and effect relationship between the "win" and their efforts. That is, the worker must feel that the win is a result of his or her actions and is not coincidental or something allotted to everyone. Employee benefits such as dental and health plans, for example, do not sustain motivation because all employees receive them regardless of their performance.

A substantial body of research indicates that a feeling of control acts as a buffer to the effects of stress. For example, a group of Harvard Graduate Business School researchers studied the job conditions of 2,000 high-status workers in three occupations: management, staff and operations. They found that while all three groups experienced equally high levels of stress, stress-related disorders and worker malaise were not shared equally.

The operations group had a preponderance of health problems, emotional distress, and job dissatisfaction. Digging deeper the researchers found that operations people reported feeling frustrated by vague goals, mutually exclusive objectives, and supervisors who were technically ignorant and couldn't be influenced.

While the management group also encountered high levels of conflict and ambiguity they reported fewer burnout symptoms. They reported less frustration, more satisfaction, and fewer illnesses.

The Harvard researchers concluded that the management group was less susceptible to stress and burnout because their decision-making power gave them a feeling that they could influence what happened to them. The U.N. Labor report came up with the same conclusion and pointed out that blue-collar workers tend to be paid less, work in harsher environments, and have less control over their jobs and lives than do white-collar workers. The U.N. Labor report also found that in country after county working women suffered more from stress than men did.

A feeling of potency—being able to do something, to make a decision, and to act—enables us to tolerate more frustration and irritation at work. Stress expert, Vittorio Martino, at the International Labor Organization headquarters, who prepared the U.N. Labor report, said employers can help by giving employees more control over their jobs. But organizations have been traditionally structured in such a way that some people have a greater sense of control than others working there. Those who feel they cannot grab their work and run with it are more susceptible to stress and worker malaise.

Management's decision-making powers provide a buffer but this does not mean that managers are immune to burnout. Within management some positions are more prone to burnout and distress than others. Middle management is one such position. Those below may feel the middle manager is betraying their concerns for company policy, while those above may look upon the middle manager as being not quite seasoned and unable to step back to grasp the big picture. Being a middle manager in a company that is restructuring or downsizing puts one at greater risk of burnout.

IS YOUR STAFF BURNING OUT?

Instructions: Using a scale from 1 to 10, with 1 being "not at all descriptive" and 10 being "very descriptive," rate how descriptive each of the following statements is of your staff.

_____ 1. Employee turnover is high.
_____ 2. People are just putting in time.
_____ 3. Drug and alcohol problems interfere with performance.
_____ 4. The absenteeism rate is high.
_____ 5. There is a lot of conflict.
_____ 6. Directives are not followed.
_____ 7. There is sabotague.

_____	8.	People cheat and steal.
_____	9.	Deadlines are not met.
_____	10.	There is a high rate of rework.
_____	11.	Back stabbing is commonplace.
_____	12.	Office politics interferes with performance.
_____	13.	Productivity is low.
_____	14.	People are confused about goals.
_____	15.	There is a sense of hopelessness.
_____	16.	There is little esprit de corps.
_____	17.	People are secretive.
_____	18.	People don't socialize much off the job.
_____	19.	Teamwork is poor.
_____	20.	Lay-offs are common.
_____	21.	There is a lot of complaining.
_____	22.	There is not much participation.
_____	23.	People are just out for themselves.
_____	24.	People have little input into management decisions.
_____	25.	Threats seem to be the best motivator.

SCORING:

25 - 75	**Comfort Level:** Your staff is exhibiting a few signs of burnout.
76 - 145	**Caution Level:** Your staff is exhibiting a moderate degree of burnout. Preventative action is advised.
146 - 200	**Chronic Level:** Your staff is exhibiting numerous signs of burnout. Ongoing corrective action is essential.
201 - 250	**Crisis Level:** Your staff is exhibiting full-blown burnout. Immediate crisis intervention is required to prevent organizational breakdown.

WHAT MANAGERS CAN DO

Empowered employees—employees who have a sense of control over their job tasks—are resistant to burnout. By empowered I mean a feeling of "I can do and I can succeed by doing." Employees who feel they can impact on their work and can "win" by doing a good job retain their enthusiasm and are more motivated. They are also an asset to the company. The challenge to management is to orchestrate the work of employees, to draw upon and develop employee talents to focus their energy and efforts, and to coordinate the interaction of numerous employees and the flow of their output.

There are four ways in which a manager can increase the feeling of controllability among staff: goal setting, feedback, reinforcement, and participation. Each encourages a feeling of mastery at work. Used in unison they are the most promising way to prevent burnout and they have a positive impact on productivity.

GOALS

Goals are important because they provide a target. Without a goal the worker is like a ship without a destination, going around and around, never making progress. A goal provides direction.

Goal setting has a highly beneficial impact upon performance when combined with quality supervision and feedback. The goal provides something to aim for and challenges people to stay focused and interested. Goals help people develop, firm up, and stretch their skill muscles. Who sets the goals and how they're set impacts on productivity. When employees participate in goal setting they typically set higher goals and reach them more often than do those who are assigned a goal. The nature of the goals is also important. Vague goals such as "do your best" or "give it your best shot" are really no goal at all and can be frustrating. Industrial research indicates that when goal setting is combined with quality supervision, production goes up; when goals are combined with poor supervision or no supervision at all, frustration and turnover is the result. In other words, goals alone are not enough.

PARTICIPATION

Participation helps make employees "burnout-resistant." The more influence people have over decisions directly related to their work, the better. All things considered, the average worker in this modern day is still treated as being not much more reliable or trustworthy than a child. While workers are adults who make important decisions about their lives and carry them out, as soon as they enter the workplace, opportunities for independent judgment are withheld. Someone else makes them. Workers are seldom treated as responsible adults who are self-

managing.

Numerous studies indicate that when given an opportunity to participate in goal setting, for example, employees set more rigorous goals and reach them more often than when they did not participate. Companies have much to gain by increasing the participation of their workforce. Participation opens communication channels. The worker knows more about his or her job and impediments to performance than anyone else. Participation provides management with the access to this vital information. Chances are employees will work harder, and the company will benefit by tapping into this reservoir of knowledge and skills. Participation, in theory, has been promoted for years; the difficulty is in implementing it.

FEEDBACK

For goals to be effective in increasing motivation, a catalyst—feedback—must be present. The worker who receives no feedback on performance is much like a blindfolded archery student. Without seeing where the arrow hits, the archery apprentice has little chance of becoming a master. Feedback is vital to learning. Without feedback goals are useless. Feedback is the yardstick we use to measure performance. It tells workers how close they've come to the bull's eye. Based on feedback the next effort can be fine-tuned. Working without feedback is much like the athlete in training for the hundred yard dash who has no watch or clock. How can one evaluate the run, tell if there's been improvement, or determine what adjustments in performance to make? Feedback facilitates learning, and giving feedback is the cornerstone of quality supervision.

ACKNOWLEDGEMENT

When and how you pay attention to employees is important. Often, managers forget about the power of personal attention, the most universally potent motivator. The effective manager is alert for and acknowledges small improvements. Acknowledgement that comes days or weeks after quality performance has little motivational clout. This is why Christmas bonuses, for example, tend to fail to influence motivation. They arrive too late. The sooner the reinforcement is administered the greater its impact on future performance.

TASC PLUS: A MODEL FOR QUALITY MANAGEMENT

The nature of supervision is probably the single largest source of burnout. No one is surprised to hear that the problem is worst with authoritarian managers who forbid any exercise of personal power whatsoever. But few realize that the manager at the other extreme—the good guy—can have an equally demoralizing effect. Equating being liked with good supervision can be a disaster. Unfortunately, most companies make the erroneous assumption that good supervision comes naturally. It does not. Being a good manager requires skills as complex as those required to be a good psychotherapist or a good defense attorney, for example. Each requires precision-tuned people skills. Managers need to know how to establish clear job standards, set specific output goals, give helpful feedback, notice and acknowledge on-task behavior, and troubleshoot performance problems before they become crises, in addition to decision-making, planning, coaching and leading skills.

Most managers are aware that implementing basic management tactics will have a dramatic impact on staff satisfaction and motivation. The problem is how to do so.

The best managers are those who function as trainers. They are not just bosses who assign tasks or just managers who oversee work; they teach people to be good performers. The best managers develop the potential within their people, creating an invaluable product for the

company—trained, motivated people. Few of us have ever had formal training in how to work. The public school system teaches how to follow orders, to walk in line, and remember facts, but not how to work, which includes determining priorities, setting goals, maintaining high motivation, and intentionally doing tasks.

When managers act as trainers (and at higher levels, when executives act as mentors) there's a hidden benefit for the company. The workforce is constantly upgraded as people are brought up through the ranks. Quality supervision develops the human resources within the company rather than squandering them.

Managing people's work requires sophisticated skills. Unfortunately, training in these skills, especially for lower level managers, is often scarce. I have developed some basic principles in managing people at work that I refer to as "TASC Plus." TASC Plus is an acronym that stands for a simple but effective managing process that incorporates four essential ingredients for quality performance: goals, feedback, participation, and acknowledgement. TASC Plus is easy to remember and easy to use.

TASC Plus is a technique that incorporates all the features necessary to sustain high motivation and productivity among performers. TASC Plus is a prescription that guides managers in communicating expectations and acknowledging on-TASC performance. Each letter in TASC Plus stands for one of the steps.

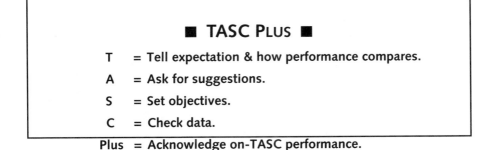

Plus = Acknowledge on-TASC performance.

TELL

T stands for *Tell*. Tell the performer your expectation which is usually meeting a particular standard, and how his or her performance compares to it. A standard is the performance goal or target that describes the specific output that the worker is responsible for producing. If no standard has been set then developing one is of primary importance. When feasible the employee should participate in the setting of the standard.

PERFORMANCE STANDARDS

A standard of performance is an invaluable tool for managers, providing a method for identifying and measuring on-TASC performance. Based upon this information, the manager knows what to acknowledge. Without standards most managers fall into the trap of looking at factors unrelated to output. For example, whether or not a design engineer comes in promptly at 8 A.M. or is chronically 15 - 20 minutes late probably has little to do with the quality of his or her design. In contrast, chronic lateness would have a definite negative impact on the performance of an on-the-air news broadcaster.

A good standard allows a manager to differentiate among people so that he or she can provide them with fair individual treatment. One person may be performing above the standard and deserve acknowledgement; another may be below the standard but making steady progress toward it and should receive acknowledgement for that progress; yet another's performance may be dropping and trouble-shooting action is needed to turn it around. Good standards make managers' decisions easier, provide a basis for individual treatment, and encourage performance rather than conformity. Unfortunately, most managers haven't set standards for the jobs they oversee.

There are a number of sources of information helpful in setting standards. You can consult the company's official job standards as a first step, but don't rely solely on these. Aside from frequently being out of date, by necessity they must be general enough to describe a job in a number of settings. Suppose, for example, "Office Assistant I" is an entry-level clerical position in any department. The job of Office Assistant I in the shipping department is likely to be very different from one in billing. It is difficult for company job standards to reflect these differences. Another source of information is the relationship between jobs. What do others need from this person to perform their own function? The answer to this question reveals the essential output of the job. With technical and professional jobs the standard is often negotiated between manager and performer.

Characteristics of a Good Standard

The job standard is a description of the individual's output, which is a part of a long and complex chain of outputs that ultimately leads to

accomplishing the overall organizational goals that usually involve making a profit by supplying a product or service.

Describe Output

The standard should describe an output. It is not a description of the behaviors or actions required to meet the standard but a statement of what result is expected. The output might be in terms of quantity, such as the number of machines inspected, number of vouchers processed, or number of complaints per quarter; of quality, such as the number of designs accepted or number of reworks; of time, such as the turn-around time, percent on-time, or response time; or of cost, such as the cost of down-time or cost per call. Standards that encompass more than one performance indicator such as specifying quality and quantity both are more effective than those relying on only one.

Specific

Good job standards are also specific. Vague standards lay the foundation for miscommunication and discontent. "Be prompt in answering the phone" is a vague standard. What is prompt? Does that mean to answer on the first ring? The third ring? Or within thirty seconds? The word "prompt" is open to interpretation. A better standard would be "Answer the phone within three rings."

Achievable

The standard must be realistic. It must be something the person can actually reach. It's best to provide a range. Reaching the low end gives the performer a feeling of success while reaching the high end provides a challenge.

Observable

The standard should be observable. At any particular time the manager as well as the performer should be able to answer "yes" or "no" to the question: "Has the standard been met?" A standard that is clearly stated in terms of observable output makes accountability (A-Count-Ability) possible.

Measureable

Finally, movement toward the standard should be easily measured. The more effort required to record an output, the less likely any data will be collected. And without counting it is difficult to determine whether or not the standard has been met.

It's not laziness or incompetence that stops managers from developing job standards. Developing a standard is a difficult and challenging task. The difficulty lies in the area of measurement. It's pretty easy, for example, to evaluate the performance of a typist. You can look at the speed of typing, the layout of the work, or the number of errors. These variables are all easy to identify and easy to measure or count. Therefore, they make A-Count-Ability simple. But what of jobs such as manager, public relations officer, or movie producer? What is the identifiable output for these jobs, and what are the observable behaviors that lead to the production of that output? Answering these questions is much more difficult but that does not mean it's impossible. When these questions aren't answered, how can people who perform these jobs tell whether or not they are performing well? And how is the manager to evaluate their performance?

Another impediment to measuring actual employee performance is the logistics of collecting the data. Managers have so many tasks that they don't have time to observe all of their employees all of the time. Some companies such as Emery Air Freight and National Semiconductor have experimented with the self-monitoring approach and report dramatic increases in productivity as a result. Basically, in this approach the performer collects data on his or her own behavior.

The figure that follows shows a data collection tool called the working graph was used on the line at National Semiconductor to monitor wafer breakage. Listed across the bottom is each function the operator performs. Each time a wafer is broken the operator places a mark in the C column representing the station where the wafer was broken. A particularly useful feature of this chart is the way it yields a bar graph. Simply by glancing at the chart manager and operator alike can determine where most wafers were broken. Information of this sort is valuable for the manager in making decisions and provides immediate feedback to the operator. The operator in turn knows where to place his or her attention to solve breakage problems as well as which efforts have been successful. Managers, for example, can use the working graph to monitor interactions with employees. This might include counting the number of interactions, rating the quality of each interaction, counting the number of acknowledging statements made during the interaction, and so forth. The next section will explain how to use data from a chart

EPI Department
Shift of: ❑ 1   ❑ 2   ❑ 3   Daily Total: ❑ M   ❑ T   ❑ W   ❑ Th   ❑ F
Week of: _____   ❑ S   ❑ Su   ❑ Weekly Total

#	Breakage Type	Loading into Carriers	Cleaning Process	Inspecting after Cleaning	Handling of Trays	Loading of Reactor	Falling off during Run	Unloading of Reactor	Data	PL Room	Inspecting Runs	Area Measuring	Bagging for Transfer	Dropped Boat	Dropped Tray	Others (Explain)
31																
30																
29																
28																
27																
26																
25																
24																
23																
22																
21																
20																
19																
18																
17														F		
16														F		
15														F		
14														Th		
13														Th		
12		F												W		
11		F								F				W		
10		F								Th				W		
9		F								Th				T		
8	Th	F						Th		Th			F	M	F	
7	Th	F						Th		W	W		F	M	F	
6	W	F				F		T	F	W	T		F	M	Th	
5	W	F				F		T	F	M	T		W	M	Th	
4	W	M				F		T	F	M	T		W	M	T	
3	W	M				F		M	Th	M	M	Th	W	M	T	
2	W	M	T			F		M	Th	M	M	Th	M	M	T	
1	T	M	T			F		M	Th	M	M	Th	M	M		

THE WORKING GRAPH

such as this to both evaluate performance and to acknowledge it.

HOW TO "TELL"

Once the standard has been determined and agreed upon, tell the individual how his or her performance compares to that standard. This feedback should be given in a simple, straightforward manner, using objective terms and avoiding judgmental, emotional, and vague words. Conciseness is important. Be clear and brief. Don't ramble, repeat, or go off on tangents that can come across as a harangue. Whenever possible use quantitative words: "Last week you were late two times" is better than "You've been late a lot." Don't defend the standard or apologize for it. Just state the expectation. Finally, deal with one standard at a time. Stringing three or four standards together will only overwhelm the person and not accomplish anything. For example, to a floor manager you can say, "Joe, one of your important functions is to motivate those you manage to peak performance. You can do this by making sure each of your people clearly understands his expected output and by checking each person's progress at least once a day. While checking the workers' charts you can let them know that you what they're doing to meet output goals *(standard)*. I've noticed that you check everyone each day and are readily available to answer questions and that you take time to make sure that they understand the answer. But I rarely hear you commenting on good work *(comparison)*."

■ **Imagine how you would respond to the following:**
Bob, I've got to talk to you about the mail. You've got to be more efficient. I've been getting a lot of complaints about you. There have been just too many delays. People want their mail on time. Got that? And another thing. The place is a dump. Why don't you ever straighten things up around here?

This is a poorly stated Tell to say the least. It is bound to lead to miscommunication, irritation, and possibly burnout of both the mail clerk and the manager. Consider this improved Tell:

> *Bob, I've got to talk to you about the mail. I've gotten*
> *some complaints about mail being delivered late. Yesterday*
> *two people said they didn't get the morning mail until after*
> *2 in the afternoon. Optimally, all the morning mail should*
> *be sorted and ready for delivery by 11:30 and by 11:45 at*
> *the latest, and between 3:30 and 3:45 in the afternoon.*

This improved Tell communicates expectations and lays the foundation for negotiations.

ASK

A stands for *Ask*. The Ask step elicits the participation of the performer. Here the manager places the problem in the lap of the performer who is the only one who can improve performance. Most people have at least some idea about what is stopping their performance and how to remove the block. The manager should avoid thinking of a solution but, instead, guide performers in developing their own solutions. This approach allows performers more responsibility and more personal power. Instead of being a disciplinarian the manager is teacher, facilitator, and coach.

The Ask step is vitally important and one that many managers tend to skip. Ask is where the participation of the performer is engaged. Ask for information about the problem and for suggestions on how to improve performance.

USE OPEN-ENDED QUESTIONS

Use open-ended questions to prompt a response. These should begin with "What," "When," "Where," "Who," "How," and "In what way." Avoid questions that begin with "Why" because why questions tend to put people on the defensive. You may have to ask a couple of times, especially when first using TASC Plus.

Continue asking questions until you've gotten all relevant information. Remember, you can't ask too many questions. A manager never looks foolish asking questions.

AVOID LEADING QUESTIONS

Avoid asking leading questions or questions that imply the answer you're seeking. It's a waste of time if the performer only tells you what he or she thinks you want to hear. Likewise, closed questions that elicit a yes/no answer are less effective. Closed questions such as "Do you...?" or "Are you...?" or "Can you...?" can feel like an interrogation. And make sure to keep an open mind. There's no point in asking for suggestions if you've already predetermined what the problem is and what is going to be done. As soon as the employees pick up on the fact that you're not really listening to suggestions, they will clam up. Pay attention to what the person is saying. Encourage him or her to talk. Genuine interest will go a long way.

ASK FOR INFORMATION AND SUGGESTIONS

The person in the job is the person who is closest to the particular work. This person knows, more than anyone else, problems that impact upon getting the job done. And this person probably has a number of good ideas for improving the way that his or her job is performed. When you tap into this wellspring of ideas, you simultaneously empower the employee. It gives people the feeling that they are important and that their input is needed. Ask the employees for information and suggestions.

"Joe, what are your ideas about using positive feedback as a motivator?"

"Bob, what suggestions do you have for getting the morning mail out by 11:45?"

When performance is below the standard, ask what can be done to bring performance up to the standard.

"Shirley, your average defect rate is 12 percent above the standard. What suggestions do you have for getting those

defects down?"

This communicates a concern with Shirley's performance without being critical or blaming. Again, the employee knows more about impediments to quality performance in his or her job than anyone else and probably has some good suggestions for solutions. Tap into this resource. By asking, you enlist participation. Again, make sure that you listen to what is suggested. If you ask and don't listen or dismiss what the employees say without careful consideration, you risk engendering a sense of futility.

When performance is above the standard, ask what will help keep performance at that high level.

> *"John, the accuracy of your cuts are exceptionally good.*
> *What can I do to help you stay at this high level?"*

SET AN OBJECTIVE

S stands for *Set Objective*. When manager and performer have clarified what is impeding performance and what actions might facilitate it, they move to the objective-setting stage, where a short-term goal is determined. The suggestions made during the Ask step are a natural springboard for setting a short-term objective aimed at achieving or surpassing the standard. What precisely will the performer do?

THE EMPLOYEE SHOULD SET THE OBJECTIVE

Once again, it's important to get the performer to set the objective. Ideally, the manager should not set the objective but guide the performer, by asking questions, in doing so. Ideally the S step is a means of teaching the worker to self-manage and self-motivate. In the early stages, the manager may have to take a more active role and teach the performer to set objectives. Over time, however the individual in the job should become more active.

TAKE SMALL STEPS

No objective is too small as long as it represents movement forward. A series of successful small steps is more effective than an objective that requires too much too soon, resulting in failure.

BE SPECIFIC

Once again, the objective should be very specific. A good objective specifies *who* will do what under which conditions (*when* and *where*) for how long. For example, Joe replied that he had learned from his father that a "swift kick" was the best motivator. He agreed, however, that a positive approach might work better than threats; but he didn't know how to start. In such a situation the manager might negotiate a small-step objective.

> *Joe, for the next week (how long), you're (who) going to pat each of your people on the back at least once a week (how much) by commenting on something he or she has done right (what). I'll come by this time next week to talk about how it worked out.*

ONE THING AT A TIME

Work on one behavior at a time. If there are two proposed actions, set two different objectives. It helps to write the objectives down. This emphasizes the importance and promotes clarity. Determine here how the behavior or outcome specified in the objective will be counted.

CHECK DATA

C is for *Check*. Periodically check how the employee is doing. After an objective has been set the manager's role becomes one of facilitating and monitoring progress toward accomplishing that objective. This is easily accomplished when a manager uses the self-monitoring working graph. The manager periodically drops in on the performer and checks the performance data on the graph. Based on this data the manager acknowledges on-TASC performance.

ACKNOWLEDGE

Plus stands for acknowledging progress toward the objective. The

rule of thumb is to look for and acknowledge what the person has done right, which I call "on-TASC performance". On-TASC performance is any action that contributes to achieving the objective. This includes gathering the data itself.

Suppose for example, the mail clerk collects data on the time that mail leaves the mail room and the number of letters returned as mismailed. Consider the following situations:

If the mail went out early and the number of returns is down, the manager should acknowledge the fact that mail went out early and that returns are down.

Bob, I see you got the mail out early today and that returns are down. Whatever you're doing to improve both of these seems to be working. This is great and I appreciate the extra effort that you've made to accomplish this. If there's anything I can do to help you keep this up, let me know.

If the mail went out on time but the number of returns exceeds the standard, the manager should acknowledge that mail went out on time and use TASC Plus to work on the returns.

> *Bob, I see that you've been getting the mail out every day on time. This is good. Let me know if there's anything I can do to assist you in keeping on schedule. I noticed that the number of returns is up to 37. As we discussed before you should keep returns to 20 or fewer per delivery (Tell). What suggestions do you have for cutting down on the number of returns (Ask)?*

If mail went out later than usual and the number of returns is up but they are both still within the acceptable range, the manager would say nothing about mail time or returns but should acknowledge that the person recorded the data. In this case, recording data is the on-TASC behavior.

> *Bob, I appreciate the efforts you have made keeping track of information like this. You've done a good job by being thorough in keeping the data charts and this is important. It helps me do my job better.*

Many managers are concerned with the honesty of the performer in accurately recording their performance. Implicit in this concern is the notion that people at work must be watched if they are to perform conscientiously. In fact, however, honesty is rarely a problem provided the manager uses TASC Plus appropriately and not as a method to penalize someone for reporting a problem. When the working graph is first introduced, understandably many people are curious, if not downright suspicious. They often think a speed-up will be demanded. However, most will record their performance accurately, at least at first. After that it depends on the manager's reaction. How the manager responds to a leveling off, a drop, or substandard performance is crucial. If the drop is criticized, you can be sure that the performer will not record substandard performance again. On the other hand, when the working graph works for the individual using it by bringing acknowledgment for performance and help in correcting problems, then people will be honest in recording their performance.

A second rule of thumb is all drops in performance should be simply ignored except when it goes below the standard. In this case, the manager should avoid criticism or threats and recycle through TASC Plus.

BENEFITS OF TASC PLUS

By following TASC Plus, managers can prompt participation as well as gave feedback and reinforcement. Substandard performance need not be criticized; instead, it can be used as an opportunity to use TASC Plus to motivate by eliciting participation in solving the problem and focusing on constructive solutions. As a secondary gain, managers who use TASC Plus experience an increase in their own sense of controllability because they gain a feeling of "I can do."

The TASC Plus approach allows employees to maximize their personal power and harness that power in the service of organizational goals. It provides managers with a road map of what to do and how to do it. In the process the manager's role is modified to one of teacher. Employees learn to set task goals and to participate in goal-setting for their own jobs and often in the definition and direction of the job itself. All organizations and the people in them are continually changing. TASC Plus provides a mechanism for on going change. Through the negotiation process expectations and directions can be modified and shaped in response to the demands of the organization and the needs of the individual. TASC Plus provides an objective basis for raises, promotions, and other organizational acknowledgement. And it takes the yearly performance review out of the manager's office and into the daily work routine. Expectations on all sides are clarified and people know how they are evaluated and what those evaluations are. Most important, TASC Plus maximizes individual responsibility and dignity.

It isn't necessary to make a big deal out of TASC Plus by calling the person in for a formal meeting. The interaction can take place casually right at the person's workstation. TASC Plus frees the manager to attend to other matters. He or she needs to occasionally check in on the performer, look at the data, and acknowledge on-TASC behavior. When workers get immediate feedback on their efforts to meet the objective they gain a sense of accomplishment for good performance and make immediate adjustments to stop problems.

TASC Plus is an effective management tool that helps the manager to keep a thumb on the pulse of the department, to identify problems, and to take corrective actions before they get out of control. It can provide a framework for a skilled manager to assist employees in making changes in their unproductive behaviors. At the setting-objective stage, for example, managers can guide employees through self-development programs. Effective coaching and other pertinent management skills and techniques are outlined in my book, *Turning Around: Keys to Motivation and Productivity.*

CHAPTER 14

FIND A PATH
WITH A HEART
THE NINTH PATH TO PERSONAL POWER

In Beating Job Burnout the emphasis has been on overcoming power-lessness at work which makes us feel unmotivated, destroys our spirit, and leads to an overall malaise—all of which makes work hell. Since job burnout is caused by feelings of powerlessness at work, the solution is to develop personal power—feelings of potency and the ability to influence situations that impact upon us.

We have looked at eight paths to personal power. Each of these paths enhance us when we follow it. If you follow the first path and PACE yourself, for example, you will use self-motivation and be more productive. If you follow the fifth path and tailor your job to your workstyle, you'll feel better when working, find work easier and accomplish more. In each case you've increased your personal power, your ability to influence your situation.

But the process of beating job burnout contains an inherent trap: the emphasis on avoidance. This is a trap because it requires that things must become bad before they can get better. To put it bluntly, it requires a "kick in the butt" to jump start us toward doing something that will improve our situations. In Chapter 4, we examined the two kinds of motivation: working for and working to avoid. Working for involves striving for goals and positives; working to avoid involves turning off negatives. By necessity, beating burnout demands a focus on avoidance motivation. If things aren't so bad, we can easily fall into a state of complacency in which we don't look for any paths to personal power until things become unbearable. We just go along waiting for negatives to come up before we start pursuing the paths to personal power which improve not just our lives at work but our lives in general.

The trap can be avoided by transfering emphasis to working for, to aiming toward something so that we don't require a negative to get us moving. That brings up a difficult question: What is the opposite of burnout? The reason we need to uncover the opposite of burnout is that if we're going to strive for a positive, we have to know what it is. If we don't know what the positive is, we can't be motivated by it.

The opposite of burnout isn't merely not being burned out. It is more than the absence of negatives. The opposite of burnout is a positive state of well-being, enthusiasm, and motivation. We experience it as contentment, joy and happiness—bliss.

Stop a moment and notice what burnout feels like. It is a feeling of being down and out, unable to perform, and unmotivated. When we suffer from burnout, we feel helpless, out of control, full of doubt, sluggish, tired, depressed, fearful, uncertain and lethargic. Now, remember when you experienced the opposite of burnout. Most people report being full of energy and having stamina, of feeling in control and able to perform with ease, of enjoying what they're doing and a sense of timelessness and being one with the activity. This is a feeling of bliss.

Psychologists call this blissful experience "the flow state." One of its most defining qualities is the feeling of "being one with what you are doing." When we are dancing, for example, we often feel like we're one with the beat of the music or the rest of the crowd or our partner. This feeling is common in various sports. When playing your best tennis, for example, you, the ball and the racket become one. You don't have to think specifically about how you will hit the ball. The racket is an extension of you, and it is you who are swinging, hitting the ball perfectly with little effort.

For over twenty years, psychologist Dr. Csikszentmihalyi researched the flow state which he described in his book, *Flow: The Psychology of*

Optimal Experience. He had people from all walks of life, races and nationalities wear beepers during their daily lives. When beeped, they made a written record of what they were doing and how they felt at the time. He found that people experienced a "flow state" which was characterized by feelings of stamina and endurance, of being in control, of timelessness and effortless creativity with highly focused attention and a feeling of being one with what they were doing. The flow state is what I am calling bliss. Think back to times when you were in the flow state, when you were performing well and things seemed to go the way you wanted. Those times were your bliss.

Being in the flow state feels good. Clearly, this is what we want more of. We want less burnout-type situations where we have to battle, avoid and overcome, and more feelings of bliss where things work for us and we perform at our peak with ease.

The final path to personal power is finding a path to your bliss. When you're following your own personal path, you discover what is good for you and what works for you. Each person is unique, and what is blissful for one person may be a burnout for another. An obvious example is that a person skilled in mathematics may be perfectly happy as an accountant, whereas a person who has trouble thinking in numerical terms would be extremely unhappy in that job situation. There are, of course, many subtle variations on this example. The point is that every person is unique, and what helps each person achieve the flow state—or bliss—will also be unique. To find your path to bliss, you must enter uncharted territory. Going into the unknown makes you a pioneer of sorts, and it requires that you develop skills as a pathfinder.

In beating job burnout, the central challenge is self-management—managing your motivation to get yourself moving and to keep moving. The eight paths to personal power for beating job burnout revolve around keeping motivation high in demotivating situations. But in finding a path to your bliss and being a pathfinder, the central challenge is leading yourself. Unfortunately, few of us have had formal training leading ourselves and don't know how to begin.

Finding your path to bliss does not mean you will be blissful every moment. It does mean there will be more moments of bliss. Your work will be experienced as more worthwhile and add meaning to your life because you know it to be something that is right for you. You perform better, get more done and function optimally more often.

In order to find bliss, we have to have a compelling image of what it is we are striving for. When we hold this picture in our minds, it exerts a magnetic force that helps us to bring about the things for which we are striving. Working to avoid exerts a repellent force that pushes us away from a negative situation. To create and sustain motivation toward something, it helps to have a compelling image to pull us to it like a magnet. The essential step in doing this is creating and sustaining that personal picture of bliss. It is important to remember that this picture will change as you travel along your path to bliss.

There are many different times when you are seeking a path. You may be seeking a career direction or a lifestyle path. To accomplish this you must be a pathfinder. At other times there may be a project you're working on that requires constant re-evaluation and adaptation as the objectives come into sharper focus. This too involves pathfinding as you move from the inception of the idea to completion of the project.

It is helpful to think of that picture of bliss as the magnet which provides attraction, and in turn facilitates the motivation to discover and travel your paths in a confident, productive manner.

In my book, *Finding a Path with a Heart: How to Go from Burnout to Bliss,* I identify twelve pathfinding tools. I've mentioned two here, the Heart Tool and Vision. The Heart Tool helps us to clarify our values and feelings so that we can differentiate between burnout and blissful situations early on.

It is with the pathfinding tool of Vision that we create a compelling picture—a vision—which is the picture of our destination. It is the picture of being in a blissful state.

Job burnout is an unpleasant and destructive process that erodes enthusiasm and damages our spirit. Every job has the potential for burnout, and no one is immune. *Beating Job Burnout* describes how to overcome burnout by following paths to personal power. Things are not all or nothing. It is always a matter of degree, and following the paths to personal power are a lifelong journey. By reading this book, you have taken the steps necessary to start on the paths to personal power. You are beginning to leave behind the energy-draining, ambition-crippling condition known as burnout. You are on your way to finding a path with a heart.

Bibliography

Bandura, Albert. *Principles of Behavior Modification,* Holt, Rinehart and Winston, New York: 1969.

Bennett, Hal Zina and Susan J. Sparrow. *Follow Your Bliss,* Avon Books, New York: 1990.

Bennett, Steven J. *Playing Hardball with Soft Skills: How to Prosper with Non-Technical Skills in a High-Tech World,* Bantam, New York: 1986.

Boe, Anne and Bettie B. Youngs? *Is Your "Net" Working?,* John Wiley, New York: 1989.

Bolles, Richard N. *What Color Is Your Parachute?,* Ten Speed Press, Berkeley, CA: 1978.

Bower, Sharon A. and Gordon Bower. *Asserting Yourself: A Practical Guide To Positive Change,* Addison-Wesley, Reading, MA: 1976.

Brief, Arthur P., Randall S. Schuler, and Mary Van Sell. *Managing Job Stress,* Little Brown, Boston: 1981.

Brothers, Joyce. "All I Wanted Was A Cadillac," in *How to Get Whatever You Want Out of Life,* Simon and Schuster, New York: 1978, p.11-18.

Brown, Barbara. *Supermind: The Ultimate Energy,* Harper & Row, New York: 1980.

Browne, Harry. *How I Found Freedom In an Unfree World,* Avon, New York: 1973.

Brunton, Paul. *The Secret Path,* Dutton, New York: 1935.

Butler, Pamela. *Talking to Yourself: Learning the Language of Self-Support,* Harper & Row, New York: 1981.

Castaneda, Carlos. *The Teachings of Don Juan,* Pocket, New York: 1968.

Castaneda, Carlos. *The Second Ring of Power,* Simon and Schuster, New York: 1977.

Charland, Jr., William A. *Career Shifting: Starting Over In a Changing Economy,* Bob Adams, Inc. Publishers, Holbrook, MA: 1993.

Chin-Lee, Cynthia. *It's Who You Know: Career Strategies for Making Effective Personal Contacts,* Pfeiffer & Company, San Diego, CA: 1993.

Coffee, Gerald. *Beyond Survival: A POW's Inspiring Lesson in Living,* Berkley Books, New York: 1990.

Colligan, Douglas. "The High Priest of Guerrilla Psych," *Omni,* March 1980, pp. 108 -115.

Connellan, Thomas. *How to Improve Human Performance: Behaviorism in Business and Industry,* Harper & Row, New York: 1978.

Coulter, Jr., N. Arthur. *Synergetics, An Adventure in Human Development,* Prentice-Hall, Englewood Cliffs, NJ: 1976.

Covey, Stephen R. *The 7 Habits of Highly Effective People: Powerful Lessons In Personal Change,* A Firestone Book, New York: 1989.

Csikszentmihalyi, Mihaly. *Flow: The Psychology of Optimal Experience,* Harper & Row, New York: 1990.

Deal, Terrence and Allen A. Kennedy. *Corporate Cultures: The Rites and Rituals of Corporate Life,* Addison Wesley, Reading, MA: 1982.

De Ropp, Robert. *The Master Game: Beyond the Drug Experience,* Delta, New York: 1968

Doore, Gary, Editor. *Shaman's Path: Healing, Personal Growth and Empowerment,* Shambhala, Boston: 1988.

Dyer, Wayne. *Pulling Your Own Strings,* Thomas Y. Crowell Co., New York: 1978.

Dyer, Wayne. *The Sky's the Limit,* Pocket Books, New York: 1980.

Ellis, Albert and Robert A. Harper. *A New Guide to Rational Living,* Wilshire Books, North Hollywood, CA: 1979.

"The Essential Hangout," Psychology Today, April, 1980. pp. 82.

Fields, Rick, with Peggy Taylor, Rex Weyler, and Rick Ingrasci. *Chop Wood, Carry Water: A Guide to Finding Spiritual Fulfillment in Everyday Life,* Tarcher, Los Angeles: 1984.

Freudenberger, Herbert J. *Burnout: The High Cost of High Achievement,* Anchor/Doubleday, New York: 1980.

Gallwey, Timothy and Bob Kriegel. *Inner Skiing,* Random House, New York: 1977.

Garfield, Charles. *Peak Performers: The New Heroes of American Business,* Avon: New York: 1986.

Gilbert, Thomas F. *Human Competence: Engineering Worthy Performance,* McGraw Hill, New York: 1978.

Gupton, Ted and Michael D. LeBow. "Behavior Management in a Large Industrial Firm," Behavior Therapy, Vol. 2. 1971, pp. 78 - 82.

Haga, William James, and Nichlos Acocella. *Haga's Law: Why Nothing Works and No One Can Fix It and the More We Try the Worse It Gets,* Morrow, New York: 1980.

Irish, Richard. *Go Hire Yourself an Employer,* Anchor Books, 1978.

Jaffe, Dennis. *Working With the Ones You Love,* Conari Press, Berkeley, CA: 1990.

Jaffee, Dennis T., and Cynthia Scott. *From Burnout to Balance: A Workbook for Peak Performance and Self-Renewal,* McGraw-Hill, New York: 1984.

Jaffee, Dennis T., and Cynthia Scott. *Take This Job and Love It: How to Change Your Work Without Changing Your Job,* Simon & Schuster, New York: 1988.

Janis, Irving L. and Leon Mann. *Decision Making: A Psychological Analysis of Conflict, Choice, and Commitment,* The Free Press, New York: 1977.

John-Roger and Peter McWilliams. *DO IT! Let's Get Off Our Butts: A Guide To Living Your Dreams,* Prelude Press, Los Angeles: 1991.

Kahn, Robert, Donald Wolf, Robert Quinn and Diedrick Snack. *Organizational Stress: Studies in Role Conflict and Ambiguity,* Wiley, New York: 1964.

Kennedy, Marilyn Moats. *Career Knockouts: How to Battle Back,* Warner Books, New York: 1980.

Keyes, Ken. *Handbook to Higher Consciousness,* Living Love Publications, Coos Bay, OR: 1978.

Keyes, Ken and Bruce Burkan. *How To Make Your Life Work or Why Aren't You Happy?*, Cornerstone Library, New York: 1976.

Lakoff, George and Mark Johnson. *Metaphors We Live By*, University of Chicago Press, Chicago: 1980.

Lazarus, Arnold. *In the Mind's Eye: The Power of Imagery Therapy to Give You Control Over Your Life*, Hawson, New York: 1977.

Lefkowitz, Bernard. *Breaktime: Living Without Work in a Nine-To-Five World*, Penguin Books, New York: 1979.

Leonard, George. *Mastery: The Keys To Success and Long-Term Fulfillment*, New American Library, New York: 1991.

LeShan, Lawrence. *How to Meditate*, Bantam Books, New York: 1974.

Lewinson, Peter, Ricardo Munoz, Mary Ann Youngren, and Antonette Zeiss. *Control Your Depression*, Prentice-Hall, Englewood Cliffs, NJ: 1978.

Marks, Linda. *Living With Vision, Knowledge Systems*, Indianapolis: 1989.

Maslach, Christina. "Burned-Out," Human Behavior, September 1976, p. 16.

Mason, L. John. *Guide To Stress Reduction*, Celestial Arts, Berkeley, CA: 1985.

Medley, H. Anthony. *Sweaty Palms: The Neglected Art of Being Interviewed*, Lifetime Learning Publications, Belmont, CA: 1978.

Mehrabian, Albert. *Public Places and Private Spaces: The Psychology of Work, Play and Living Environments*, New York: Basic Books, 1976.

Miller, Emmett E. and Deborah Lueth. *Feeling Good: How to Stay Healthy*, Prentice-Hall, Englewood Cliffs, NJ:1978.

Miller, Lyle H., and Alma Dell Smith. *The Stress Solution: An Action Plan To Manage The Stress In Your Life*, Pocket Books, New York: 1993.

Moreau, Daniel. *Take Charge of Your Career: How to Survive and Profit from a Mid-Career Change*, Kiplinger Books, Washington D.C. : 1990.

Morehouse, Laurence E. and Leonard Gross. *Maximum Performance*, Pocket Books, New York: 1978.

Nair, Keshavan. *Beyond Winning: The Handbook For The Leadership Revolution*, Paradox Press, Phoenix: 1990.

Ostrander, Sheila, Lynn Schroeder and Nancy Ostrander. *Super-learning*, Delacorte Press, New York: 1979.

Health Care Worker Burnout: What It Is, What to Do About It, An Inquiry Book, (Blue Cross Association) Chicago: 1981.

Pearce, Joseph Chilton. *The Crack in the Cosmic Egg: Challenging Constructs of Mind and Reality*, Pocket Books, New York: 1971.

Potter, Beverly A. "Managing Authority: How to Give Directives" in *Turning Around: Keys to Motivation and Productivity*, Ronin Publishing, Berkeley, CA: 1987.

Potter, Beverly A. *Preventing Job Burnout*, Crisp Publications, Menlo Park, CA: 1986.

Potter, Beverly A. "Self-Management" in *Turning Around: Keys to Motivation and Productivity*,

Ronin Publishing, Berkeley, CA: 1987.

Potter, Beverly A. *The Way of the Ronin: Riding the Waves of Change at Work,* Ronin Publishing, Berkeley, CA: 1987.

Reps, Paul, editor. *Zen Flesh, Zen Bones: A Collection of Zen and Pre-Zen writings,* Doubleday, New York.

Rosen, Gerald. *The Relaxation Book,* Prentice Hall, Englewood Cliffs, NJ: 1977.

Scheele, Adele M. *Skills For Success: A Guide to the Top,* Morrow, New York: 1980.

Schumacher, E. F., and Peter N. Gillingham. *Good Work,* Harper & Row, New York:1979.

Seligman, Martin E. P. *Helplessness: On Depression, Development, and Death,* W. H. Freeman & Co., San Francisco: 1975.

Simon, Sidney B. *Getting Unstuck: Breaking Through Your Barriers to Change,* Warner Books, New York: 1988.

Sinetar, Marsha. *Do What You Love, The Money Will Follow: Discovering Your Right Livelihood,* Paulist Press, New York: 1987.

Shah, Idries. *Tales of the Dervishes,* New York: Dutton, 1970.

Shapiro, Dean H. Jr. *Precision Nirvana,* Spectrum Books, Englewood Cliffs, NJ: 1978.

Sheehy, Gail. *Passages: Predictable Crisis Of Adult Life,* Bantam, New York: 1976.

Sher, Barabra. *Wishcraft: How To Get What You Really Want,* Ballantine, New York: 1979.

Silva, Jose, and Philip Miele. *The Silva Mind Control Method,* Simon & Schuster, New York:1977.

Smith, Manuel. *Kicking The Fear Habit,* The Dial Press, New York: 1977.

Stevens, Paul. *Stop Postponing The Rest of Your Life,* Ten Speed Press, Berkeley, CA: 1993.

Truch, Stephen. *Teacher Burnout and What to Do About It,* Academic Therapy Publications, Novato, CA: 1980.

Veninga, Robert L. and James P. Spradley. *The Work Stress Connection: How to Cope with Burnout,* Ballantine, New York: 1981.

Waitley, Denis and Reni L. Witt. *The Joy of Working: The 30-Day System to Success, Wealth, and Happiness on the Job,* Ballantine, New York: 1985.

Wassmer, Arthur, C. *Making Contact: A Guide To Overcoming Shyness, Making New Relationships and Keeping Those You Already Have,* The Dial Press, New York:1978.

Watson, David L. and Roland G. Tharp. *Self-Directed Behavior: Self-Modification for Personal Adjustment,* Brooks/Gale, Monterey, CA: 1972.

West, Ross. *How to Be Happier in the Job You Sometimes Can't Stand,* Boradman, Nashville: 1990.

Woods, David Lee. *My Job My Boss and Me: Gaining Control of Your Life,* Lifetime Learning Publications, Belmont, CA: 1980.

Young, Jeffrey, E., and Janet S. Klosko. *Reinventing Your Life: How To Break Free From Negative Patterns,* Dutton, New York: 1993.

Zaleznick, Abraham, Manfred frets de Writs, and John Howards: "Stress Reactions in Organizations: Syndromes, Causes, and Consequences," *Behavioral Science* (Vol. 22), pg 77.

Zastrow, Charles. *Talk To Yourself Using the Power of Self-Talk,* Spectrum Books, Englewood Cliffs, NJ: 1979.

INDEX

FINDING A PATH WITH A HEART
How To Go From Burnout To Bliss
Dr. Beverly Potter

In today's workplace you must solve problems rather than just complete repetitive tasks, and lead yourself rather than wait to be told what to do. *Finding A Path With A Heart* shows how to become a self-leader—a pathfinder—finding a way to your bliss in your work.

When following a path with a heart you feel at one with what you are doing. Attention is highly focused and actions seem effortless, almost spontaneous. You can achieve optimal performance, be more innovative and get your job done while experiencing many moments of bliss.

Finding A Path With A Heart is an engaging guide sprinkled with drawings, stories, exercises and quotes. You'll learn why you're more likely to experience bliss while at work than in leisure, how you can increase your potential for achieving it, and discover 12 self-leadership tools for finding your path to more bliss in work and play while performing at your peak.

Business/Careers
3 66 pp
Illustrations
Appendix
$14.95
ISBN 0-914171-74-7

"Cock-full of good ideas, interestingly put together...tremendously informative and helpful.."
— Mihaly Csikszentmihalyi
**author of *Flow: The Psychology
of Optimal Experience***

"Worth reading!!!"
—Marty Edelson
president, Boardroom, Inc.

*"...practical, readable, imaginative, non-linear,
creative and filled with doable ideas."*
—John D. Krumboltz
professor, Stanford University

FROM CONFLICT TO COOPERATION
How To Mediate A Dispute
Dr. Beverly Potter

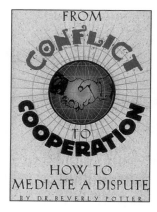

From Conflict To Cooperation presents techniques for mediators to resolve disputes—powerful tools for all managers, supervisors, coaches, parents, teachers, neighborhood leaders, politicans, and police officers.

This sensible manual shows how to intervene to control hostility while uncovering each party's perspective on the issues involved. It then demonstrates how to mediate an agreement on what should be done, who should do it, and when.

From Conflict To Cooperation's hands-on methods and realistic scenarios were adapted from police training designed to handle domestic disputes and developed in workshops for the staff at Stanford University.

Management/Self-help
194 pp
Illustrations
$14.95
0-914171-79-8

"A superb guide to mediating disputes that will appeal to many readers . . . This excellent source can serve as a basic training manual for those involved in mediating disputes . . . Potter's handbook is highly recommended."

—Library Journal

"A valuable addition to the library of any person who wants to build more harmonious relationships."

—Napra Review

THE WAY OF THE RONIN
Riding The Waves Of Change At Work
Dr. Beverly Potter

Ronin or "wave-men" were masterless samurai who had been thrown into the waves of chaos. *The Way of the Ronin* tells how to surf the waves of chaos, how to be excellent and self-mastering like a warrior, and how to deal with "corporate feudalism"—a rigid system that that tries to squelch your spirit.

The Way of the Ronin draws upon the wisdom of philosophers, the findings of trend watchers, the latest research of management experts and the technology of behavior psychology to create an inspiring strategy for handling change while performing excellently in today's workplace.

"Intelligent and inspiring book."
—*ALA Booklist*

"One of the best business books of the year."
—*Library Journal*

Career/Self-help
252 pp
Illustrations
Appendix
$9.95
0-914171-26-7

PREVENTING JOB BURNOUT
A Workbook
Second Edition
Dr. Beverly Potter

Preventing Job Burnout is a hands-on workbook which guides you step-by-step through the change process. Filled with checklists and worksheets, this power-packed workbooks allows individuals to progress at thair own pace. It is an excellent resource for groups and classes. Very practical.

"If it's possible to cure burnout with a book, this one could do it."
— *Savvy Magazine*

Careers/Self-Help
112 pp
Worksheets
Questionnaires
$9.95
ISBN 1-56052-357-3

TURNING AROUND
Keys To Motivation And Productivity
Beverly Potter, Ph.D.

Turning Around shows step-by-step how to assure top performance from yourself and all those on your team. It explains the most complex techniques in down-to-earth terms.

Turning Around explains behavior psychology and how to apply the techniques to daily supervision situations. It is a valuable reference to return to when faced with difficult management questions. *Turning Around* tells how to:

- Use behavior modification
- Conduct interviews
- Lead meetings
- Mediate conflicts
- Manage authority
- Manage yourself.

Turning Around focuses strictly on objectives and how to achieve them day-in and day-out. It makes your job easier and your career progress more satisfying.

"Best book on the topic."

—Personnel Psychology

"Fresh insight in the area of motivation by kindness and compassion."

—Special Libraries

**Management/
Psychology**
292 pp
Illustrations
Appendix
Index
$9.95
0-914171-16-X

BEATING JOB BURNOUT
How To Increase Job Satisfaction
Dr. Beverly Potter

A lively and informative interview in which Dr. Potter describes the symptoms and causes of job burnout and what to do about it. Based on Dr. Potter's book *Overcoming Job Burnout.* Originally produced by *Psychology Today* Cassette Program.

$9.95

Audio cassette, 60 minutes

ISBN 0-914171-41-0

MAVERICK AS MASTER IN THE MARKETPLACE
The Way of the Office Warrior
Dr. Beverly Potter
Interview by Michael Toms

An inspiring interview with Dr. Beverly Potter by Michael Toms, host of New Dimensions Radio, featured on over 100 National Public Radio shows. *Maverick As Master in the Marketplace* provides insights to empower the independent minded to rise above corporate feudalism and get ahead while enjoying it more.

$9.95

Audio cassette, 60 minutes

ISBN 0-914171-42-9

THE WORRYWART'S COMPANION

Twenty-One Ways to Soothe Yourself and Worry Smart

Dr. Beverly Potter

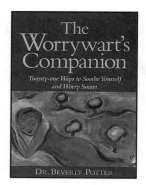

The Worrywart's Companion includes twenty-one simple things you can do to soothe yourself when you feel a worry coming on, such as

Psychology/Self-Help
174 pp
Suggested Reading
$11.95
1-885171-15-3

- Talk to yourself like a good friend would
- Breathe deeply
- Take a walk
- Distract yourself
- Take a warm bath
- Imagine a happy ending
- Smile and Laugh
- Say a little prayer

Instead of worrying yourself sick, *The Worrywart's Companion* shows how to soothe yourself so that you can think more clearly, deal with the worry at hand, and then let it go.

Positive, easy to understand, and fun to read, *The Worrywart's Companion* is a revolutionary little book that explores the roots of worry and explains how worry is a behavior that is *learned.* The good news it that it can be *unlearned.*

Do you lie awake at night mulling over things that *could* happen? Do you automatically expect the worst? Have you worried obsessively about things only to have everything turn out okay? If so, *The Worrywart's Companion* can help.

For the millions of people who lie awake at night worrying. *The Worrywart's Companion* offers peace of mind and a good night's sleep!

*D*r. **Beverly Potter's** work blends humanistic psychology and Eastern philosophies with principles of behavior psychology to create an inspiring approach to the many challenges encountered in today's workplace. Beverly earned her Master's of Science in vocational rehabilitation counseling from San Francisco State and her Doctorate of Philosophy in counseling psychology from Stanford University. She was a member of the staff development team at Stanford for nearly twenty years. Beverly is a dynamic and informative speaker. Her workshops have been sponsored by numerous colleges including University of California at Berkeley Extension, San Francisco State Extended Education, DeAnza and Foothill Colleges Short Courses, as well as corporations such as Hewlett-Packard, Cisco Systems, Genentech, Sun Microsystems, Becton-Dickinson, and Tap Plastics; government agencies like California Disability Evaluation, Department of Energy, IRS Revenue Officers; and professional associations such as California Continuing Education of the Bar, Design Management Institute, and International Association of Personnel Women. Beverly has authored many books and is best known for her work on job burnout.